RIT - WALLACE LIBRARY
CIRCULATING LIBRARY BOOKS

OVERDUE FINES AND FEES FOR <u>ALL</u> BORROWERS

*Recalled = $1/ day overdue (no grace period)
*Billed = $10.00/ item when returned 4 or more weeks overdue
*Lost Items = replacement cost+$10 fee
*All materials must be returned or renewed by the duedate.

D1413947

OPERATIONAL PROFITABILITY

OPERATIONAL PROFITABILITY

SYSTEMATIC APPROACHES FOR CONTINUOUS IMPROVEMENT

SECOND EDITION

ROBERT M. TOROK

PATRICK J. CORDON

JOHN WILEY & SONS, INC.

Library of Congress Cataloging-in-Publication Data:

Torok, Robert M.
 Operational profitability : systematic approaches for continuous improvement / Robert M. Torok, Patrick J. Cordon.—2nd ed.
  p. cm.
 Includes index.
 ISBN 0-471-21473-6 (cloth : alk. paper)
 1. Management audit. 2. Performance—Evaluation. I. Cordon, Patrick J. II. Title.
HD58.95.T67 2001
658.4—dc21

                                                                 2001046920

Printed in the United States of America.

10 9 8 7 6 5 4 3 2 1

DEDICATION

Kevin and Bradley
Bright young sons, Lighting Minds and Hearts

Robert Torok

This book is dedicated to Jesus Christ, Lord and Savior of the world.

Patrick Cordon

ABOUT THE AUTHORS

Robert M. Torok, CPA, CFE, MBA Shareholder of the Accounting firm of Zalick Torok Kirgesner Cook and Co. CPAs.

Patrick (Pat) J. Cordon is an RAB/IRCA Registered Quality Systems Lead Auditor, an AIAG/Supplier Quality Requirements Task Force Certified QS-9000 (recertified) and QS-9000-TE and ISO TS 16949 Quality Systems Auditor, an IATCA Senior Auditor, and an ICBC Certified Business Counselor who provides ISO 9000:2000, ISO Guide 25/17025, Q1/QOS, AS9100, ISO 9000/QS-9000/QS-9000-TE/ISO TS 16949 Quality Management Systems Registration Auditing, and Auditor Training. In addition, he provides warehousing quality assurance evaluations, financial/operational auditing and systems implementation for tooling and equipment, manufacturing, distribution, and logistics companies worldwide.

CONTENTS

PREFACE

The Operational Profitability concept has its basis in understanding and eliminating costs and improving margins in a business process. Data on profitability forms the basis of a metric, or standard of measurement, used to determine the performance of that process. When measured over time, you can make short-term performance predictions and establish stretch goals to drive continued improvement. When you standardize performance definitions between processes and define complexity between them, you can establish benchmarks through comparative analysis, identifying high performance processes and opportunities for improvement. You can then use established tools and techniques to drive the necessary improvements once you identify lower performing processes.

The Operational Profitability concept systematically measures profitability within processes, determines performance levels, establishes benchmarks for best practices, and utilizes existing tools and techniques to drive process improvement toward the achievement of stretch goals. This system leads toward the vision of Operational Profitability: elimination of all bottlenecks within a process.

THE HISTORY OF OPERATIONAL PROFITABILITY

In the mid-1980s, many companies started the movement toward excellence in manufacturing when they adopted a new philosophy of margin management. They worked toward this ideal by thoroughly reviewing their customers' needs, and by analyzing their processes and the abilities of their suppliers. By doing this they were able to produce a product that was reliable and allowed them to meet the needs of the customer. The philosophy, measure, and methodology of Operational Profitability form a framework that helps an organization to focus on reducing costs while improving their processes, thereby yielding higher margins.

A number of companies have since adopted the philosophy of Operational Profitability. They discovered that designing and manufacturing a product without profitability was not only possible, but essential to remain viable in a highly competitive marketplace. Removal of costs in any process eliminates rework and reduces cycle time which reduces the cost of doing business.

Most manufacturing companies adopted the Operational Profitability methodology and discovered not only a manufacturing application, but a universal application in all their processes. They proved the Operational Profitability concept was applicable anywhere one could collect and analyze customer satisfaction, process, and supplier data. The Operational Profitability approach demonstrated the profitability reduction and increased efficiency characteristics.

PHILOSOPHY

The philosophy of Operational Profitability includes six elements: (1) a common goal, (2) teamwork promotion, (3) a common language, (4) synergism, (5) comparison capability, and (6) desire for improvement. Each element is vital toward achieving the desired end result—"excellence in all we do."

- **A Common Goal:** Improved process performance through profitability reduction. Every process has one commonality. They all contain profitability. When focusing on profitability, everyone is working toward that common goal. This commonality also leads toward the desire for a common metric.
- **Teamwork Promotion:** Many operations within a company are task oriented, or based on an individual performing just that part of the process for which they are responsible without regard for other tasks or individuals in the process. Operational Profitability drives a process focus requiring individuals to team together to improve the overall process. Also, by measuring the process, supplier performance, and customer satisfaction, individuals team with those customers and suppliers to identify everyone's needs and requirements.
- **A Common Language:** Using Operational Profitability as the basis for all process measures within an organization, leaders and managers can more easily understand process performance without having to interpret numerous types of charts for different processes.
- **Synergy:** Reduction of costs is not the only benefit of Operational Profitability. When we reduce costs, we also reduce the cost of rework as well as the cycle time required to deliver the product to the customer. The result is a product or service that costs less, takes less time to produce, and yields a higher profit.
- **Comparison Capability:** By providing variance for process complexity, you can compare similar processes to determine overall performance and improvement opportunities.
- **Desire for Improvement:** Current metrics are reactive in nature. When we don't meet a desired standard, we make changes to the process or metric to achieve the standard. The Operational Profitability concept is proactive in nature by communicating current performance, allowing stretch goals to be established for continuous improvement.

Today's businesses need a new mindset that focuses on providing a value-added product or service to the customer. The philosophy demands a cultural change from the

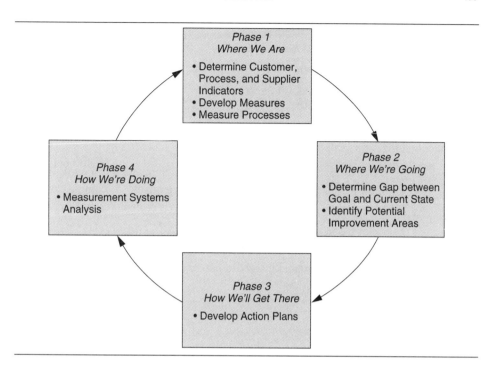

attitudes of the past. Organizations must move away from the current attitude of an "acceptable profitability level," to a point where they actively seek out information on profitability in order to eliminate costs. It is a culture change that does not allow measures to drive improvement, but instead makes the desire for improvement the motivating agent. Firms must cultivate improvement by actively searching out and eliminating system profitability sources at the root and preventing their recurrence to save the limited resources. The new philosophy demands a change in attitude from focusing on individual tasks to focusing on the processes as a whole. We must progress from "look good" metrics to ones that enable organizations to perform better.

Essential elements must be included in order to operationalize profitability fundamentals in daily operations. In the end, state the vision for the culture. Organizations must link mission to the strategic focus at all levels. The diagram above shows how closely the strategic planning process aligns with Operational Profitability.

Operational Profitability drives a measure of key output areas and then uses these measures to plan for the future. In order to have meaningful goals, organizations must have a measure that gives business owners an accurate picture of their current process profitability and capability (Where we are). With this information, they can determine where they want to go as an organization and see exactly where the gaps exist between where they are and where they want to be (Where are we going?). This drives goals that aim for higher effectiveness and efficiency to the customer without overtasking the process of the suppliers to produce beyond their capacity or ability.

We don't know what we don't know.

We can't act on what we don't know.

We won't know until we search.

We won't search for what we don't question.

We don't question what we don't measure.

From here organizations can make action plans that focus on reducing these gaps (How will we get there?) then monitor progress toward reaching the established goals (How are we doing?).

Operational Profitability addresses another aspect of the end state vision by encouraging teamwork to fix problem areas, leveraging innovative solutions, and benchmarking to find the best way to provide high profitability products and services for the customer with reduced cost. By including process workers in formulating process improvement strategies, we get valuable insight to how the process actually works.

Robert M. Torok and Patrick J. Cordon

OPERATIONAL PROFITABILITY

1

THE BASIC APPROACH

This book explains in detail how to maximize your Business System through the use of effective experienced-based financial, business analysis approaches, and profit strategies. You get the benefit of over 1,500 company analyses and 50 profitability system implementations for large, medium, and small companies just like yours.

Operational Profitability explains in detail the basic and advanced techniques of profitability analysis and profit strategies, what it involves, how to set it up, how to revitalize your system, and how to establish a clear set of organizational goals. This book will explain:

1. How to rethink and rebuild the business from the bottom up;
2. How to use a full range of real, value-added analytical tools for improving problem areas throughout the company;
3. What a complete business analysis requires;
4. An overview of the analysis approach;
5. Supply-chain strategy until the year 2005;
6. International expansion;
7. The impact of technology;
8. The effectiveness of systems and the efficiency of business operations;
9. Practical advice on profitability;
10. A typical "process" analysis trail; and
11. Business assessment.

In addition to profitability tools, there are a number of assessment tools in this book; these tools are designed to help you measure your operations and improve your profitability. This is a "how to" book, not a book on modern profitability theory. Complete the quick assessment of your business in Exhibit 1.1 and see if you're currently measuring your operations. These questions are some of the key indicators and rivers behind your success or lack of success in your profitability. If you are not assessing

EXHIBIT 1.1   Quick Assessment of Your Business

	Yes	No
1. Are we measuring the right thing?		
• Does the set of measures address improvement in performance of objectives?		
• Does the set of measures use a small set of significant performance measures that provide a clear basis for assessing accomplishment, facilitate decision making, and focus on accountability?		
• Does the set of measures assess the "value-added" contribution made by the _____?		
• Does the set of measures capture the requirements of internal and external customers?		
Quality % Defect reduction (incoming shipments and work center output) % Scrap value reduction % Product returns or warranty claims reduction % Unscheduled downtime reduction % Supplier reduction % Inspector operations eliminated % Reduction in time between defect detection and prevention		
Cost % Capacity utilization % Efficiency % Productivity % Inventory turnover increase % Average setup time improvement per product line % Total product cost as a function of lead time % Reduction of employee turnover % Reduction in total number of data transactions per product (logistical, balancing, quality, and change) % Improvement in labor/desired labor		
Flexibility % Increase in average number of direct labor skills % Increase in average number of setups per day (% Average lot size reduction) % Decrease in the number of bottleneck work centers % Increase in vendor inputs obtainable in x days or less % Increase in multipurpose equipment % Increase in portion of product made for which a specified level of slack time exists		

EXHIBIT 1.1 *(Continued)*

	Yes	No
Dependability		
% Reduction of lead time per product line % Reduction in average service turnaround per warranty claim % Increase in portion of delivery promises met % Reduction in purchasing lead time % Improvement in output/desired output		
Innovation		
% Increase in annual investment dollars in new product and process research and design % Reduction in material travel time between work centers % Increase in annual number of new product introductions % Increase in common parts per product		
• Does the set of measures address the external performance of the functional area?		
• Does the set of measures address the benefits, costs, and schedules?		
2. Do we have the right measures?		
• Are most measures linked to a clear outcome (results rather than inputs or outputs)?		
• Is the set of measures understood at all levels that have to evaluate and use the measures?		
• Is the set of measures effective in prompting action?		
• Is the set of measures accurate, reliable, valid, verifiable, and cost effective?		
• Does the set of measures include, along with long-term measures, short-term measures or goals that show interim progress?		

your business using similar indicators, perhaps you will give some consideration to reading this book completely and to conducting a comprehensive assessment to strengthen your overall operations and profitability.

How well did you do? Are there some things missing in your measurement system? Now take a detailed assessment of your business control processes by completing Exhibit 1.2. These controls develop the accuracy of your reporting system that you will put in place.

EXHIBIT 1.2   Assessment of Business Control Process

General Controls	Yes	No	N/A	Comments
1. Chart of accounts				
2. Accounting procedures manual				
3. Organizational chart to define responsibilities				
4. Absence of entries direct to ledgers				
5. Posting references in ledgers				
6. Review of journal entries				
7. Use of standard journal entries				
8. Use of prenumbered forms				
9. Support for all journal entries				
10. Access to records limited to authorized persons				
11. Rotation of accounting personnel				
12. Required vacations				
13. Review of system at every level				
14. Appropriate revision of chart of accounts				
15. Appropriate revision of procedures				
16. Separation of record keeping from operations				
17. Separation of record keeping from administration and sales				
18. Record retention policy				
19. Bonding of employees				
20. A conflict of interest policy				
Cash Funds Controls	**Yes**	**No**	**N/A**	**Comments**
1. Completeness of vouchers				
2. Personnel responsible for fund				
3. Reimbursement checks to order of Personnel				
4. Surprise Analysis				

EXHIBIT 1.2 *(Continued)*

Cash Funds Controls	Yes	No	N/A	Comments
5. No employee check cashing				
6. Physically secure				
7. Personnel has no access to cash receipts				
8. Personnel has no access to accounting records				
Cash Receipts Controls	**Yes**	**No**	**N/A**	**Comments**
1. Detail listing of mail receipts				
2. Restrictive endorsement of checks				
3. Special handling of postdated checks				
4. Daily deposit				
5. Cash Personnel bonded				
6. Cash Personnel apart from negotiable instruments				
7. Bank accounts properly authorized				
8. Handling of returned NSF items				
9. Comparison of duplicate deposit slips with cash book				
10. Comparison of duplicate deposit slips with detail A/R				
11. Banks instructed not to cash checks to company				
12. Control over cash from other sources				
13. Separation of cashier personnel from accounting duties				
14. Separation of cashier personnel from credit duties				
15. Use of cash registers				
16. Cash register tapes				
17. Numbered cash receipt tickets				

(continued)

EXHIBIT 1.2 *(Continued)*

Cash Receipts Controls	Yes	No	N/A	Comments
18. Outside salesmen cash control				
19. Daily reconciliation of cash collections				
Cash Disbursements Controls	**Yes**	**No**	**N/A**	**Comments**
1. Numbered checks				
2. Sufficient support for checks				
3. Limited authorization to sign checks				
4. No signing of blank checks				
5. All checks accounted for				
6. Detail listing of checks				
7. Mutilation of voided checks				
8. Specific approval of unusually large checks				
9. Proper authorization of persons signing checks				
10. Control over signature machines				
11. Check listing compared to cash book				
12. Control over interbank transfers				
13. Prompt accounting for interbank transfers				
14. Checks not payable to cash				
15. Physical control of unused checks				
16. Cancellation of supporting documents				
17. Control over long outstanding checks				
18. Reconciliation of bank account				
19. Independence of person reconciling bank statement				
20. Bank statement direct to person reconciling				
21. No access to cash records or receipts by check signers				

EXHIBIT 1.2 *(Continued)*

Investments Controls	Yes	No	N/A	Comments
1. Proper authorization of transactions				
2. Under control of Personnel				
3. Personnel bonded				
4. Personnel separate from cash receipts				
5. Personnel separate from investment records				
6. Safety deposit box				
7. Record of all safety deposit visits				
8. Access limited				
9. Presence of two required for access				
10. Periodic reconciliation of detail with control				
11. Record of all aspects of all securities				
12. Availability of brokerage advices, etc.				
13. Periodic internal analysis				
14. Securities in name of company				
15. Proper segregation of collateral				
16. Physical control of collateral				
17. Periodic appraisal of collateral				
18. Periodic appraisal of investments				
19. Adequate records of investments for application of equity method				
Accounts Receivable and Sales Controls	**Yes**	**No**	**N/A**	**Comments**
1. Sales orders prenumbered				
2. Credit approval				
3. Credit and sales departments independent				

(continued)

EXHIBIT 1.2   *(Continued)*

Accounts Receivable and Sales Controls	Yes	No	N/A	Comments
4. Control of back orders				
5. Sales order and sales invoice comparison				
6. Shipping invoices prenumbered				
7. Names and addresses on shipping invoice				
8. Review of sales invoices				
9. Control over returned merchandise				
10. Credit memoranda prenumbered				
11. Matching of credit memoranda and receiving reports				
12. Control over credit memoranda				
13. Control over scrap sales				
14. Control over sales to employees				
15. Control over COD sales				
16. Sales reconciled with cash receipts and A/R				
17. Sales reconciled with inventory change				
18. A/R statement to all customers				
19. Periodic preparation of aging schedule				
20. Control over collections of written-off receivables				
21. Control over A/R write off, e.g., proper authorization				
22. Control over A/R written off, i.e., review for possible collection				
23. Independence of sales, A/R, receipts, billing, and shipping personnel				
Notes Receivable Controls	**Yes**	**No**	**N/A**	**Comments**
1. Proper authorization of notes				
2. Detailed records of notes				

EXHIBIT 1.2 *(Continued)*

Notes Receivable Controls	Yes	No	N/A	Comments
3. Periodic detail to control comparison				
4. Periodic confirmation with makers				
5. Control over notes discounted				
6. Control over delinquent notes				
7. Physical safety of notes				
8. Periodic count of notes				
9. Control over collateral				
10. Control over revenue from notes				
11. Personnel of notes independent from cash and record keeping				
Inventory and Cost of Sales Controls	**Yes**	**No**	**N/A**	**Comments**
1. Periodic inventory counts				
2. Written inventory instructions				
3. Control over count tags				
4. Control over inventory adjustments				
5. Use of perpetual records				
6. Periodic comparison of G/L and perpetual records				
7. Investigation of discrepancies				
8. Control over consignment inventory				
9. Control over inventory stored at warehouses				
10. Control over returnable containers left with customers				
11. Preparation of receiving reports				
12. Prenumbered receiving reports				
13. Receiving reports in numerical order				
14. Independence of personnel from record keeping				

(continued)

EXHIBIT 1.2   *(Continued)*

Inventory and Cost of Sales Controls	Yes	No	N/A	Comments
15. Adequacy of insurance				
16. Physical safeguards against theft				
17. Physical safeguards against fire				
18. Adequacy of cost system				
19. Cost system tied into general ledger				
20. Periodic review of overhead rates				
21. Use of standard costs				
22. Use of inventory requisitions				
23. Periodic summaries of inventory usage				
24. Control over intracompany inventory transfers				
25. Purchase orders prenumbered				
26. Proper authorization for purchases				
27. Review of open purchase orders				
Prepaid Expenses and Deferred Charges	**Yes**	**No**	**N/A**	**Comments**
1. Proper authorization to incur				
2. Authorization and support of amortization				
3. Detailed records				
4. Periodic review of amortization policy				
5. Control over insurance policies				
6. Periodic review of insurance needs				
7. Control over premium refunds				
8. Beneficiaries of company policies				
9. Physical control of policies				
Intangibles Controls	**Yes**	**No**	**N/A**	**Comments**
1. Authorization to incur				
2. Detailed records				

EXHIBIT 1.2   *(Continued)*

Intangibles Controls	Yes	No	N/A	Comments
3. Authorization to amortize				
4. Periodic review of amortization				
Fixed Assets Controls	**Yes**	**No**	**N/A**	**Comments**
1. Detailed property records				
2. Periodic comparison with control accounts				
3. Proper authorization for acquisitions				
4. Written policies for acquisition				
5. Control over expenditures for self-construction				
6. Use of work orders				
7. Individual asset identification plates				
8. Written authorization for sale				
9. Written authorization for retirement				
10. Physical safeguard from theft				
11. Control over fully depreciated assets				
12. Written capitalization—expense policies				
13. Responsibilities charged for asset and depreciation records				
14. Written, detailed depreciation records				
15. Depreciation adjustments for sales and retirements				
16. Control over intracompany transfers				
17. Adequacy of insurance				
18. Control over returnable containers				

(continued)

EXHIBIT 1.2 *(Continued)*

Accounts Payable Controls	Yes	No	N/A	Comments
1. Designation of responsibility				
2. Independence of A/P personnel from purchasing, cashier, receiving functions				
3. Periodic comparison of detail and control				
4. Control over purchase returns				
5. Clerical accuracy of vendors' invoices				
6. Matching of purchase order, receiving report, and vendor invoice				
7. Reconciliation of vendor statements with A/P detail				
8. Control over debit memos				
9. Control over advance payments				
10. Review of unmatched receiving reports				
11. Mutilation of supporting documents at payment				
12. Review of debit balances				
13. Investigation of discounts not taken				
Accrued Liabilities and Other Expenses Controls	**Yes**	**No**	**N/A**	**Comments**
1. Proper authorization for expenditure and incurrence				
2. Control over partial deliveries				
3. Postage meter				
4. Purchasing department				
5. Bids from vendors				
6. Verification of invoices				
7. Cash account				
8. Detailed records				
9. Responsibility charged				

EXHIBIT 1.2 *(Continued)*

Accrued Liabilities and Other Expenses Controls	Yes	No	N/A	Comments
10. Independence from G/L and cashier functions				
11. Periodic comparison with budget				

Payroll Controls	Yes	No	N/A	Comments
1. Authorization to employ				
2. Personnel data records				
3. Tax records				
4. Time clock				
5. Supervisor review of time cards				
6. Review of payroll calculations				
7. Comparison of time cards to job sheets				
8. Imprest payroll account				
9. Responsibility for payroll records				
10. Compliance with labor statutes				
11. Distribution of payroll checks				
12. Control over unclaimed wages				
13. Profit-sharing authorization				
14. Responsibility for profit-sharing computations				

Long-Term Liabilities Controls	Yes	No	N/A	Comments
1. Authorization to incur				
2. Executed in company name				
3. Detailed records of long-term debt				
4. Reports of independent transfer agent				
5. Reports of independent registrar				
6. Otherwise adequate records of creditors				
7. Control over unissued instruments				

(continued)

EXHIBIT 1.2 *(Continued)*

Long-Term Liabilities Controls	Yes	No	N/A	Comments
8. Signers independent of each other				
9. Adequacy of records of collateral				
10. Periodic review of debt agreement compliance				
11. Record keeping of detachable warrants				
12. Record keeping of conversion features				
Shareholders' Equity Controls	**Yes**	**No**	**N/A**	**Comments**
1. Use of registrar				
2. Use of transfer agent				
3. Adequacy of detailed records				
4. Comparison of transfer agent's report with records				
5. Physical control over blank certificates				
6. Physical control over treasury certificates				
7. Authorization for transactions				
8. Tax stamp compliance for canceled certificates				
9. Independent dividend agent				
10. Dividend account				
11. Periodic reconciliation of dividend account				
12. Adequacy of stockholders' ledger				
13. Review of stock restrictions and provisions				
14. Valuation procedures for stock issuances				
15. Other paid-in capital entries				
16. Other retained earnings entries				

INDICATORS OF A PROFITABLE BUSINESS OPERATING SYSTEM

Now let's take a look at what an effective business enterprise does.

- Management is involved and committed in the process;
- Return on operating assets and inventory turns remain high from quarter to quarter;
- Cash flow and net income remain positive and consistent;
- There is management enforcement of declared aims;
- There is enforcement of a monitoring system;
- Analyses are carried out to get to the root cause of problems;
- Analyses are reviewed and acted on appropriately;
- An audible system is provided that can be verified by external analysis;
- Management helps to successfully implement the feedback loop;
- There is focus on customer needs;
- You apply a supplier/customer relationship with well-defined and mutually agreed-upon requirements;
- A prevention attitude is developed throughout the company, accompanied by an early detection and correction system;
- Clearly understood documented procedures are established for everyone involved;
- Procedures are deployed;
- There is control of all appropriate documents and data;
- Adequate quality training is provided for everyone that includes general comprehension of what quality means and training in the use of specific financial, operating, and quality tools;
- You foster a good working relationship with external analysis; and
- All corrective actions are closed out to prevent reoccurrence.

Manufacturing Effectiveness

- Forecasting is centered around customer production demand;
- Bill of materials is accurate; material shortages are nonexistent;
- Sales and operations management planning is accurate and coordinated with inventory planning for every product;
- Set up times are reduced; inventory buffers are reduced;
- Time and the amount of processes are synchronized;
- Products are produced to what is needed at the time needed;
- Work flow is synchronized during work-in-process so that stocks don't accumulate during work-in-process;

- There is a balancing of uneven work flows with flexible workers and equipment;
- Transport and material movement is removed as much as possible;
- Set up times are shortened and lead time is reduced;
- Waste is reduced or eliminated;
- Motion and walking is minimized;
- The manufacturing process is designed to prevent defects; and
- Manufacturing and vendor lead times are reduced.

WHAT THIS BOOK WILL DO FOR YOU

Operational Profitability; Systematic Approaches for Continuous Improvement, Second Edition will teach you in detail how to maximize your business through the use of effective financial, operational, and analysis approaches and effective business strategies, whether your company is profitable or becoming profitable.

This book presents a common sense, experienced-based approach for improving business and covers:

Process Timing—The aspects of a process's activities are modeled to identify bottlenecks and reduce the overall duration of a business process.

Costing—A true picture of the costs incurred by an organization is given by attributing expenses to the activities that consume resources.

Process Scenarios—Business processes by nature do not follow the same path each time they are performed. Differing paths through a process are identified to compare alternatives.

Process Analysis—Simulation results are examined to identify opportunities to improve productivity, decrease response time, lower costs, and so forth. Because the analysis is model based, parameters can be changed and the process rerun.

Exhibit 1.3   Process Timing

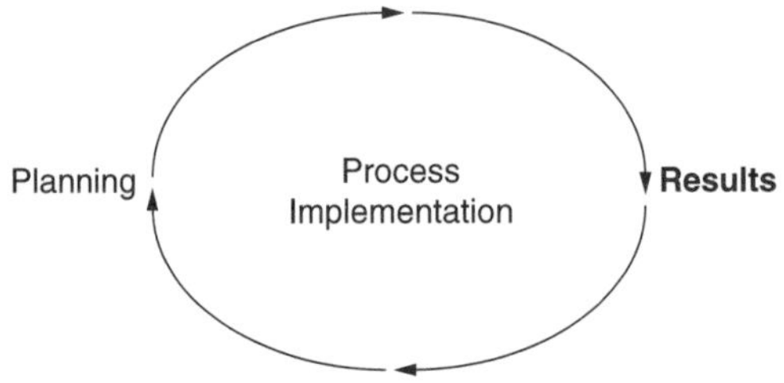

2

A History of American Business and the Impact on Profitability

Forty-five years ago American industrial strength was the best in the world. Fortified by a strong manufacturing base, a vast reservoir of technical expertise, and the temporary weakness of Europe and Japan, the United States dominated the global economy. Following World War II, the United States accounted for roughly half of the world's gross national product. Since 1950, the U.S. economy has adapted to some big changes. The 1950s saw the economic shift from war to peace, then exploded as the country tried to satisfy pent-up demand. The 1960s saw a rapidly expanding consumer economy and an overhaul of the nation's infrastructure. Additional rapid growth was caused by major expansions in the use of metal. Complicating this picture for U.S. producers was the growth of imported products from 4 percent to 14 percent of domestic consumption.

An erratic marketplace with significant inflation, stagnation, and a roller coaster ride of alternating growth and recessionary periods marked the 1970s. The 1980s saw a maturing U.S. economy. Financial markets created new capital sourcing opportunities and the economy enjoyed an 8-year period of uninterrupted growth. However, product consumption actually declined by the end of the decade and import penetration increased to 26 percent—as high as 50 percent in some product lines.

In the 1990s American business (particularly medium and small businesses) have experienced a highly charged, competitive environment identified by:

- Changing product markets;
- Management of investments and assets;
- Profit margin pressure;
- Complex issues in cost control;
- Appreciable capital and technological investment;
- Lower skilled workforce;
- Complex legal issues;
- Global partnerships;
- Fluctuating growth trends;

17

- Complex customer and analysis relationships;
- Greater competitive intensity;
- Significant consolidation;
- Increased foreign product sold in the U.S. domestic markets;
- Fragmentation of the marketplace and an influx of niche competitors, causing companies to carry narrower or broader lines to meet customer needs;
- More demanding customers;
- Effectiveness and efficiency of operations;
- Reliability of financial, operational, and quality reporting;
- Compliance with applicable laws and regulations;
- Higher costs of doing business;
- Difficulty of finding and keeping good employees;
- Push for increased quality and productivity;
- Uncertain and in some cases unreliable supply; and
- Rapidly expanded and costly value-added service requirements to maintain market share to meet increasing customer demands.

GLOBAL MARKETS

Transition from National to Global Capital Markets

We are fast approaching—if not already there—a global capital market system. Powerful strategic forces are driving the globalization of business, the worldwide integration of financial markets, and the growing interdependence among national and regional economies. Sophisticated observers judge that these trends are irreversible. A new world political paradigm of "reciprocity" has emerged. Consider the following: The European Monetary Union (EMU), the North American Free Trade Agreement (NAFTA), and the Association of Southeast Asian Nations (ASEAN), provide overwhelming evidence that a growing number of sovereign nations are subordinating some of their national policies and goals to regional agreements. The de facto enforceability of harmonized regional policy structures and controls is, without doubt, a major global breakthrough as we begin the new millennium.

Innovative Technologies.   The huge breakthroughs in information technology that have come our way in the past three decades are an everyday fact for hundreds of millions of people. Satellite and fiber-optic technology permit global communication at high speed and low cost. These technological advances have contributed greatly to global interdependence. Two specific consequences are: (1) the rise of the multinational corporation and (2) borderless financial markets.

Multinational Corporations (MNCs).   Multinational, transnational, international, global, stateless—no matter what the descriptor, these enterprises, large and

small, view the entire world as one market in which to produce and sell goods and services. MNCs have become the most effective international transfer agents ever known.
All indications are that MNCs have become a permanent feature of the world economy.

Cross-Border Deal Making.   The term "mergers and acquisitions" has assumed
new meaning and significance. Hardly a week goes by without an announcement of yet
another cross-border mega merger. Shareholders appear to support cross-border deals.
Regulators, by and large, seem to have few objections and consumers appear supportive.

Wide Globalization of Markets.   While most recognized markets are turning increasingly global, none equals the internationalization of financial markets. There is
now an almost autonomous world economy of money, credit, and financial investments.
This economy is based strictly on information, and new records are literally set in international financial markets every day. More than ever, the growth and success of
today's manufacturers directly depend on whether their customers expand and prosper. In effect, the same is often true for customers themselves, whose ability to meet
their customers' demands rests on reliable analysis to provide high-quality, competi-
tively priced goods in a responsive manner. Today, major industrial companies rely on
far fewer analysis, sometimes known as preferred analysis, as a way to control costs,
ensure replenishment of supply, and maintain quality.

Supply-Chain Strategy into the Year 2005

Increased supply-chain implementation is widely recognized today as the stream of
business processes through which materials, components, and parts flow from source
to end-consumer. Whether manufacturers supply goods to the public, to other manufacturers, to retailers, or to wholesaler/distributors, customers of all sizes and types
demand more value from the products and services they buy. As the sum of all their
parts, products can only promote customer satisfaction and loyalty if their features,
availability, serviceability, reliability, and price meet that customer's expectations. It
then becomes the job of each supply-chain participant to strive for and achieve these
goals. Nevertheless, while preferred-supplier relationships provide companies with the
opportunity to increase sales, the commitment can involve considerable investment to
comply with customer requirements, such as electronic communication systems and inventory-management techniques. There is also significant risk as companies commit
their energies, resources, and entire futures to the success of fewer customers. Achieving and sustaining profitability is more critical than ever.

Even after many manufacturers become preferred suppliers, companies do not always exchange information on a constant basis. Only 44 percent of preferred suppliers
frequently engage in performance measurement and comments with major customers.
Such measures should include all of the major service levels, such as inventory turns,
on-time deliveries, fill rates, quality, and invoicing accuracy. Generally speaking,
these reviews should occur at least quarterly in order to be effective.

Among the services that large companies, particularly those in the electronics sec-
tor, require from preferred suppliers is inventory consignment. Additionally, some customers demand that suppliers implement vendor-managed inventory (VMI) systems.

This more advanced inventory-management technique takes consigned inventories a step further by making the supplier responsible for gauging, tracking, and actually replenishing its customers' inventories, often at the production site.

All these findings suggest that, for manufacturers' customers, preferred-supplier relationships probably result in lower unit costs and some additional services. However, neither customers nor analysts appear to be leveraging these arrangements to the fullest. Companies are often caught in the crossfire between unceasing customer demands and the inability to control when and if their suppliers' goods arrive correctly and on time. To be effective as preferred suppliers, companies must place the same demands for price, quality, and delivery on their own suppliers to ensure prompt and cost-effective replenishment.

International Expansion

Despite all of these sound, growth-inspiring reasons to expand internationally, 46 percent of manufacturing companies continue to see the United States as their primary market. The fact that nearly half of American manufacturers continue to rely on the domestic marketplace to fuel their growth is not, in and of itself, surprising. There are some industry sectors that view the United States as a largely untapped market for their products. In addition, many companies have applied product improvements and operational efficiencies to recapture domestic customers previously lost to foreign competitors. By strengthening a domestic thrust, these manufacturers can reap the rewards for as long as the potential exists without the distractions of cultivating brand-new markets in unknown places. The maturing U.S. economy is forcing all automotive and other consumer goods analysis to focus on improving quality, delivery performance, operations/cost effectiveness, new product/service development, and product warranty costs all at the same time. Some examples of what will be seen in the future are shown below.

The Impact of Technology

The need for well-educated analysis and control professionals is increasing, thanks to technology's potential to dramatically change organizations and business practices, reduce costs, and create new opportunities.

Technology has affected the business environment in three significant ways. First, it has increased our ability to capture, store, analyze, and process tremendous amounts of data and information, as well as to change production and service processes. This has greatly empowered the business decision maker. Second, technology has significantly affected the control process. While control objectives have remained constant, except for some that are technology specific, technology has altered the way in which systems should be controlled. Safeguarding assets, as a control objective, remains the same whether manual or automated. However, the manner by which we meet the control objective is certainly impacted. Third, technology has affected the analysis profession in terms of the knowledge required to draw conclusions and the skills to perform an analysis.

Due to the rapid diffusion of computer technologies and the ease of information accessibility, knowledgeable and well-educated analysts are needed to ensure that effective controls are in place to maintain data integrity and to manage access to information. It has influenced what can be done in business in terms of information and as a business counselor. It has increased the ability to capture, store, analyze, and process tremendous amounts of data and information, which has increased the empowerment of the business decision maker. Technology has also become a primary counselor to various production and service processes. It has become a critical component to business processes. There is a residual effect in that the increased use of technology has resulted in increased budgets, increased successes and failures, and increased awareness of the need for control.

What Does the External Environment Consist of?

The business's external environment consists of three main sectors: the Remote Environment, the Industry Environment, and the Operating Environment. All of these environmental sectors affect the business's operations both on an international and domestic level.

The Remote Environment comprises five factors that are not influenced by a single firm. The main factors are economic, social, political, technological, and ecological. The business must consider these factors when working with the market.

The Industry Environment is made up of the entry barriers, supplier power, buyer power, substitute availability, and competitive rivalry. These contending forces are of the greatest importance to the business in strategy formulation.

In dealing with the threat of entry there are six major barriers: economies of scale, product differentiation, capital requirements, cost disadvantages independent of size, access of distribution channels, and government policies.

These can be overcome or dealt with individually, but some companies are not able to handle them and fail.

A supplier becomes powerful when it purchases in large quantities, the products purchased are not differentiated, the products purchased represent a significant cost of their product, the product does not save the buyer money, or the buyer poses a credible threat of backward integration. A buyer becomes powerful if it is concentrated or purchases in large volume, the product purchased is standard or undifferentiated, the product purchased represents a significant portion of the cost, it earns low profits, quality is not a factor, the product purchased does save the buyer money, or the buyer poses a credible threat of integrating backward.

What Is Competitive Advantage?

Competitive advantage is a company's ability to outperform its competitors. Competitive advantage can be achieved through low cost and differentiation. A company is said to have achieved competitive advantage when its profit rate is higher than the average for its industry. The profit rate is based on return of sales (ROS) or return of assets (ROA). The most basic determinant of a company's profit rate is the gross profit margin. There are three reasons why a company's gross profit margin may be higher: the unit price is higher, unit cost is lower, or it has both a higher price and a lower unit cost. The building blocks of competitive advantage are efficiency, quality, innovation, and customer responsiveness. These building blocks are generic in that they provide four basic ways to lower cost and achieve differentiation. Any firm can adopt these no matter what industry it is in or what product or service it provides.

Efficiency is based on the cost of inputs required to produce a given output. The more efficient a company, the lower the cost of its inputs required producing a given output. Efficiency helps a company attain a low-cost competitive advantage. Employee productivity can be the key to efficiency.

The impact of high product quality on competitive advantage is the creation of a brand name reputation, greater efficiency, and, thus, lower costs. This enhanced reputation allows the business to charge a higher price. At the same time, the costs are down so profits are much higher, producing a higher competitive advantage. Quality has become imperative for survival in some companies.

To achieve customer responsiveness a company must deliver exactly what the customer wants when the customer wants it. A company must do everything it can to identify and satisfy customer needs. Steps taken to improve quality and efficiency are consistent with the goal of high customer responsiveness. There may be a need to customize goods and services to meet the demands of individual customers. Customer response time has become a big factor in increasing customer responsiveness. Other areas that aid in achieving higher customer responsiveness are superior design, superior service, and superior after-sales service and support. Distinctive competencies come from two sources: resources and capabilities. These sources are both tangible and intangible. To achieve distinctive competency, a company's resources must be both unique and valuable. A company's capabilities refer to its ability to coordinate resources and put them to productive use. A company needs to develop strategies that build on existing resources and capabilities as well as build additional resources and capabilities. The durability of a company's competitive advantage depends on three factors: the height of barriers to imitation, capability of competitors, and dynamism of the industry. Barriers to imitation are the factors that make it difficult for a competitor to copy a company's distinctive competencies. The major determinant of the capability of a competitor is its prior strategic commitments. A dynamic industry changes rapidly, thus it has a high rate of product innovation.

Companies fail for three related reasons: inertia, prior strategic commitments, and also when it becomes so dazzled by its early success that it believes more of the same effort is the way to future success. To avoid failure a company might focus on the building blocks of competitive advantage. It must identify the best practice and adopt it. In order to determine the best industrial practice, companies should reevaluate their operations and apply best practices, and implement integrated ERP/MRP systems and industry benchmarking.

3

THE EFFECTIVENESS
OF SYSTEMS AND THE EFFICIENCY
OF BUSINESS OPERATIONS

BUSINESS IMPROVEMENT APPROACH

What a Complete Business Analysis Requires

Realistically, it will take you 2 weeks to 2 months to gather the information, another month to develop action plans, and possibly two more months to see the results of your improvements—a 4- to 5-month project. However, by doing so you can realize substantial benefits of 35 percent to 45 percent profit improvement, operational effectiveness, and increased market reputation. This approach might be just the opportunity to improve your business, increase your competitive advantage, and increase your market share; it has worked for thousands of companies. First you have to rethink your approach to your management control system, specifically:

- To determine whether the management system is documented comprehensively;
- To ensure that the documentation meets the intent of the requirements (addressing all the mandatory requirements);
- To verify that the system is effectively implemented using records checking, interviews, and observations, taking into account that no one analysis source or company determines overall system functioning; and
- To verify that the System is effective (Is it accomplishing its intended purpose?) through trends and patterns in customer satisfaction, cost improvements, measurements, and records history.

The Effectiveness of Systems and the
Efficiency of Business Operations

Simply stated, an effective management system is "a business mechanism that ensures that company financial and operational goals are met over time and customer requirements and expectations are realized consistently over time through the effective use of people and internal/external resources; it is a viable concern." The formula for effective operational and management analysis is Economic Evaluation + Management Evaluation + Financial Evaluation = Company Performance. The company might ask itself four key questions:

- Do the systems, as they are designed, have the potential to succeed?
- Are the systems implemented as designed?
- Are the systems achieving their intended results?
- Are the systems maximizing profits?

In order to achieve and maintain an effective management system, it is important to realize that a strong element of management control and employee involvement works together in tandem to protect its viable concern, that is, the "effectiveness and efficiency of operations" which includes the safeguarding of assets, or "the prevention or timely detection of unauthorized acquisition, use, or disposition of the company's assets." Preventive action to protect company assets depends on a unique and consistent reliability of financial, operational, and quality reporting and compliance with applicable laws and regulations. This is accomplished with internal control.

Internal control is much more than an internal check. An internal check can best be understood as being an internal cross check, which is certainly an important element of most effective systems of internal control. The system of internal control is the totality of methods and measures that management has introduced to provide reasonable assurance of the achievement of objectives and the avoidance of unwanted outcomes. As such, internal control is the essence of good management. The classic view of management is that it comprises effective goal setting and planning, organizing, staffing, directing, and controlling. Each of these must be done well if there is to be effective internal control.

Hidden in every sizable company are a wealth of innovative techniques that will improve its competitiveness—if they are recognized and diffused to the rest of the organization. How do you find the pearls? How do you get the rest of the organization interested in something they did not invent?

Mobilizing embedded corporate knowledge is a cornerstone of profitability. If a company is going to accelerate its proactive and reactive capabilities, it cannot afford to reinvent the same solutions over and over again, it cannot afford to make the same mistakes over and over again, it cannot afford large changes when small ones will do, and it cannot afford to ignore the pearls begging for recognition. Leverage comes from reusable knowledge, reconfigurable for different applications across the entire corporation.

The principle asset in a corporation today is its collective knowledge—something that does not show on the balance sheet. The value of that asset is multiplied by its mobility within the corporation. Most companies today have not thought about that knowledge base, how it changes, and how it gets deployed at points that need it while it still has something to offer.

1. **Organizational Structure**—Discuss the organization relative to its structure. How are responsibilities compartmentalized? What are the organizational units

and subunits? What are the standard mechanisms and events of interunit interaction? How are decisions and approvals obtained? What is organizationally rigid and what is fluid? Are teaming concepts employed? What about cross-functional teams? When was the last reorganization and what was its nature?

2. **Human Resources**—Discuss the human factors for all employees, management and labor alike. What forms of training and education exist? Is cross-functional training available? To what degree are people empowered? How is hiring and downsizing accomplished? What mobility exists within the plant, within the corporation, and within the community for employees? Are there unique, difficult, or rare skill sets involved? When an open or new position is filled, is there a ripple effect among other employee positions? What is the general access-to-information situation? What surprise events have occurred in this area in the last 24 months that required a response?

3. **Operating Procedures**—Discuss standardized policy and operating procedures. Is there a standard procedure for new product start-up, or for factory conversion? What operating procedures apply to the production activity? What requires approval signatures and how long do they take? What events have caused procedures to be implemented and/or modified? What performance metrics are used within the plant, and what by corporate? Discuss work rules and speed of responsiveness to unexpected production needs.

4. **Information Automation**—Discuss the management information system (MIS) and decision support computer-related environment. What kind of operating and management reports are available? What kind of general information is accessible? To what degree are personnel supported with desktop access? How often have these been updated and modified? What kind of shop-floor reporting exists? What role does simulation and modeling play? What project management tools used? Describe an event where a change to the system was desired but did not (could not) occur. What forms of electronic communication exist—and between whom? How are engineering changes dealt with? Are suppliers and customers tied electronically to the plant in any way?

5. **Control Automation**—Discuss the automation control environment. What systems, hardware, and software are in use? Discuss a case where an improvement was implemented. Discuss the backlog of unimplemented improvements and corrections. How is control code developed and maintained? How do new controls enter the plant? How are controls and their systems maintained? How is training for new technology accomplished?

6. **Facility**—Discuss the physical plant facility relative to its fixed and flexible nature. Has the plant ever been reconfigured? What restrictions exist in adding equipment and processing capabilities? Discuss the utilities (electric, gas, steam, sewage, toxic disposal, etc.) required by the production process, and their fixed and flexible nature. Discuss the procedures involved in relocating or obtaining new utility service in the physical plant. How is equipment that was initially installed removed or relocated?

7. **Material Movement/Management**—Discuss material, work-in-progress (WIP), and finished goods movement and storage within the facility. Discuss just-in-time (JIT) implementation and examples of when it fails—such as when material is not available when needed from both internal and external sources.

8. **Production Process**—Discuss production process issues. What is the capacity utilization of the processes in place? Do capacity requirements fluctuate? How is the plant scheduled? How does installed process technology compare to the state of the art? What changes in process technology are occurring and what does the future require? When was the process last changed and why and with what procedure? Are workstations or work areas ever idled because of upstream or downstream stoppages? What forms of flexibility exist in the process? What is the human role in the process? What kind of process characterization knowledge exists? What is the role, if any, of simulation and modeling?

9. **Production Equipment**—Discuss the general state of production equipment. What degree of automation exists? What degree of flexibility exists? What range of materials can be accommodated? What unique single-point equipment has caused the biggest problem when it is down? How does installed equipment compare to the state-of-the-art equipment? What is the turnover and upgrade of equipment technology? What does the future require that is not present now? Are unique and/or rare skills required for any equipment? What is the nature and state of operator and maintenance training? What are equipment utilization and failure rates? Where would you like to make a change but cannot? What kind of process characterization knowledge exists? What is the role, if any, of simulation and modeling? What degree of variation and commonality exists among equipment types?

10. **Changeover/Setup System**—Discuss the changeover and setup processes. How often do they occur? What are the procedures? How is equipment utilization affected? What are the cycle times? How is a new product introduced to the production environment and how frequently does this occur?

11. **Supply Chain**—Discuss the supply chain and supporting logistics. How stable is the supply chain? What is the procedure for gaining new suppliers? What is supplier turnover? Describe an unexpected supplier failure that was costly. How flexible are supplier contracts? What is JIT situation and performance history?

12. **Distribution Chain**—Discuss the customer interface and logistical support. How is business obtained? How is the customer interface conducted? How are product orders obtained and received? How often do product orders get modified and with what lead time? What are the trends in this area? What are sizes and frequencies of orders? How many product types are there? What shipping alternatives exist? What finished-goods inventory exists? What are the customer delivery-time expectations and trends?

Any of the following will complicate and/or compromise plant efficiency:

- Absenteeism of key people with unique skills;
- Externally imposed production schedule changes;

- Bad materials/subassemblies received from supplier;
- Key supplier insolvency;
- Mandatory short-notice engineering changes;
- Market demand increases/decreases;
- New performance/cost/staffing metrics imposed;
- Discovery that shop floor control has a major bug;
- New product needs new materials or new process;
- Process technology breakthrough becomes available;
- Major process/equipment/die failure; and/or
- Regulatory procedure/process change mandated.

Business Analysis and Analysis Sampling

Business analyses are designed to maximize the efficiency of operations by exposing redundant and inefficient procedures and processes, to measure the effectiveness of operating practices and their outcomes, and to determine that the practices and procedures are suitable and in compliance with those prescribed by the customer and management. They are also designed to prevent fraud, waste, and ensure the reliability of management data. The functions in Exhibit 3.1 benefit most from business analysis.

Determining Sampling Methods

Sampling is used extensively by analysts in their work. Samples are portions of a whole (or population) that are used to represent the whole. The sample is used to obtain

EXHIBIT 3.1   Functions Benefiting from Business Analysis

Operational Area	Degree of Benefit for Customer Satisfaction
Purchasing	90%
Inventory control	60%
Billings and collections	60%
Electronic data processing	60%
Capital expenditures	50%
Manufacturing and production	45%
Shipping and receiving	30%
Marketing	30%
Financial and debt management	10%

information about the whole. A sample is preferred over an analysis of the whole because the information can be obtained cheaply and quickly. There are many types of samples and they can be grouped conveniently into two main categories, judgmental samples and statistical samples. The usual goal for a sample is for it to be "representative" of the population. Analysts may use subjective methods of sample selection in the belief that they are able to assure a representative sample by the exercise of judgment. Such a sample is selected with the intention of being representative, but it is usually drawn without the knowledge of the probabilities involved. Many factors influence the success in getting a sample on this basis. A judgment sample is one that was under the control or influence of factors other than chance. Are there conditions where judgment samples are entirely appropriate? All samples furnish statistics, but the use of objective probability methods in selection is characteristic of what is called statistical sampling. Samples are those in which the items were selected under a procedure excluding the influence of nonchance factors. The use of probability can, in many analyses, offer real advantages. Judgmental sampling performs satisfactorily when statistical sampling is not warranted. Judgmental sampling occupies a prominent place in the analysis' sample and evaluation procedures. Nevertheless, analysts should know when and how to use it. Judgmental sampling may be used to select examples of deficiencies to the analysis' contention that a system is weak. They may make a search for defective or improperly processed items to confirm suspicions, or support their position that the system is not capable of identifying improprieties. This is a valid use of judgmental sampling. It should not be used to estimate the number or value of such items in total population, because not every item in the population was given a chance of selection. Judgmental sampling can provide analysts with some clues as to whether to proceed with a statistical sample. If they encounter a well-designed system, good management, well-trained employees, and feedback that highlights errors, it would be extravagant to spend a great amount of time performing extensive transaction tests. A small random sample to obtain some reasonable representation of the many will suffice. If no errors are found, the analyst may be able to determine no basis for examining the population further for any material error. He may not say that he has adequate proof that the population is truly error free, or even reasonably error free. He has no statistical basis for such a statement. However, what he can say about the functioning of the system may be sufficient for the specific objective. Judgmental sampling has its place, so long as the analyst is aware of it. If the analyst's objectives are fully met by a judgmental sampling, there is no valid reason to insist on the discipline of added support.

Statistical Sampling

The main advantages of statistical (probability) sampling over judgmental sampling are based on the fact that there is a significant body of accepted to support and explain probability sampling. It is not necessary to all of the theory to use it and benefit from it. Because theoretical support exists, probability sampling is widely accepted. Reasonable conclusions based on probability sampling will be accepted when the sampling plan has been explained. One of the attractive aspects of probability sampling is that it is used to measure the reliability of the estimates computed from the results. It can

EXHIBIT 3.2   Sampling Analysis Sampling Sizes

Desired Degree of Analysis Assurance	Sample Size of the Total Analysis Samples	Confidence Level of Controls, and System Effectiveness
High	7–15 (Broad-Based Historical Samples)	99%
Moderate	5–7 (Broad-Based Samples)	95%
Low	3–5 (Broad-Based Samples)	85% to 90%

provide an estimate of the number of orders issued to sole sources, but it will not give an estimate of value. That, too, is the function of variables sampling. Determining sample sizes is relatively easy. The first determines the population size, the desired confidence, the desired precision, and the expected error rate.

BUSINESS ANALYSIS

Overview of Business Analysis

Business analysis is often used to identify a variety of activities: to describe evaluations of management's performance, detailed technical operations, and management's planning and control systems.

Management analysis, performance analysis, modern internal analysis, and operations analysis are used to describe activities very similar to what others refer to as business analysis. The distinction between operational, financial, and compliance analysis is often confused. For example, business analysis is described as an attitude— a manner of approach, analysis, and thought—and it is said that it differs very little, if any, from traditional analysis. Recognizing that advancements in the theory and practice of business analysis require a workable definition, we define business analysis as follows:

Business analysis is a systematic process of evaluating an organization's effectiveness, efficiency, and economy of operations under management's control and reporting to appropriate persons the results of the evaluation along with recommendations for improvement. Its objectives are to provide a means for evaluating an organization's performance and to enhance performance by making recommendations for improvements. Business analysis requires measuring the degree of correspondence between actual performance and acceptable criteria and focuses on management's planning and control system. Both the adequacy of the system and the degree of compliance with its established policies and procedures are evaluated. Evaluation requires an analyst who is independent of the activity being evaluated to obtain and evaluate evidence which, in the analyst's judgment, is relevant to the effectiveness, efficiency, and economy of operations.

Important Characteristics of Business Analysis

By emphasizing the improvement of future operations, business analysis is distinguished from financial analysis and compliance analysis, both of which have historical perspectives. Financial analysis is concerned with reporting past economic activity, and compliance analysis is concerned with past adherence to established requirements. Business analysis is concerned with improving future performance and focuses on management's policies, planning and control systems, and decision-making processes. Internal analysts must determine that such policies, systems, and processes exist and are being complied with and must evaluate the quality and the degree to which they contribute individually and collectively.

Practical independence is necessary if the potential benefits of business analysis are to be realized. It is that degree of independence that protects analysts from having to compromise their analysis objectives. Such independence requires that analysts be:

- Free of personal involvement or responsibility for operations of an analyzed unit;
- Able to develop analysis programs without undue influence;
- Able to gain full access to evidential matter and operating personnel as necessary;
- Objective in gathering and evaluating evidence; and
- Able to include in an analysis report all matters deemed necessary.

The importance of practical independence cannot be overemphasized; it must be established by organizational policy, reflected in organizational status, and maintained by professional performance. Management must understand and accept the necessity for analysis independence. The potential benefits of business analysis will not be realized unless competent analysts have the confidence and support of executive management and are allowed to exercise professional judgment in all analysis matters. Restricting the work scope of analysts and assigning them mundane tasks are self-defeating. Essential to practical independence are the personal integrity and objectivity of analysts, requiring that they demonstrate courage of conviction rather than subordinating their professional judgment to others and that they be unbiased in their evaluation of relevant evidence.

Systematic Approach. Business analysis is a rational, systematic evaluation for which there is a consistent methodology. A well-planned and systematic approach to business analysis is both feasible and necessary and involves a comprehensive understanding of the analysis environment, establishing objectives, determining what evidence is available to satisfy these objectives, accumulating and evaluating evidence, developing conclusions, reporting to management, and following up on the analysis report. These elements will be more fully developed later in this chapter.

Phases of an Business Analysis

A systematic approach to accomplish a business analysis consists of a series of well-planned phases. A brief review of each phase will put the process of business analysis in proper perspective. Each phase is designed to achieve certain objectives and is dependent on the results of the preceding phases. Each phase is briefly explained below and is discussed more fully in subsequent chapters.

Preliminary Preparation. Business analysis requires a thorough understanding of the business environment. Analysts must study and evaluate available information to gain an appreciation of the history and current status of an organization. Knowledge of the industry, the business's input markets, production technology, output markets, and applicable government controls and regulations is essential to understand the unique characteristics of the organization's and the management's styles and values, organizational structure, geographic distribution of facilities, production processes, and major planning and control systems. This knowledge should be reasonably complete before a business analysis is attempted in any functional area or organizational unit.

During the preliminary preparation, the analysis file containing background information on the unit, activity, or function is reviewed, brought up-to-date, and evaluated. Information includes the objectives of the production processes, resources used (financial, material, and human), organizational elements, and major controls systems employed. Up-to-date files will provide analysts with a grasp of the what, why, and how of a company's operation. Sources of information for this file include company charters, organizational charts, policy and procedure statements, budgets, financial and operating reports, systems descriptions, applicable governmental and regulatory requirements, analysis reports, and memoranda. Trade publications, such as journals and statistical summaries, are also an important resource.

Field Survey. The field survey determines the scope and emphasis of a business analysis. During this phase, analysts use what they have learned in the earlier phase as a guide to asking questions of operating management, in reviewing reports and outputs of control systems, and in observing operations. The survey is conducted on the premises of the unit being analyzed and results in a more precise identification of problem areas, sensitive functions or activities, and operations that are crucial to the success of the analysis. These aspects emerge more clearly as analysts review the output of control systems, discuss operations with line management, and observe operations.

Having completed the field survey, analysts will have sufficient knowledge of operations to identify important issues and problems, if any exist, and to decide where analysis efforts should be concentrated. With the information gathered during the preliminary preparation and the field survey, analysts prepare a systematic plan for the conduct of the analysis: an analysis program.

Program Development.   A written analysis program documents analysis planning and provides a guide for the systematic accumulation and evaluation of evidence and consists of the detailed steps for collecting and analyzing appropriate evidence to achieve stated objectives. Analysis programs must be consistent with the scope and objectives of the analysis and contain the procedures to apply. A written program must be developed for each individual analysis; it is a valuable quality-control device when carefully planned and followed by field analysts.

In the program-development phase, analysts write analysis programs for obtaining and analyzing evidence concerning the specific areas of interest that will have been identified in the prior phases. The literature on business analysis contains some excellent, illustrative programs that analysts may use for guidance. Nevertheless, all business analysis programs should be individually designed and take into consideration the analysts' environment, objectives, available evidence, and appropriate techniques. These programs usually include one or more statements about analysis objectives, sources of evidence, and some indication of how the evidence is to be obtained and analyzed.

A written analysis program is a valuable control tool without which efficiency and effectiveness will certainly suffer. Some have viewed written analysis programs as too constraining for business analysis. Nothing could be further from the truth. Writing an analysis program that logically links objectives with available evidence and techniques provides a discipline of thought and action that is essential for a systematic evaluation. Without such imposed discipline, it is almost certain that the analysis will be inefficient and that voids in coverage will inadvertently occur. Properly managing a business analysis or an activity that practices business analysis requires management's planning and control techniques which include the use of written, specifically designed analysis programs.

Analysis Application.   Analysis application usually takes place on a company's premises and involves the step-by-step completion of each element of the analysis program to gather and analyze evidence, draw conclusions, and develop recommendations. During this phase, analysts complete an in-depth review of the company's operations previously identified as appropriate analysis subjects. Normally, this step is the most time-consuming phase of the analysis. Analysts must also identify specific problems, gather and analyze sufficient evidence to demonstrate cause and effect, and develop recommendations for improvement during the application phase. They use appropriate techniques to accumulate sufficient, reliable evidence to ensure that:

- Identified problems are real, not imaginary;
- Related problems are identified;
- Specified cause-and-effect relationships are valid; and
- Recommended changes are feasible, relevant, and cost effective.

During the application phase, each step or instruction in the analysis program must be completed and documented in the working papers to show clearly the methodology employed, evidence accumulated, and conclusions reached. Documentation of the logic, evidence, conclusions, and recommendations is important because analysts might, at a later date, need to convince a higher level of management that the findings, conclusions, and recommendations are valid. In other words, analysts may have to "sell" the results of an analysis.

Although stressing that each step of the analysis program must be completed during the application phase, analysts should have flexibility in completing their work. Certainly, it is appropriate to modify a program in light of new information coming to their attention during this work. Experienced analysts must be free to deviate from the program whenever conditions indicate that more or different evidence is required. Furthermore, unanticipated discoveries may lead to the decision to pursue matters that were not considered earlier. An analysis program provides a guide, not a straitjacket.

Reporting and Following Up. Reporting is the most critical phase of a business analysis and will not be successful unless it accurately communicates to management the operating deficiencies and practical recommendations for improving operations. Good analysis reports state facts (findings) precisely and clearly, support conclusions with findings, and give practical recommendations that address the problems described. During the analysis, analysts must clearly establish facts, closely scrutinize conclusions and recommendations, and discuss the report with management. A logically structured report with sections on background information, scope, opinions, findings, and recommendations enhances both the report and the communication process. Extensive editing for grammar, style, spelling, and technical accuracy will facilitate communication.

Analysis reports should reflect that due professional care was exercised throughout all analysis phases and must be firmly supported by documented evidence and recorded in the working papers. When discussing draft reports with employees, analysts are often called on to support their conclusions, findings, and recommendations. Working-paper documentation provides an invaluable record of the processes employed to gather evidence and the logic used to analyze the findings and draw conclusions. Working papers provide documented support for all findings and recommendations, reflect planning and control aspects of the analysis, and show the rational and systematic process that culminated in the analysis report.

Well-written analysis reports bring to management's attention an objective review of current conditions and provide the basis for management's decision on the need to take action. They also provide suggestions and available alternatives for improving the company's activities.

The reporting phase includes following up the analysis report to determine what, if any, action was taken in response to the report. Follow-up is essential because there is the possibility that deficiencies revealed by the analysis will continue uncorrected. Normally, the analyst's findings should result in management's action to correct deficiencies identified in the report. Whether to formally consider the material defects in managerial or operational controls identified in the analysis must not be allowed to be a matter of choice. Nevertheless, management should reserve the right to take the actions recommended, to devise solutions other than those recommended, or not to take action if the cost–benefit trade-off is unacceptable. To achieve desired results, executive management must establish a policy requiring timely written responses to analysis reports and clearly delineating the responsibilities of the entity to improve processes.

The analysis department's responsibility for follow-up should also be established by a policy that may stipulate that the analysis report remain "open" until the analyst is satisfied that management has taken appropriate steps to correct deficiencies. That approach may result in the analyst acting in a management capacity which may effectively destroy his or her independence. Another alternative is to require that higher management approve the company's proposed action to correct the conditions reported by the analysis. When this arrangement is used, the analysis department receives a copy of the response and sends management a written summary of its evaluation of the appropriateness of the response. Because business analysis is by nature a service to management (or organization) and depends heavily on its operational independence, the second alternative is clearly preferable.

Requirements for Effective Business Analysis

If business analysis is to achieve optimum benefits for management, several conditions must be consciously developed and maintained along with the efforts and attention of both management and analysts. Business analysis requires continuous support from the organization as a whole, especially from executive management, which includes establishing appropriate organizational status and practical independence as well as providing adequate resources. It also requires recognition and acceptance of its services by users and the acceptance of responsibility by analysts themselves. Status is granted by management in the analysis charter, but analysts must continually earn it.

Independence is a mental attitude and should be continuously emphasized in training programs, performance evaluations, and reporting. Independence may be granted by policy and organizational status, but analysts must assume responsibility for maintaining it. Independence from management is especially important for business analysis, despite the fact that business analysis provides a valuable service to management.

Human-Relations Aspects of Business Analysis

The very nature of analysis creates some sensitive human-relations problems. Sometimes analysts encounter irritation or hostility because their job creates inconveniences or additional work for some personnel. There is a tendency for employees to be anxious or defensive because analysis reports will undoubtedly be given to one or more managers who have authority over them. Employees want to look good in the eyes of the readers of analysis reports, whereas analysts are likely to find and report deficiencies in the company's control systems. Analysts, of course, are obligated to report all material deficiencies in the planning and control systems reviewed, not the personal performance of employees. The significance of that distinction is very important but not always apparent to the company's personnel.

Business analysts often become involved in areas and operations previously not subject to analysis. Despite the fact that objective standards are employed as much as possible, subjectivity comes into play more in business analysis than in financial or compliance analysis. Subjectivity, of course, increases the possibility of conflict between analysts and employees. For business analysts to be successful, they must understand the human-relations implications and deal effectively with them.

Internal analysis is an independent appraisal activity within an organization for the review of operations as a service to the organization. It is a managerial control that functions by measuring and evaluating the effectiveness of other controls. The objective of internal analysis is to assist management in the discharge of its responsibility. Attaining this objective involves a wide variety of activities including appraising the design and function of accounting, financial, and operating controls; evaluating the degree of compliance with established policies, plans, and procedures; determining whether assets are properly accounted for and safeguarded; evaluating the reliability of management data; appraising the quality of performance; and recommending operating improvements.

The burden of developing and maintaining proper relationships with operating or line managers rests squarely on business analysts who must understand the internal analysis environment, including the management's style and expectations concerning business analysis. Operating management and others will react to business analysis and analysts based on their perceptions of the analyst's relevance, responsibility, and performance. If business analysts are viewed as qualified persons performing a valuable service with integrity and objectivity, operating management and others will cooperate by readily providing needed information, by relying on the business analyst's work, and by implementing their recommendations. However, if the analyst is perceived as unqualified or as lacking integrity or objectivity, cooperation will be withheld. The manner in which the analyst conducts his or her assignment has a direct effect on the deference and status of business analysis in the organization.

Good human relations and positive attitudes can be cultivated through the analysis report. The purpose of the analysis report is to improve the organization's overall performance, not to point out mistakes or criticize individuals. The tone of analysis reports reflect the analyst's attitudes and can generate positive or negative reactions from readers. Insofar as possible, analysis reports should be positive in nature and give credit for good performance. Because business analyses primarily evaluate management's planning and control systems, analysis reports should address the performance of such systems and not an individual's performance.

Process Analysis Matrix

One of the most effective methods to verify that procedures are used, records are kept, and that the quality operating system is effective is using analysis trails. Analysis trails help the analyst understand the design and operating process a company deploys to ensure the customer product quality requirements; it also helps determine whether the process is actually in use once it is in operation.

A typical "process" analysis trail to assess the effectiveness of the business analysis process is shown in Exhibit 3.3.

EXHIBIT 3.3 Business Analysis Process

Determine Measurements	Define Improvement Objectives	Map Existing Business Processes	Look for Gaps, Trends, and Patterns as Well as Opportunities for Improvement; Analyze Problem Solve Data
Net income as a % of sales	Waste elimination	Request for quote	Variance analysis identify value-added time
Average time to market for new products	Lead time reduction	Customer sales concept	Reduce or eliminate non–value-added time
New product sales dollars as a % of total sales	Productivity gains	Feasibility review	Determine internal and external organization
% first time quality	WIP reduction	Development	Analyze parallel vs. sequential work
Actual vs. planned production	Delivery improvement	Forecasting	Investigate the application of information technology
Unit cost	Set up reduction	Purchasing	Identify mistake proofing opportunities
Production, order, shop cycle time	Quality improvement	Monthly production plan	
Day's supply of finished-goods inventory	Machine uptime	Material requirement plan	
Sales forecast accuracy	Improved cycle time	Inspection plan	
Sales dollars and % growth	*Conduct Variance Analysis:*	Staffing plan	
Market share %	ROE	Kanban plan	
Employee satisfaction index	Cash flow	Manufacturing capacity plan	
Customer satisfaction index	ROA/ROS	Material handling	
Cash flow from operations	Capacity variance	Packaging	
Return on net assets	Capacity utilization	Delivery	
Profitability ROI	Ratio delay	Installation/servicing plan	
	Inventory turnover	Customer satisfaction	
	Time studies		
	Analyze process for continuous improvement		
	Track metrics		
	Determine future trends		

Financial Analysis: General Planning	Objective Evidence
Review and assessment of internal control structure	*General* Analyze financial statements Schedule supporting footnote disclosures and other reports Consolidation and combination of adjusted trial balance List of general ledger balances Adjust journal entries and reclassify entries Analyze unrecorded differences Financial statement disclosure checklist

EXHIBIT 3.3   *(Continued)*

Financial Analysis: General Planning	Objective Evidence
	Letter of representations
	Subsequent events review documentation
	Commitments and contingencies, including lawyers' letters
	Board of directors and related committee minutes
	Reports on internal control
	Notes for management letter comments
	Review and approval checklist
	Tax return information and worksheets
	Planning and Administration
	Company acceptance and retention evaluation form
	Analysis planning analysis checklist
	Internal control structure Analysis checklist
	Analytical review
	Analysis program
	Engagement letter
	Analysis time budget and control
	Control of schedules
	Assets
	Cash
	Marketable securities and related income
	Other investments and related income
	Trade accounts receivable
	Notes receivable and related income
	Allowance for doubtful accounts and notes receivable
	Inventory and production costs
	Prepaid expenses
	Other current assets
	Property, plant, and equipment
	Intangible assets
	Other noncurrent assets
	Liabilities
	Accounts payable
	Notes payable and related interest expense
	Accrued payroll and related liabilities
	Other accrued liabilities
	Income taxes
	Other current liabilities

(continued)

EXHIBIT 3.3   *(Continued)*

Financial Analysis: General Planning	Objective Evidence	
	Long-term debt and related interest expense (including capitalized lease obligations)	
	Other long-term liabilities	
	Equity	
	Capital stock	
	Additional paid-in capital	
	Retained earnings	
	Operations	
	Systems walkthrough	
	Tests of controls	
	Revenues	
	Cost of sales	
	Selling, general, and administrative expenses	
	Other operating expenses	
	Nonoperating income and expense	
Management Systems	**In the Case of a Tooling and Equipment Analysis (Operational)**	**Analysis Strategies: Analysis Should Review the Core Business Processes of**
Management	Contract	*Quality Goals and Objectives as They Relate to the Business Plan:*
Responsibilities/financial/ operating	Methods	Sales
Measurements/customer	Quality policies	Design
Satisfaction/management review/continuous improvement/business planning/training/technical resource activities	Feasibility reviews	Purchase
	Design methods	Manufacture
	Life cycle costing	Testing
	Mean time between equipment failures	Packing
Quality policy implementation, company goals and objectives based on customer requirements	Mean time to repair equipment	Delivery
	Cross-functional teams	Service
Strong performance metrics	Failure mode and effects analysis	Determine market conditions, business goals, and customer requirements and analysis requirements
Continuous improvement in cost, quality, throughput, delivery	Quality planning/reliability and maintainability	
	Tooling systems	*Analyst Should Review the Documents of:*
Defect detection and prevention	Control planning	
	Critical path scheduling	Results/measurements
Waste/variation reduction	Timing plan management	System administration
Closed-loop system with effective follow through	Project management	Personnel
Cost-reduction requirements	Purchasing methods	Training

38

EXHIBIT 3.3   *(Continued)*

Management Systems	In the Case of a Tooling and Equipment Analysis (Operational)	Analysis Strategies: Analysis Should Review the Core Business Processes of
Delivery requirements	Calibration and gauge repeatability and reproducibility systems	Internal analysis
Contract review methods		The closed-loop system
Feasibility capability review		System effectiveness
Quality planning/special characteristics	Product identification	*Determine the Balance between System Elements:*
	Machine run-offs	
Design methods, control and verification	Process control and capability	Planning
		Implementing
Advanced product quality planning implementation	SPC approaches	Control
	Inspection identification	Follow-up
Production part approval	Handling and packaging methods	Reporting
Purchasing methods		Evaluation
Incoming inspection methods	Delivery requirements	Cost reduction?
Product identification/ traceability/work-in-process inspection	Training records	Product quality?
	Servicing requirements and capability	On-time delivery?
		ROAs?
Inspection/test status methods	50/20 dry run	Capacity?
	Reliability methods	Capability?
Tooling setups/process control/calibration/work-in-process inspection/ preventive maintenance	20-hour dry run	Advanced quality planning?
		Customer requirements?
Statistical methods		*Current System:*
Reaction/containment plans		Prepare a paper/work flow of the existing system in force; break the system down from input (planning) to execution (implementation of the plan) to the reporting stage (what was accomplished) and when.
Final inspection/inspection identification		
Internal analysis/corrective and preventive action		
Control of nonconforming product		Obtain live copies of all documents used in the area and write the purpose of each on the reverse side of the documents and number each document to identify the position in the flow cycle of the existing system.
Handling/storage/packaging/ preservation/delivery methods		
Shipping methods		*Product Flow:*
Delivery requirements		Indicate the flow of finished products/materials through the area, starting with the first stage of activity moving through the area, routing

(continued)

EXHIBIT 3.3 *(Continued)*

Management Systems	In the Case of a Tooling and Equipment Analysis (Operational)	Analysis Strategies: Analysis Should Review the Core Business Processes of
		movement through the department through the final output from the area.
		Major Operating Problems:
		What are the major operating problems existing in the department as described by the supervisor?
		What changes are contemplated in the department? When will they take place? What effect will they have on the department's function/workload?
		Definition of change
		Timetable
		Effect of change
		What is the relationship of these plans/changes to the planned installation of the pending system?
		Physical Layout:
		Obtain copies of the physical layout (blue prints, flow diagrams, etc.) or draw one; indicate area designations, major pieces of equipment, furniture, etc. Denote names of areas that surround this department as they exist.
		Personnel Roster:
		Complete personnel roster, indicating employees names, hired dates, shifts, job classification, and positions as well as appropriate pay rates and vacations in weeks for the total department.
		Flexibility Chart:
		List employees names, functions, critical skill levels, and if they were transferred into another area or department.

EXHIBIT 3.3   *(Continued)*

Management Systems	In the Case of a Tooling and Equipment Analysis (Operational)	Analysis Strategies: Analysis Should Review the Core Business Processes of
		Equipment List and Location within the Department:
		List all the major machines and equipment located in the department; their limitations and normal operating output speeds in units per hour.
		Quantity
		Name of equipment or machine
		Limitations maximum output per hour
		Normal operating speed output per hour

4

Case in Point Using the Business Assessment

Two years ago, XYZ Manufacturing Company, a tier one supplier to General Motors and Ford, decided to improve their overall business operations in one facility and was entering the final stages of a 2-year restructuring of operations. Its target was to expand sales by 30 percent while increasing both its profitability and return on assets. As they attempted to augment and manage their growth, XYZ Manufacturing encountered many questions and decisions that could have advanced—or impeded—their future. The preceding sections of this report discussed some of the critical issues they faced: What other markets should XYZ pursue? When and how should they implement emerging technologies? How could they maximize customer and analyst relationships? Additionally, questions about product development, internal operations, and capital formation were discussed. The $50 million manufacturer of automotive parts and truck parts had downsized; closed, consolidated, and divested various facilities; relocated its Indiana headquarters; and revamped its entire supply-chain methods. The alternatives to these goals were to increase the current system to meet the new objectives or to invest in a process that would maximize its earnings. In order to reach the new sales target of $65 million through additional processes, XYZ Manufacturing would have had to invest in assets of $15 million, meaning equipment, construction, and inventory would have had to increase by the same amount as the projected growth.

Realizing that they had already invested heavily in their system, they decided to maximize their system with effective business analysis techniques. The new analysis process cost the company $25,000 (including additional training and employee compensation). Because of a 40 percent improvement in overall operational efficiency, customer's approval significantly increased and within a year the word got out about XYZ's improved business processes. The company was able to increase sales by the projected 30 percent and save over $14 million in operating and inventory costs. Once known for overpromising and underperforming, XYZ Manufacturing had improved operating earnings from their 1996 to their 1997 fiscal year through the use of effective analysis techniques and a fundamentally strong management commitment to operational improvement. Internal analysis operations experienced perhaps the most pronounced changes because of XYZ Manufacturing's finance and operational overhaul. The group reduced the time spent on bureaucratic functions and management oversight by redefining its administrative processes. In addition, they eliminated non–value-added reporting requirements, cut the time requirements for reporting from 10 to 2 hours per quarter, and reduced the administrative head count by 66 percent and the management head count by 50 percent. The company's mandate to the internal analysis group was the same he gave to other finance areas: Justify yourselves. One of the first things XYZ Manufacturing did was evaluate whether or not internal analysis should be outsourced. XYZ Manufacturing benchmarked what other companies were doing and realized that they already had the skill sets within the organization to do the job effectively.

To achieve a clearer, strategic approach to analysis, XYZ created operating teams in the areas of information technology, finance retail/wholesale, manufacturing, quality, administration, and training. Each member of the analysis staff became a member of one of the teams. The teams set overall analysis approaches and programs, maintained and enhanced the department's knowledge base and expertise, and developed training programs. In addition, they communicated with the group's internal customers on an ongoing basis, built best practices databases, and identified data interrogation opportunities.

Internal analysis teams were paired with other parts of the organization to address specific objectives. For example, the IT (Information Technology) team worked with XYZ Manufacturing's risk management department to develop a worldwide, standardized disaster recovery plan.

They organized and trained multifunctional teams to shorten cycle time for all manufacturing processes, thus reducing order to ship cycle time by 50 percent. They:

- Leveraged common data, common processing, and risk-focused authorization to obtain greater efficiency and service gains;
- Used a common data source and a standard authorization and routing process for its payroll and employee reimbursement processes;
- Reduced initial inventory by 30 percent;
- Used statistical samples to assess error rates and transaction dollar amounts to determine authorization requirements;
- Used electronic workflow and authorization to empower XYZ Manufacturing users to access real-time information, initiate actions electronically, and approve transactions electronically;
- Used automated time-collection tools and sophisticated algorithms to verify time of processes;
- Standardized payroll cycles and calendars by the hour for hourly employees and monthly for salaried employees;
- Employed a single common employee information database for both human resources and payroll;
- Direct-deposited employee paychecks fort least 80 percent of all employees;
- Processed all travel and entertainment expense reporting through a single system;
- Used data interrogation software tools to identify transactions to be analyzed;

- Before each analysis, completed a general risk assessment to determine the scope of the analysis;

- Waged significant effort to quantify the dollar impact of a risk;

- Employed analysis-based software to perform a full review of transactions, as opposed to the previous practice of analyzing only small samples of a given population;

- Shifted the bulk of their effort to performing business analysis;

- Moved the majority of accounts receivable confirmation testing and all of the information systems testing from the external analysis to internal analysis;

- Created a "Guide to Best Fiscal Practice" for use by finance personnel globally, outlining tax compliance processes and listing resources available for different situations;

- Set clear tax policies regarding transfer pricing, capital movements, corporate structure, and employee contracts;

- Upgraded systems so that tax data is captured from accounting systems and validated at the transaction level;

- Established an up-front consulting relationship, better corporate tax staff, and the business units on new business and changes in business, to assess tax implications and strategies;

- Developed a comprehensive, worldwide, multi-year tax strategy, incorporating most recent business unit plans and legal-entity reviews;

- Developed tax department bottom-line contribution goals, and presented them to senior management;

- Provided customers with a single point of contact for inquiries;

- Developed a seamless interface, XYZ Manufacturing order entry, billing, and credit;

- Used summary statements for a high volume of transactions;

- Consolidated invoice printing and distribution to take advantage of bulk-mail discounts;

- Reduced year-to-year purchasing costs by 5 percent;

- Routed orders electronically to managers when approval was required;

- Transformed credit and collections into customer service–oriented functions;

- Implemented an effective dispute-management process;

- Set days sales outstanding (DSO) goals according to best experience;

- Electronically received and posted customer payments and data;

- Implemented a client/server integrated financial system worldwide, enabling the establishment of one common general ledger;

- Implemented strict, self-imposed reporting guidelines to achieve 100 percent consistency in XYZ Manufacturing internal and external reports;

- Developed information to permit rapid dissemination of critical information at reduced cost;
- Reduced head count by 42 percent, resulting in annual savings of $9.9 million;
- Developed "Cost Management Competency Network" to focus on the design and introduction of cost management processes;
- Balanced priorities of liquidity, profitability, and growth by emphasizing return on invested capital and reduced cash conversion metrics;
- Invited employees, vendors, and customers into its educational campaign to develop cash conversion strategies;
- Designated its asset management team responsible for reengineering the financial services training curriculum to improve functions and reduce errors in order processing and collections;
- Centralized the treasury function for domestic and foreign operations;
- Made business units fully responsible for credit and collections processes;
- Developed systems to improve vendor processing, customer processing, and accounting processing in tandem with the reengineering of treasury operations;
- Used a procurement card;
- Rationalized the supply chain by consolidating and analyzing vendors;
- Moved approvals and data validation up front;
- Trimmed processing chores with blanket purchase orders;
- Developed online catalogs and online requisitioning;
- Processed all accounts payable through one system;
- Eliminated manual check generation and signatures;
- Integrated the purchasing, payable, and receivable systems and processes; and
- Created a data warehouse and used it to analyze the supply chain, forecasted needs, and supplies costs.

5

PROFITABILITY IN
TODAY'S MARKET

The push is on across organizations to not only operate, but also to thrive in an environment that is increasingly more competitive. Improving the competitive posture involves raising the quality of the goods and services provided to customers, designing and producing these goods and services more quickly, and doing so in a manner that minimizes costs and increases revenue. To accomplish these competitive objectives an organization must look internally to optimize its operations.

Optimizing organizational operations requires a model of the business (see Exhibit 5.1). This profit model represents the composition of the business and reflects the competitive issues of timeliness, cost, and quality. Its components must be able to be adjusted and the model analyzed to examine the effect of changes. Modeling allows the organization to experiment with change, and succeed or fail before implementing change. This capability is key for organizations considering significant transformations such as becoming an e-business.

Historically, business models have been a hierarchical representation of the organizational structure, which related little to these timeliness, cost, and quality issues. True business improvement is driven by optimizing the processes that a business performs.

BUSINESS MODELS

The Impact of Recession

Economic slowdowns and recessions come in all sizes and shapes. In most instances, however, their impact on sales is actually rather modest. The problem is that even a modest drop in sales penetrates the company's profitability resulting in dramatically reduced profits or even losses.

The typical effects of a recession include:

- Sales volume declines 3 to 5 percent;
- Gross margin has a $\frac{1}{2}$ to 1 percentage point reduction;
- Inventory turnover is $\frac{1}{4}$ to $\frac{1}{2}$ turn slower;

EXHIBIT 5.1 Planning Model

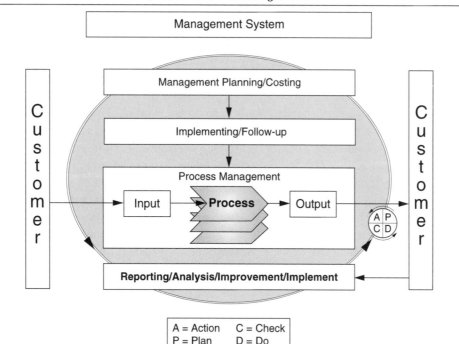

- Accounts receivable collection period is 3 to 5 days slower; and
- Net profit declines 40 to 60 percent.

At the same time, investment levels tend to build up. Inventory generally can be controlled (although with reduced sales, inventory turnover falls), but accounts receivable balances increase as customers take longer to pay. All of this culminates in a return on assets that falls appreciably and a diminished cash flow position.

Management's challenge is to understand these potential pressures and counter them directly. In an environment as uncertain as the present, it is also imperative to plan for a potential downturn without foregoing the ability to move forward should the economy prove resilient. Management must have a much more flexible planning process than has normally been employed throughout the period of extended economic growth.

Sales Up or Sales Down

In planning for the short-term environment, management must pay attention to three essential areas: (1) the relationship between sales and expenses, (2) the gross margin percentage, and (3) investment levels. In each of these areas, a strong degree of contingency planning is required. In reality, the management actions to be taken in these three areas should be the same in good economic times and bad. All that is different is the way the actions are implemented.

Sales and Expense Balancing

The single most important factor that must be understood in the variable-planning model is that sales and expenses must always be planned together. What management needs to do, regardless of the health of the economy, is generate a degree of sales productivity.

The reality is that in good times sales productivity gains are easy, often almost automatic. Generating greater sales while incurring slightly greater expenses is an achievable goal for almost every company. On the downside, however, reducing expenses as sales fall proves to be a very difficult undertaking. In large part, this is due to a lack of anticipation of the imminence of sales declines. Management is left in a reactive, defensive mode. As companies plan for next year they should bring two ideas to bear on their planning—expense creep and contingency planning. The assumption must not be made that a line item will increase simply because it has always increased in the past. Every expense increase should be challenged. Contingency planning, planning for various uncertainties, is what management is supposed to do. Contingency planning has largely been abandoned in favor of a one-way view of expense planning. Namely, how much do expenses need to be increased to support increased sales?

When the ideas of expense creep and contingency planning are brought to the planning table, they really represent a return to what was once known as "zero-based budgeting." That means that every expense must be justified in absolute dollars, not just in percentage increase form. It also means that management should have a checklist of every contingent activity indicating which expenses will be eliminated, should sales fall.

Gross Margin Maintenance

With the rampant price competition that emerges in a recession, gross margins usually decline. However, there is no real need to accept a decline. In fact, except in the most brutal of economic downturns, some companies have actually been able to engineer improved gross margins. Three factors come into play: buying, asset utilization, and cost.

Buying

There are always selected opportunities to buy at advantageous prices. In a slow-growth environment, both the number and magnitude of these opportunities are increased. The most successful companies are always positioned to capitalize on these situations.

Internal Controls.   In good times systems and controls are never maintained as vigorously as they should be. Attention to detail on control systems can prevent markdowns, inventory shrinkage, and other gross margin leaks. In tough times, training is one of the first causalities; maybe rightfully so. One training expense that must be maintained is sales training to ensure that sales personnel are fully prepared to sell in difficult times. Often the problem is not customers who are truly challenging prices, but employees who are too quick to cut deals when they do not have to.

Product Mix. The issue of product mix management becomes much more important in a slow-growth environment. When core products are under price pressure, it is essential to get the full order, including fringe items where margins are more attractive.

Asset Utilization

Far too many companies approach asset utilization the wrong way in a recession. In particular, they attempt to reduce inventory and curtail credit terms, both of which are counterproductive.

Inventory turnover is virtually impossible to improve during a recession. In an attempt to do something about turnover, many companies simply stop buying. This does nothing more than create out-of-stock situations on the best selling items with disastrous sales results. Other companies try to reduce dead inventory. This is a great idea in good times. In recessions, though, nobody wants to buy somebody else's problems.

It is not recommended that companies just let inventory slide. However, they should do little more than monitor inventory and try to hold the dollar level constant during the recession. The result will be lower turnover given lower sales. However, the strategy will not hurt sales volume, and cash flow will not be impacted.

Accounts receivable represent somewhat the same situation. In down times there is a tendency to cut terms that can also have negative sales results. A more successful strategy is to give greater attention to collection with more frequent collection calls and much earlier calls. It is also a time to get everybody involved in the collection process. Goods that are sold properly and perform for the customer represent far less of a collection problem. If management works on balancing sales and expenses, on trying to increase gross margin, and on controlling investment properly, the company can maintain profits during a recession. A select group of companies will even be able to enhance profits. Those same actions will also prove beneficial if growth continues unabated.

Costs Involved in the Design Process

The primary coordinates of value appear to be quality and cost. Market timing is also important but can be viewed as the dynamic nature of quality. Quality is defined by customer desires. Quality Function Deployment (QFD) is a process by which one can deploy quality into the product; into the system to bring forth, sustain, and retire the product; and into the enterprise as a whole. Within QFD, we deploy quality to ensure that the customer gets what is desired. But what about cost?

From the perspective of an individual, cost is a measure of value in that a consumer is willing to trade money for value. From the perspective of a project, a project is driven by value, which is potential energy. As time proceeds, the cost of a project grows and the residual value to be realized decreases. If too much cost is incurred relative to the initial value of the project, measured in terms of what the customer is willing to spend, then the residual value at the end of the project is negative. Simply put, cost deployment is a means of designing for cost.

THE BUSINESS PROCESS

Business Process Flow-1

A business process represents how work gets done in the organization. Rather than looking at the organization vertically (using a hierarchy), the correct view of the business is taken horizontally, by analyzing the business processes that flow across organizational boundaries. By nature, a business process is initiated by an event, consumes resources, performs activities, and produces goods or services. The event component of the business process allows for the analysis of timeliness issues. The resources consumed allows for the analysis of associated costs. The activities performed leads to analysis targeting process quality. Finally, the resulting goods and services lead to the analysis of product quality.

Continuous Improvement Process

The Continuous Improvement Process (CIP) allows for the implementation of improvements using data. The methods simplify targeting those elements that can create

EXHIBIT 5.2   Continuous Improvement Process

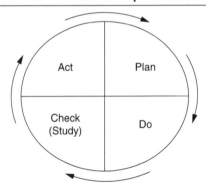

PLAN	Do
• Select Project	• Record/Observe/Collect Data
• Define Problem and Aim	• Examine/Prioritize/Analyze
• Clarify/Understand	• Justify/Evaluate Cost
• Targets/Schedules	• Develop/Test Most Likely Causes
• Inform and Register the Project	• Investigate/Determine Most Likely Solutions
• Solve/Come Up with Most Suitable Recommendation	• Test and Verify/Determine Costs and Benefits

CHECK	ACT
• Consolidate Ideas	• Plan Installation/Implementation
• Select Next Project	• Install/Implement Approved Project/Training
• Seek Approval from Management	• Maintain/Standardize

significant improvement, and lays out the processes for trial runs and verifying and adopting improvements. The seven steps of the CIP are the PDCA (Plan, Do, Check, Act) cycle of the improvement model.

CIP is a systems approach. While the implementation of improvement is process-by-process, the overall effect on the system must be watched. Many times a process optimized in isolation will, in fact, reduce the overall efficiency of the organization.

The seven steps of the CIP are described as follows.

Step 1. Identify the Improvement Opportunity

Objective: To select the appropriate process for improvement.

This step establishes the logic to carry the team through the improvement process. A process for improvement is selected based on the organization's plan, priorities, and data. Tools such as flow charts, run charts, and control charts help a team understand why the process was selected and how the improvement effort supports the organization's goals.

Step 2. Evaluate the Process

Objective: To select a challenge/problem and set a target for improvement.

This step enables the team to focus the scope of the improvement effort identified in Step 1. The team will collect and interpret data on the process using tools such as checksheets, Pareto charts, histograms, run charts, and control charts.

EXHIBIT 5.3   Identify Improvement Opportunity

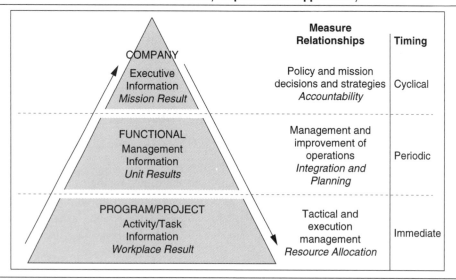

Step 3. Analyze

Objective: To identify and verify root cause(s).

The analysis stage helps teams focus on root cause(s) rather than symptoms. This step employs tools such as the cause and effect (also known as Ishikawa and Fishbone) diagram, scatter diagram, Pareto charts, and histograms. These tools logically demonstrate the selection and verification of the root cause(s).

Step 4. Take Action

Objective: To plan and implement actions that eliminate the root cause(s).

This step enables the team to propose actions that eliminate root causes. Teams evaluate the possible actions on the basis of effectiveness in eliminating the root cause and feasibility of being implemented. Performing a force field analysis aids a team in developing a plan to implement these solutions, that is, reducing the problem causing factors and increasing the problem-solving factors.

Step 5. Check Results

Objective: To confirm that the actions taken achieved the target.

This step verifies whether the actions taken have been effective in achieving the desired objective. Teams should use the same measurements that identified the improvement opportunity to study the results of their efforts. Pareto charts, run charts, control charts, and histograms can be used to show the data before and after the improvement effort.

Step 6. Standardize the Solution

Objective: To ensure that the improved level of performance is maintained.

This step ensures that the team's improvement effort becomes part of daily operations through control charts and standardizing procedures with revised flow charts of the process (see Exhibit 5.4). Additionally, this step provides opportunities to repeat, transfer, or share this improvement with other organizations.

Step 7. Plan for the Future

Objective: To plan what is to be done with any remaining problems and evaluate the team's effectiveness.

The final step in the CIP allows the team a chance to review their effort, plan future actions to continually improve the area the team started on, and evaluate the team's effectiveness. Additionally, the team should review lessons learned related to their problem-solving skills and group dynamics. An analysis form is shown in Exhibit 5.5.

EXHIBIT 5.4   Revised Flow Chart

A = Action	C = Check
P = Plan	D = Do

Profit Improvement

Although companies want to act prudently in planning, they do not want to miss any continued sales growth opportunities. The profit improvement approach's ultimate goal is to ensure that the company not only survives, but also prospers during whatever economic conditions prevail. See the profit improvement model in Exhibit 5.6.

Business Process Improvement Approach

The broad categories of analysis are shown in the diagram in Exhibit 5.7.

EXHIBIT 5.5   Continuous Improvement Analysis

Location of Event:

Date of Event or Date Begun: Date Completed:

Date Locally Approved: Date Report Submitted:

Departments Impacted by Event	
Team Leader:		Team Facilitator:	

Information Needed	Person(s) Responsible

Cost Source	Cost
Personnel Salaries	
Personnel Benefits	
External Consultants	
Material	
Lost Revenue	
Other: Describe expense	
Total	

Possible Contributors

Date	Time	Sequence of Events

EXHIBIT 5.5 *(Continued)*

	Corrective Action		Measurement Strategy	
	Person(s) Responsible	Action Due Date	Person(s) Responsible	Follow-Up Date
	Person(s) Responsible	Action Due Date	Person(s) Responsible	Follow-Up Date
Contributor or Improvement Opportunity				

EXHIBIT 5.6   Profit Improvement Model

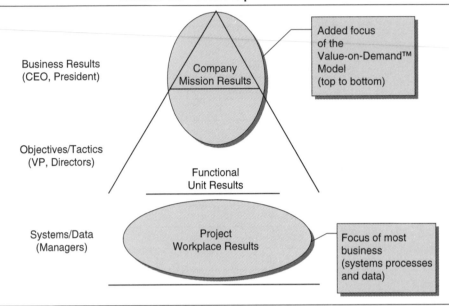

Business Results
(CEO, President)

Company
Mission Results

Added focus
of the
Value-on-Demand™
Model
(top to bottom)

Objectives/Tactics
(VP, Directors)

Functional
Unit Results

Systems/Data
(Managers)

Project
Workplace Results

Focus of most
business
(systems processes
and data)

EXHIBIT 5.7   Performance Measures

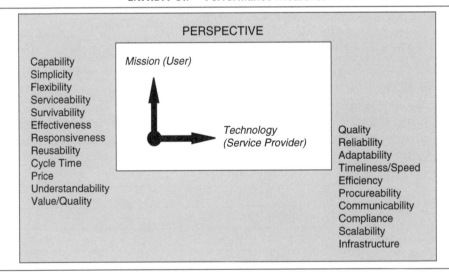

PERSPECTIVE

Capability
Simplicity
Flexibility
Serviceability
Survivability
Effectiveness
Responsiveness
Reusability
Cycle Time
Price
Understandability
Value/Quality

Mission (User)

Technology
(Service Provider)

Quality
Reliability
Adaptability
Timeliness/Speed
Efficiency
Procureability
Communicability
Compliance
Scalability
Infrastructure

6

TYPES OF
FINANCIAL STATEMENTS

FINANCIAL STATEMENTS

In the process of financial capability analysis, a great variety of formal and informal data are normally reviewed and tested for their relevance to the specific purpose of the analysis. The most common form of basic financial information that is available for publicly held companies is the set of financial statements issued under the guidelines of the Financial Accounting Standards Board (FASB) of the public accounting profession and governed by the U.S. Securities and Exchange Commission (SEC). These statements, prepared according to Generally Accepted Accounting Principles (GAAP), usually include balance sheets, income statements, and statements of cash flow.

To obtain a good representation of a company's performance, the business manager needs to focus on the business's past and current financial statements. These statements report the results of financing, investing, and operating activities and serve as a basis for assessing the success of corporate strategies. These statements also show important elements such as changes in sales, inventory, and expenses over the years and also levels of accounts receivable, fixed assets, and debt.

Because financial statements are the basis for much of the analytical effort, their nature, coverage, and limitations must first be understood before the business manager can use the data and observations derived from these statements for analytical judgments.

The Balance Sheet

The balance sheet is a snapshot of the company. It is a convenient means of organizing and summarizing what a company owns (assets), what a company owes (its liabilities), and the difference between the two (equity) at a given point in time. The balance sheet reflects conditions as of the date chosen for reporting purposes. These balance sheet accounts also represent the cumulative effects of all decisions and transactions that have taken place since the inception of the business.

Financial accounting rules require that all transactions be recorded at cost and retroactive adjustments to recorded values are made only in limited circumstances. As a consequence, balance sheets display assets and liabilities, acquired or incurred at different times, at the historical cost. Because the market value of assets can change, particularly in the case of longer-lived items, the costs stated on the balance sheet probably do not reflect the market value.

Some additional points regarding the balance sheet are worth noting. It is important to recognize the difference between cash and other assets. All the assets on the balance sheet are stated in terms of dollars, but only cash represents actual money. Cash is considered a current asset because it is ready immediately for payment of goods and services. The other assets listed as current on the balance sheet represent accounts that can quickly be converted to cash, usually within one year. All other assets listed on the balance sheet are considered noncash assets because they are not expected to be converted to cash within the period of one year from the date on the balance sheet.

The Income Statement

The income statement measures the results of the operating activities of a business for a specified period of time, usually one year. Simplistically represented, it is Revenues − Expenses = Net Income. It reflects the effect of management's operating decisions, as well as externalities beyond management's control, such as changes in market demand, changes in material prices, and the impact these have on business performance. The income statement is presented in such a way that allows the business manager to examine profits or losses after each expense item has been deducted.

An income statement that has been prepared using GAAP will show revenue when it accrues. This may differ from the time that revenue is actually collected. Financial managers have several options when it comes to revenue recognition. However, regardless of the method used, GAAP must be followed. A company can choose to recognize revenue and expenses at different times, varying year to year results. However, when aggregated, the net effect is zero.

The Statement of Cash Flows

The statement of cash flows summarizes the business's sources and uses of cash over a specified period. This statement captures both the current operating results and the accompanying changes in the balance sheet. It gives the business manager a dynamic picture of the ultimate changes in cash relating to operating, investing, and financing activities for a given period of time. An example is included in Appendix C. The statement of cash flows explains the change in cash between the beginning and end of the accounting period. Because it also explains the major investing and financing activities of the period, it helps explain changes in various items on the balance sheet. The statement of cash flows also relates to the income statement in that it shows how operations affected cash during the period.

Analyzing a contractor's cash flows is important because cash is often necessary to pay subcontractors or to maintain operations. As a result, business managers must examine and understand the difference between the accrual income reported on the income statement and the related cash flow from revenues and expenditures. Over the life of a company, in any particular year, cash inflows and outflows may deviate from accruals on the income statement by a wide margin. Over a period of several years, a cash-based income statement should begin to approach the true income generated by the business. The business manager must consider a series of annual flows to obtain a meaningful image of how the business is operating. If a company cannot generate cash in sufficient amounts and at the right times, it faces financial difficulty and even bankruptcy. Since financing cash flows are not an indefinite source of funds, the business must generate cash internally from operations to grow and to stay financially responsible.

The analysis and interpretation of a statement of cash flows centers on the basic question of what sources and uses of cash are likely to recur in the future. The statement of cash flows, like the balance sheet and the income statement, is historical in focus, but the business manager must attempt to use this data to predict the future cash flows of the company. Analysis of any statement of cash flows should focus on the current and projected adequacy of the Cash Flow from Operations (CFO), as this is the one cash source that the business must ultimately use to repay the principal and interest of a loan or dividends on an equity investment. A second objective should be the identification of the actual free cash flow for the current period and a projection of the expected future recurring free cash flows.

The first step in any cash flow analysis should involve a comparison of the CFO with the net income for the same period. The CFO is effectively a measure of the accrual net income of a company on a cash basis. This measure is of significance not only because of its relationship to dividend and debt payments, but also because it is a relatively invariant measure, far less easily manipulated by a company's executives. The CFO is a complex number and deserves detailed analysis because it can substantially differ from accrual net income.

After comparing CFO to net income, the business manager must relate the past, as reflected in the historical statement of cash flows, to expectations regarding the future. Some very simple rules, coupled with these classifications, can make cash flow analysis relatively straightforward:

- Long-term cash sources should be used to fund long-term cash uses. In general, the term of cash sources should always exceed the term for the cash uses.
- Long-term cash sources may be used to fund short-term cash uses; however, short-term cash sources should never be used to fund long-term cash uses.
- Recurring cash sources should be used to fund recurring uses.
- Recurring cash sources may be used to fund nonrecurring uses; but nonrecurring sources should never be used to fund recurring uses.

These rules follow sound business logic. If, for instance, the operations line is truly the only source of cash flow to draw on for loan or investment repayment, then operations must occur before payback can take place. If a company fails to follow the above rules, it may lead to a situation in which operations will be inadequate to generate needed cash flows on a timely basis, thus necessitating the acquisition of cash from other sources (e.g., investors, creditors, or via asset sale). The business manager's objective is to determine whether a company follows these rules and if the business does not, to estimate the impact of the risk on the business's financial stability.

FINANCIAL STATEMENT ANALYSIS

Financial Statement Review Using Ratio Analysis

Although a glance at the financial statements may highlight areas of concern, it is often difficult to interpret all of the information presented on these statements. For example, knowing that there is a large amount of inventory in the warehouse is not as helpful as knowing how quickly the company is turning over its inventory compared to others in the industry (i.e., use of the inventory turnover ratio). Ratios have been developed to provide a comprehensive way to absorb the data disclosed on financial statements. Ratios, in general, involve a process of standardization. Ratios measure a company's crucial relationships by relating inputs (costs) with outputs (benefits) and facilitate comparisons of these relationships over time and across companies. Traditional ratio analysis provides insightful information to the business manager by summarizing data from financial statements and placing it into an easily understood format.

The easiest job the business manager will have is calculating the ratios. The availability of financial analysis packages and computerized databases permit the business manager to do much of the analytical work on the computer. The important and challenging part of the analysis is the interpretation of the results. These interpretations require the business manager to understand the reason for the analysis, to identify the current conditions facing the industry, and to understand the important accounting principles underlying the financial statements.

The business manager can perform two different forms of ratio analysis: time-series analysis (comparing ratios for the same firm over time) and cross-section analysis (comparing ratios for the same period with other companies in the industry). A time-series analysis of a particular firm's financial statement ratios provides a historical tracking of the trends and variability in the ratios over time. The business manager can study the impact of economic conditions (i.e., recession or inflation), industry conditions (e.g., shift in regulatory status, new technology), and firm-specific conditions (e.g., shift in corporate strategy, new management) on the time pattern of these ratios.

Using cross-sectional analysis, the business manager can make comparisons between the contractor being analyzed and other related companies. The business manager needs to be very selective when identifying the companies with which to compare. The business manager should select companies with similar products, strategies, and size. Also, the business manager must keep in mind differences in accounting methods, operations, financing, and so forth. Because this is often difficult, a common approach is to use average industry ratios as benchmarks.

Industry norms may be calculated directly through the use of computerized databases such as Standard & Poor's Database. Alternatively, industry profiles are available from sources such as Robert Morris Associates (RMA) and Dun & Bradstreet's (D&B) Industrial Handbook. These sources provide common-size balance sheets, income statements, and selected ratios on an industry and company basis.

The broad categories of analysis that measure such relationships are listed as follows.

Liquidity analysis measures the adequacy of a company's cash resources to meet its near-term cash obligations.

Ratios:

- Current ratio
- Quick ratio
- Cash ratio
- Cash flow from operations ratio
- Defensive interval
- Net working capital to total assets ratio

Asset utilization analysis evaluates the levels of output generated by the assets employed by the business.

Ratios:

- Total asset turnover ratio
- Fixed assets turnover ratio
- Inventory turnover ratio
- Average number of days inventory in stock
- Receivables turnover ratio
- Average number of days receivables are outstanding

Profitability analysis measures the net income of the company relative to its revenues and capital investments.

Ratios:

- Gross profit margin ratio
- Net profit margin ratio
- Pretax margin ratio
- Basic earning power ratio
- Return on assets ratio
- Return on equity ratio

Debt utilization analysis examines the business's capital structure in terms of the mix of its financing sources and the ability of the company to satisfy its longer-term debt and investment obligations.

Ratios:

- Debt to equity ratio
- Total debt to total assets ratio
- Times interest earned ratio
- Cash coverage ratio
- Debt to total capital ratio

Profitability affects solvency, and the efficiency with which assets are used (as measured by asset utilization analysis) impacts the analysis of profitability. In measuring these relationships, ratios provide a profile of a contractor. An analysis of the ratios can provide insight into a contractor's performance, economic characteristics, competitive strategies, and abilities.

Ratio analysis should be fairly comprehensive. Each ratio included in this chapter will assist the business manager in focusing on a particular aspect of the company. At times, a full analysis is not possible due to time constraints or limited information. In this case, a "condensed" ratio analysis can be applied.

Liquidity Analysis

Liquidity analysis is used to assess the risk level and ability of a company to meet its current obligations. Satisfying these obligations requires the use of cash resources available as of the balance sheet date and the cash generated through the operating cycle of the company.

The concept of working capital relies on the classification of assets and liabilities into "current" and "noncurrent" categories as shown in Exhibit 6.1. Current assets include cash and other assets that the business expects to convert to cash or consume within one year from the date of the balance sheet. Current liabilities are liabilities the business expects to pay within one year. Net working capital is simply current assets minus current liabilities. On the typical balance sheet, there are a variety of current assets and current liabilities.

The ratios used in short-term liquidity analysis evaluate the adequacy of the company's cash resources relative to its cash obligations. Its cash resources can be measured by (1) the business's current cash balance and potential sources of cash or (2) its net cash flows from operations. The business's cash obligations can be measured by either (1) its current obligations or (2) the cash outflows arising from operations. Conceptually, the ratios differ in whether levels (amounts shown on the balance sheet) or flows (cash inflows and outflows) are used to gauge the relationships. It is important to distinguish between marketable securities and long-term investments. Marketable securities are securities such as stocks or bonds that are actively traded on national exchanges and have bid and ask prices (buy and sell prices). Long-term investments are investments in stocks or bonds that are either not marketable, or are not meant to serve as a cash resource.

EXHIBIT 6.1   Current Assets and Liabilities

Current Assets	Current Liabilities
• Cash and cash equivalents • Marketable securities • Accounts receivable • Inventories • Prepaid expenses	• Short-term debt • Accounts payable • Accrued liabilities

A more conservative measure of liquidity, the quick ratio, excludes inventory from cash resources, recognizing that the conversion of inventory to cash is less certain both in terms of timing and amount. The other assets in the numerator are "quick assets" because they can be quickly converted to cash. The quick ratio is a variant of the current ratio.

The use of the current or quick ratio implicitly assumes that the current assets will eventually be converted to cash. Realistically, however, it is not anticipated that companies will actually liquidate their current assets to pay their current liabilities. Certain levels of inventories and receivables, as well as payables and accruals (which finance inventories and receivables), are always needed to maintain operations. If all current assets and liabilities are reduced to zero, the business will cease to operate. It is assumed that the process of generating inventories, collecting receivables, and so on is ongoing. These ratios, therefore, measure the "margin of safety" provided by the cash resources relative to obligations.

The cash ratio is the most conservative of these measures as it includes only actual cash and cash equivalent balances (marketable securities) to measure cash resources. It excludes possible poor receivable or inventory ratios, which will be discussed in the next section.

The cash flow from operations ratio addresses the issues of convertibility to cash, turnover, and the need for minimum levels of working capital (cash) to maintain operations by measuring liquidity through a comparison of actual cash flows (instead of current and potential cash resources) with current liabilities.

The defensive interval provides an intuitive "feel" for a company's liquidity, albeit a most conservative one. This measure is essentially a "worst case" scenario that tells us how many days the business could maintain its present level of operations with its present cash resources without the generation of any additional revenues. It compares the currently available "quick" sources of cash (cash, marketable securities, and accounts receivable) with the estimated outflows needed to operate the business (projected expenditures). There are various forms of the defensive interval as well as various methods one can use to arrive at the projected expenditures. The calculation of the defensive interval uses the current year income statement data as the estimate of projected expenditures.

The net working capital to total assets ratio is a good indicator of a company's liquidity. A low ratio may indicate low levels of liquidity. Liquidity analysis is not independent of asset utilization (activity) analysis. Poor receivables or inventory turnover (how many times per year inventory is sold off) limits the usefulness of the current and quick ratios, since the reported amounts of these components of current assets may not truly represent sources of liquidity. Also, obsolete inventory or uncollectable receivables are unlikely to be sources of cash. Consequently, short-term liquidity ratios should be examined in conjunction with turnover ratios.

Asset Utilization (Activity) Analysis

To carry out operations, a company needs to invest in both short-term (inventory and accounts receivable) and long-term (property, plant, and equipment) assets. Activity ratios describe the relationship between the business's level of operations (usually defined as sales) and the assets needed to sustain the activity. The higher the ratio, the more efficient the business's operations, as relatively fewer assets are required to maintain a given level of operation (sales). By monitoring the trends in these ratios over time and comparing them to other companies in the industry, the business manager can point out potential trouble spots or opportunities. Although these ratios do not measure profitability or liquidity directly, they are ultimately an important factor affecting those performance indicators.

Activity ratios can be used to forecast a company's capital requirements (both operating and long term). Increases in sales may require investments in additional assets. Activity ratios enable the business manager to forecast these possible requirements and to assess the business's ability to acquire the assets needed to sustain the forecasted growth.

An overall activity measure that relates sales to total assets is the total asset turnover ratio. This relationship provides a measure of overall investment efficiency by aggregating the joint impact of both short- and long-term assets. Lower total asset turnover ratios indicate longer shelf life for inventory and slower collection of receivables, assuming cash balances and other short-term investments are not unusually high. This indicates a cutback in demand for a company's products or sales to customers whose ability to pay is uncertain. This might signal one or more of the following:

- The business's income is overstated;
- Future production cutbacks may be required; or
- Potential liquidity problems may exist.

The fixed assets turnover ratio measures the efficiency of long-term capital investment and reflects the level of sales maintained or generated by investments in productive capacity. The business manager must consider changes in its level over time. These changes can be a function of a number of subtle factors. Sales growth is normally continuous, albeit at varying rates. However, increases in capacity to meet that sales growth are discrete, depending on the addition of new factories, warehouses, stores, and so forth.

The life cycle of a company or product includes a number of stages: start-up, growth, maturity, and decline. Start-up companies' initial turnover may be low, as their level of operations (sales) is well below their productive capacity. As sales grow, however, turnover will continually improve until the limits of the company's initial capacity are reached. However, the increase in capital investment needed to maintain the growth will then impact unfavorably on that ratio until the business's growth satisfies the new capacity. This process will continue until the business matures and its sales and capacity level off, only to reverse when the business enters its decline stage.

Additional problems can result from the timing of a company's purchase of assets. Two companies with similar operating efficiencies, the same productive capacity, and the same level of sales may show differing ratios depending on when the companies' assets were acquired. The business with the older assets would show a higher turnover ratio, as the accumulated depreciation would tend to lower the carrying value of that firm's assets. In other words, the accumulation of depreciation expense would result in improving the ratio (especially if the business uses accelerated depreciation methods or short depreciable lives) even if actual efficiency did not change.

An offsetting and complicating factor is that the productivity of assets also depends on their acquisition date. Newer assets, while purchased at higher prices, probably operate more efficiently. The use of gross asset value (before depreciation) rather than net fixed assets would alleviate this shortcoming.

The inventory turnover ratio indicates the efficiency of the company's inventory management. A higher ratio indicates that inventory does not languish in warehouses or on the shelves but rather turns over rapidly as it moves from time of acquisition to sale. Inventory turnover can be used to calculate the days' sales in inventory ratio (the average number of days that inventory is held until it is sold). The cost of goods sold is simply the cost of the inventory. The average inventory number is calculated by adding the inventory number from the balance sheet to the inventory number from the previous year's balance sheet, and dividing by two.

The average number of days inventory are in stock (days' sales in inventory ratio) tells the business manager how many days inventory sits before it is sold. Obviously, the shorter the time inventory sits before it is sold, the more times it can be turned over, thus resulting in more sales.

The receivables turnover ratio and the days' sales in receivables (the average number of days that receivables are outstanding) are calculated in a similar manner. The average accounts receivable number is calculated in the same way as average inventory, as explained previously. This ratio gives an indication of how many times a company collected on its credit sales during the year.

The average number of days receivables are outstanding (days' sales in receivables ratio) shows how many days on average it takes to collect from credit sales. This ratio is also called the average collection period. A large number may indicate either poor collection policies or leeway given to customers in order to establish above-average customer satisfaction. These receivables ratios (1) measure the effectiveness of the company's credit policies (loans to its customers) and (2) indicate the level of investment in receivables needed to maintain the business's level of sales.

Profitability Analysis

Stockholders invest with the expectation that the business will earn profits. Profits are also required to ensure the business's long-term growth and staying power. A company's profitability can be measured in several differing but interrelated dimensions. First, there is the relationship of a company's profits to sales, for example, what is the residual return to the business per sales dollar? The second type of measure, return on investment (ROI), relates profits to the investment required to generate them. The following section briefly defines these measures and then elaborates on their use in financial statement analysis.

One measure of a company's profitability is the relationship between the business's costs and its sales. The greater a company's ability to control costs in relation to its revenues, the more its earnings power is enhanced. The gross profit margin ratio captures the relationship between sales and manufacturing costs. It is a measure of the raw earning power of the company. The net profit margin ratio shows how many dollars of bottom line net income are generated per dollar of sales. This ratio takes into account all expenses and taxes that the business has to pay out, as well as all revenues coming in to the company. The pretax margin ratio is calculated after financing costs (interest) but prior to income taxes. EBT stands for earnings before taxes, and serves as the numerator in the formula. The basic earning power ratio shows the earning power of a company's assets without regard to taxes or financing. This ratio should be examined in conjunction with turnover ratios to help pinpoint potential problems regarding asset management. Return on assets (ROA) measures a company's performance in using assets to generate earnings. In actuality, the number can be interpreted as profit per dollar of assets.

It should be noted that the ROA measure is sometimes computed "after interest" as either net income or earnings before taxes (EBT) over assets. Preinterest measures of profitability facilitate the comparison of companies with different degrees of leverage. Using postinterest measures of profit negates this advantage and makes leveraged companies appear less profitable by charging earnings for payments (interest) to some capital providers (lenders) but not others (stockholders). Ratios that use total assets in the denominator should include total earnings (before interest) in the numerator. The ROA measure can be interpreted in two different ways. First, it is an indicator of management's operating efficiency (how well management is using the assets at its disposal to generate profits). Alternatively, it can be viewed as the total return accruing to the providers of capital, independent of the source of capital.

The second commonly used ROI measure focuses on the returns accruing to the business's common and preferred shareholders. A more general definition of this relationship computes the return on total stockholders' equity (ROE).

Both ROA and ROE are commonly cited numbers measuring performance over a prior period. The relationship between ROA and ROE can be understood in terms of the company's relationship to its creditors and shareholders. The creditors and shareholders provide the capital needed by the business to acquire the assets needed for the business. In return, they expect to be rewarded with their share in the business's profits. The business manager should compare both ratios to the company's historical performance measures and to industry ratios to verify if there have been any substantial operating changes.

Debt Utilization Analysis

A company's financing is obtained from debt and equity. The greater the proportion of debt relative to equity, the greater the risk to the business as a whole. Two important factors should be noted when analyzing the capital structure of a company: (1) the relative debt levels themselves and (2) the trend over time in the proportion of debt to equity.

Total debt is simply the total liabilities account on the balance sheet. Total capital is defined as total equity + total debt. The business manager should be aware that since total assets = total liabilities + owner's equity, total capital is the same as total assets.

The higher the debt ratio, the riskier the business. As with other ratios, however, industry factors play an important role both in the level of debt as well as in the nature of the debt, whether short or long term, variable or fixed, and the relative proportion of different maturities. Capital-intensive industries tend to have high levels of debt because debt is needed to finance property, plant, and equipment. To manage the debt, the maturity of debt should match the level of the assets acquired.

In addition to servicing debt, internally generated cash flows are also needed for purposes of investment. The liquidity ratios do not take this aspect into consideration. Cash Flow from Operations is calculated without any deduction for the cost of operating capacity. Net income, with its provision for depreciation, reflects the use of assets. However, even with minimal inflation rates, over their relatively long service life, replacement costs of these assets tend to be significantly higher, and historical cost depreciation cannot adequately account for their replacement. Neither net income nor cash from operations makes any provision for the capital required for growth. A company's long-term solvency is a function of (1) its ability to finance the replacement and expansion of its investment in productive capacity and (2) the amount of cash left for debt repayment after paying for capital investments.

The debt to equity ratio shows the proportion of debt (both short and long term) to equity within the capital structure of the company. The higher this number, the riskier the business, all else being equal.

The total debt to total assets ratio takes into account all debts of all maturities to all creditors. This ratio shows how much debt a company has per dollar of assets.

The times interest earned ratio is a measure of how well a company can cover its interest expense with its pretax and preinterest dollars.

The cash coverage ratio adds back depreciation to the numerator in the times interest earned ratio. The numerator is now earnings before interest and taxes (EBIT) + depreciation, which is a basic measure of the company's ability to generate cash from operations. The cash flow from operations, as discussed before, is used as a measure of cash flow available that can be used to meet various obligations.

The debt to total capital ratio captures the relationship between the amount of debt a company has and the total capital of the company.

Analysis of a company's capital structure is essential to the evaluation of its long-term risk and return prospects. Leveraged companies accrue excess returns to their common shareholders so long as the rate of return on the investments financed by debt exceeds the cost of debt. The benefits of financial leverage bring additional risks, however, in the form of fixed costs that adversely affect profitability if demand declines. Because priority is given to interest and principal payments to debt holders, these claims can have a severely negative impact on a company when adversity strikes. The inability to meet these obligations can lead to default and possibly bankruptcy. In this sense, financial leverage works in two ways: It enhances the return to shareholders during profitable years, but during periods when sales are low, the leverage works the other way and produces returns that are worse than would be expected without the borrowing.

An example of how financial leverage affects a company is shown in Exhibit 6.2.

For ease of illustration, taxes have been ignored in this example. Currently, Company ABC has no debt in its capital structure. The company is considering a restructuring of

EXHIBIT 6.2   Example of Financial Leverage Affects on Company ABC

Current and Proposed Capital Structures for Company ABC

	Current	Proposed
Assets	$8,000,000	$8,000,000
Debt	$ 0	$4,000,000
Equity	$8,000,000	$4,000,000
Debt/equity ratio	0	1
Share price	$ 20	$ 20
Shares outstanding	400,000	200,000
Interest rate	10%	10%

Current Capital Structure: No Debt

	Recession	Expected	Expansion
EBIT	$ 500,000	$1,000,000	$1,500,000
Interest	0	0	0
Net income	$ 500,000	$1,000,000	$1,500,000
ROE	6.25%	12.50%	18.75%
EPS	$ 1.25	$ 2.50	$ 3.75

Proposed Capital Structure: Debt = $4,000,000

	Recession	Expected	Expansion
EBIT	$ 500,000	$1,000,000	$1,500,000
Interest	$ 400,000	$ 400,000	$ 400,000
Net income	$ 100,000	$ 600,000	$1,100,000
ROE	2.50%	15.00%	27.50%
EPS	$ .50	$ 3.00	$ 5.50

its capital structure that would involve $4,000,000 of debt, which would be used to re-purchase 200,000 shares of stock ($4,000,000/$20 per share), leaving only 200,000 shares outstanding. After the restructuring, the company would now have a debt to equity ratio of 1 (50 percent debt and 50 percent equity). The interest expense at a 10 percent rate would now be $400,000. The three scenarios described involve different assumptions regarding the business's EBIT (earnings before interest and taxes). Notice the ROE and earnings per share (EPS) numbers for the no debt capital structure compared with those of the capital structure with debt. The EBIT numbers are the same, of course, under both structures. When debt is used, the company has an interest expense to pay each year. This lowers net income for each of the three scenarios: recession, expected, and expansion. However, because there are fewer shares outstanding, the return on equity and the EPS are improved when the expected and expansion scenarios occur. Note what happens during the recession scenario—the capital structure with no debt achieves better numbers. This is because interest expense is simply too much to handle with an EBIT of $500,000. This really brings to life leverage and the risks involved in using it. During good times, when demand is high and revenues are large, returns are *greater* than without leverage. However, if the economy turns sour, and sales drop off, returns are *worse* than without leverage.

Debt Covenants

To protect themselves, long-term creditors often impose restrictions on the borrowing company's ability to incur additional debt as well as on dividend payments. The debt covenants that control these activities are often expressed in terms of working capital, cumulative profitability, and net worth. It is, therefore, important to monitor various ratios to ensure that their levels are in compliance with the debt covenant specifications. Violations of debt covenants are frequently an "event of default" under loan agreements, making the debt due immediately. When covenants are violated, borrowers must either repay the debt (not usually possible) or obtain waivers from lenders. Such waivers often require additional collateral, restrictions on the business's operations, or higher interest rates.

The Prediction of Bond Ratings

Bond ratings are issued by bond rating agencies, the most prominent of which are Moody's and Standard & Poor's. The ratings attest to the creditworthiness of the company. The probability that adverse conditions will result in financial difficulties is taken into consideration in assessing the likelihood of the company defaulting on its interest or principal payments and is, therefore, reflected in its bond ratings. In addition, the bond indentures and the degree of protection afforded in the event of bankruptcy are considered when the ratings decision is made.

Market Value Analysis

When assessing the financial capability of a publicly held company, there are two other important ratios to examine. The price/earnings ratio (PE) shows how much investors are willing to pay for a dollar of company earnings. Care is needed in the interpretation of this number. A high PE might mean investors are willing to pay more now for future growth, or the company has very little earnings. Similarly, a low ratio may indicate an undervalued company with average earnings, or an appropriately valued company with little earnings. This is an important ratio to compare to others in the same industry.

The other market value ratio is the market/book ratio. This number compares the market value of a company's investments to their historical costs, as shown on the balance sheet. The book value per share is simply the business's common equity divided by the total number of shares outstanding. The market/book ratio gives a good indication of how investors regard the business. High ratios would normally describe a company that has high returns on equity, therefore, investors are willing to pay more for these high returns.

Accounting for the Different Reporting
Periods of Ratio Components

The business manager needs to be aware of a certain problem when using ratio analysis. When a ratio contains a numerator from the income statement and a denominator from the balance sheet, an adjustment needs to be made. The income statement measures performance over a period of time, usually one year, while the balance sheet shows results as of a particular date. The balance sheet data need to be converted to a yearly number by averaging current year data and the previous year's data. For example, the total asset turnover ratio, which was discussed earlier in the chapter, requires the conversion. It is calculated by dividing sales by average total assets. The sales number appears on the income statement, and the total asset account is on the balance sheet. To obtain an average total asset number, simply add the current year number with the previous year's total asset number and divide by two. However, when comparing to industry averages, using the number as it appears on the balance sheet (current year) is preferred because most industry numbers are calculated in that manner. The business manager simply needs to be aware of the calculation methods used for the industry numbers, so that apples are compared with apples.

Industry norms are used to compare the ratios of a company to the relative performance of its competitors. However, the industry benchmark may have limited usefulness if the whole industry or major companies in that industry are doing poorly. The industry benchmark should be used only with an understanding of the industry's overall performance and potentials. The business manager compares the relationship of the ratios within the company as well as between the company and its industry over time in order to analyze occurring trends. As long as the business continues its operations in the same manner that resulted in its financial status to date, the trends will likely illustrate the business's future. Of course, this is also dependent on a constant environment. If the business's ratios are worse or deteriorating against the industry ratios, the business may be in serious trouble. Other considerations are the specific industry's opportunities and obstacles. Even if a company fits well within its industry, the aggregate industry must still be profitable and stable in order to provide the business with a beneficial benchmark. Therefore, a company's financial trends, objectives, and managerial plans (how the business plans to operate) in comparison to its industry and the economy in general, essentially determine the business's strength and enduring capabilities.

Information for Analysis

Financial information is obtainable from a wide array of sources. Information sources can range from the daily newspaper to managed databases to the Internet. The key is to obtain the information that is most applicable and relevant to the analysis. For financial statements, ratio calculations, and industry benchmarks, a *Dun and Bradstreet Financial Record Report* would be beneficial. For analysis of specific corporate credit risk, the business's specific financial statements, SEC filings, and investment advisory services such as Moody's and Standard & Poor's are the best sources of information.

ADVISORY SERVICES

The Securities and Exchange Commission

The SEC has the power to regulate trading on the stock exchanges and to require corporate disclosure of information relevant to the stockholders of publicly traded companies. Furthermore, the SEC has the power to dictate accounting conventions. Information available through the SEC consists of corporate income statements, balance sheets, detailed support of accounting information, and internal data not always found in a company's annual report. In addition, companies are required to file 10-K, 8-K, and 10-Q forms with the SEC. The annual 10-K report is perhaps the most widely known and can usually be obtained free of charge directly from the company, rather than paying the SEC a copying charge. This report should be read in combination with the business's annual report, as it contains the same type of information but in greater detail. The 8-K report must be filed when the corporation undergoes some important event that stockholders should know about such as changes in control, bankruptcy, resignation of officers or directors, and other material events. 10-Q statements are filed quarterly, no later than 45 days after the end of the quarter. This report includes quarterly financial statements, changes in stockholdings, legal proceedings, and other matters. There are many other SEC reports, but these three are the most relevant.

Data used to compute ratios are available only at specific points in time, primarily when financial statements are issued. For annual reports, these points in time correspond to the end of a company's operating cycle, and the reported levels of assets and liabilities generally do not reflect the business's level of normal operations. As a result, certain ratios will not reflect the actual (short-term) operating relationships, especially in the case of seasonal businesses. For example, inventories and accounts payable will most likely be below the average operating levels at the end of the operating cycle. This results in companies trying to look more profitable by pumping up income over assets used. Reference to interim statements is one way of alleviating this problem.

The timing of accounting entries leads to another problem. Transactions at year end by management can lead to manipulation of the ratios to show them in a more favorable light. For example, a company with a current ratio (current assets/current liabilities) of 1.5 ($3 million/$2 million) can increase it to 2.0 ($2 million/$1 million) by simply using cash of $1 million to reduce accounts payable immediately prior to the end of period.

Investment Advisory Services

The first investment information service, Moody's, is owned by Dun & Bradstreet. This service publishes several databases that analyze a variety of corporations. Moody's Manuals are widely used and present historical financial data on listed companies, on their officers, and on the companies' general corporate condition. The Manuals are divided into several categories (Banks and Finance, Industrial, Municipals and Government, Over the Counter [OTC] Industrial, Public Utility, and Transportation). Each manual has a biweekly news supplement that updates quarterly earnings, dividend announcements, mergers, and other news of interest. *Moody's Bond Record,* a monthly publication, contains data on corporate debt ratings. Corporate bond information includes the interest coupon, payment dates, call price, Moody's rating, yield to maturity, and other market-related data.

The second major source of information is the Standard & Poor's Corporation, a subsidiary of McGraw-Hill. Standard & Poor's has comprehensive coverage of financial data. Standard & Poor's Corporate Records are similar to Moody's Manuals, except the former are organized alphabetically rather than by trade categories. The Corporate Records are published monthly and updated daily with supplements. Information found in the volumes includes historical company background, financial statements, news announcements, earnings updates, and other news of general interest. Ratings for a corporation's debt are located in *Standard & Poor's Bond Guide.*

The financial statements are the core information source for financial analysis, but the investment services provided by Moody's and Standard & Poor's are helpful for focusing the analysis. Business managers should review this information for a summary assessment of a company before analyzing the business's financial statements. In addition, discussions with the business's management will provide further clarity to important issues used for assessing the managerial direction of the corporation, its goals, and obstacles.

Summary

The preceding sections covered many aspects of financial capability analysis including financial statements, formulas for ratios, and sources of financial data. Throughout the chapter, four sources of financial data were mentioned: Moody's, Standard & Poor's, Dun & Bradstreet, and individual companies. All of the topics covered, such as financial statements (see Exhibits 6.3 through 6.5 for examples of Financial Statements), ratio analysis (as shown in Exhibit 6.6 and 6.7), leverage, agency credit ratings, and review of any other financial/business data are interrelated and provide insight from various points of interest.

EXHIBIT 6.3   The XYZ Manufacturing Company

Assets	1998	1999
Current		
Cash and cash equivalents	$ 2,994,000	$ 2,868,000
Marketable securities, at cost (approximate market)	$ 240,000	$ 321,000
	$ 3,234,000	$ 3,189,000
Trade accounts receivable, less allowances of		
117,000 in 1999 and 99,000 in 1998	$ 3,630,000	$ 3,165,000
Finance subsidiary—receivables	$ 99,000	$ 93,000
Inventories	$ 3,147,000	$ 3,057,000
Prepaid expenses and other assets	$ 3,192,000	$ 3,240,000
Total current assets	$13,302,000	$12,744,000

EXHIBIT 6.3 *(Continued)*

Assets	1998	1999
Investments and other assets		
Investments		
XYZ Enterprises, Inc.	$ 1,494,000	$ 1,554,000
XYZ Limited	$ 1,776,000	$ 1,644,000
Other	$ 3,375,000	$ 3,291,000
Finance subsidiary—receivables	$ 678,000	$ 285,000
Long-term receivables and other assets	$ 2,604,000	$ 1,911,000
Total Investments and other assets	$ 9,927,000	$ 8,685,000
Property, plant, and equipment		
Land	$ 591,000	$ 609,000
Buildings and improvements	$ 4,848,000	$ 4,587,000
Machinery and equipment	$10,140,000	$ 9,411,000
Containers	$ 1,209,000	$ 1,122,000
Total property, plant and equipment	$16,788,000	$15,729,000
Less allowance for depreciation	$ 5,601,000	$ 5,151,000
Fixed assets	$11,187,000	$10,578,000
Goodwill and other intangible assets	$ 1,647,000	$ 1,149,000
Total assets	$36,036,000	$33,156,000
Current liabilities		
Accounts payable and accrued expenses	$ 6,651,000	$ 6,759,000
Loans and notes payable	$ 4,227,000	$ 5,901,000
Finance subsidiary	$ 732,000	$ 315,000
Current maturities of long-term debt	$ 57,000	$ 45,000
Accrued taxes	$ 3,846,000	$ 2,889,000
Total current liabilities	$15,513,000	$15,909,000
Long-term debt	$ 4,284,000	$ 3,360,000
Other liabilities	$ 2,175,000	$ 1,977,000
Deferred income taxes	$ 339,000	$ 246,000
Total liabilities	$22,311,000	$21,492,000
Shareholders' equity		
Common stock .75 par value-		
Authorized: 8,400,000,000 shares;		
Issued: 5,110,578,897 shares in 1999;		
5,088,608,520 shares in 1998	$ 1,278,000	$ 1,272,000
Capital surplus	$ 3,258,000	$ 2,613,000
Reinvested earnings	$28,374,000	$24,495,000
Unearned compensation related to outstanding		
restricted stock	$ (255,000)	$ (300,000)
Foreign currency translation adjustment	$ (1,260,000)	$ (813,000)
	$31,395,000	$27,267,000
Less treasury stock, at cost (1,218,218,451 common		
shares in 1999; 1,168,294,866 common shares		
in 1998)	$17,643,000	$15,603,000
Stockholders' equity	$13,752,000	$11,664,000
Total liabilities and shareholders' equity	$36,063,000	$33,156,000

EXHIBIT 6.4   The XYZ Manufacturing Company

Year Ended December 31,	1999	1998	1997
Net operating revenues	$41,871,000	$39,222,000	$34,716,000
Cost of goods	$15,480,000	$15,165,000	$13,947,000
Gross profit	$26,391,000	$24,057,000	$20,769,000
Selling, administrative, and general expenses	$17,085,000	$15,747,000	$13,812,000
Operating income	$ 9,306,000	$ 8,310,000	$ 6,957,000
Interest income	$ 432,000	$ 492,000	$ 525,000
Interest expense	$ 504,000	$ 513,000	$ 576,000
Equity income	$ 273,000	$ 195,000	$ 120,000
Other income (deductions)—net	$ 12,000	$ (246,000)	$ 123,000
Gain on issuance of stock by subsidiaries	$ 36,000	$ 0	$ 0
Income before taxes and changes in accounting principles	$ 9,555,000	$ 8,238,000	$ 7,149,000
Income taxes	$ 2,991,000	$ 2,589,000	$ 2,295,000
Income before changes in accounting principles (transition effects in accounting principles)	$ 6,564,000	$ 5,649,000	$ 4,854,000
Postemployment benefits	$ (36,000)	$ 0	$ 0
Postretirement benefits other than pensions			
Consolidated operations	$ 0	$ (438,000)	$ 0
Equity Investments	$ 0	$ (219,000)	$ 0
Net income	$ 6,528,000	$ 4,992,000	$ 4,854,000
Preferred stock dividends	$ 0.00	$ 0.00	$ 3.00
Net income available to common shareholders	$ 6,528,000	$ 4,992,000	$ 4,851,000
Income (loss) per common share before changes in accounting principles (transition effects on changes in accounting principles)	$ 5.04	$ 4.29	$ 3.63
Postemployment benefits	$ (0.03)	$ 0.00	$ 0.00
Postretirement benefits other than pensions			
Consolidated operations	$ 0.00	$ (0.33)	$ 0.00
Equity investments	$ 0.00	$ (0.18)	$ 0.00
Net income per common share	$ 5.01	$ 3.78	$ 3.63
Average common shares outstanding (in thousands)	3,906,000	3,951,000	3,999,000

EXHIBIT 6.5 The XYZ Manufacturing Company

Consolidated Statements of Changes in Financial Position (Dollars in thousands)

Year Ended December 31,	1999	1998	1997
Operating activities			
Net income	$6,528,000	$4,992,000	$ 4,854,000
Transition effects of changes in accounting principles	$ 36,000	$ 657,000	$ 0
Depreciation and amortization	$1,080,000	$ 966,000	$ 783,000
Deferred income taxes	$ (186,000)	$ (81,000)	$ (282,000)
Equity income, net of dividends	$ (105,000)	$ (90,000)	$ (48,000)
Foreign currency adjustments	$ 27,000	$ 72,000	$ 198,000
Gain on sale of businesses and investments before income taxes	$ (252,000)	$ 0	$ (105,000)
Other noncash items	$ 234,000	$ 309,000	$ 99,000
Net change in operating assets and liabilities	$ 162,000	$ (129,000)	$ 753,000
Net cash provided by operating activities	$7,524,000	$6,696,000	$ 6,252,000
Investing activities			
Decrease (increase) in marketable securities	$ 87,000	$ (156,000)	$ 9,000
Additions to finance subsidiary receivables	$ (531,000)	$ (162,000)	$ (630,000)
Collections of finance subsidiary receivables	$ 132,000	$ 762,000	$ 156,000
Purchases of investments and other assets	$(2,448,000)	$(2,151,000)	$(1,197,000)
Proceeds from disposals of investments and other assets	$1,863,000	$ 741,000	$ 540,000
Purchase of property, plant, and equipment	$(2,400,000)	$(3,249,000)	$(2,376,000)
Proceeds from disposals of property, plant, and equipment	$ 936,000	$ 141,000	$ 132,000
All other investment activities	$ (294,000)	$ (3,000)	$ (6,000)
Net cash provided by (used in) investing activities	$(2,655,000)	$(4,077,000)	$(3,372,000)
Net cash provided by operations after reinvestment	$4,869,000	$2,619,000	$ 2,880,000
Financing activities			
Issuance of debt	$1,335,000	$4,143,000	$ 2,970,000
Payment of debt	$(1,701,000)	$(1,296,000)	$(3,738,000)
Preferred stock redeemed	$ 0	$ 0	$ (225,000)
Common stock issued	$ 435,000	$ 393,000	$ 117,000
Purchases of common stock for treasury	$(2,040,000)	$(3,777,000)	$(1,197,000)
Dividends (common and preferred)	$(2,649,000)	$(2,214,000)	$(1,920,000)
Net cash used in financing activities	$(4,620,000)	$(2,751,000)	$(3,993,000)
Effect of exchange rate changes on cash and cash equivalents	$ (123,000)	$ (174,000)	$ 0
Cash and cash equivalents			
Net increase (decrease) during the year	$ 126,000	$ (306,000)	$(1,113,000)
Balance at beginning of year	$2,868,000	$3,174,000	$ 4,287,000
Balance at end of year	$2,994,000	$2,868,000	$ 3,174,000

EXHIBIT 6.6   Ratios

Liquidity Ratios	
Current ratio	$\dfrac{\text{Current assets}}{\text{Current liabilities}}$
Quick ratio	$\dfrac{\text{Current assets} - \text{Inventory}}{\text{Current liabilities}}$
Cash ratio	$\dfrac{\text{Cash} + \text{Marketable securities}}{\text{Current liabilities}}$
Cash flow from operations ratio	$\dfrac{\text{Cash flow from operations}}{\text{Current liabilities}}$
Defensive interval	$365 \times \dfrac{\text{Cash} + \text{Marketable securities} + \text{Accounts receivable}}{\text{Projected expenditures}}$
Net working capital to total assets	$\dfrac{\text{Net working capital}}{\text{Total assets}}$
Asset-Utilization Ratios	
Total asset turnover ratio	$\dfrac{\text{Sales}}{\text{Average total assets}}$
Fixed asset turnover ratio	$\dfrac{\text{Sales}}{\text{Average fixed assets}}$
Inventory turnover ratio	$\dfrac{\text{Cost of goods sold}}{\text{Average inventory}}$
Average number of days inventory in stock	$\dfrac{365}{\text{Inventory turnover ratio}}$
Receivables turnover ratio	$\dfrac{\text{Sales}}{\text{Average receivables}}$
Average number of days receivables are outstanding	$\dfrac{365}{\text{Receivables turnover ratio}}$

EXHIBIT 6.6 *(Continued)*

Profitability Ratios	
Gross profit margin ratio	$\dfrac{\text{Gross profit}}{\text{Sales}}$
Net profit margin ratio	$\dfrac{\text{Net income}}{\text{Sales}}$
Pretax margin ratio	$\dfrac{\text{EBT}}{\text{Sales}}$
Basic earning power	$\dfrac{\text{EBIT}}{\text{Average total assets}}$
Return on assets (ROA)	$\dfrac{\text{Net income}}{\text{Average total assets}}$
Return on equity (ROE)	$\dfrac{\text{Net income}}{\text{Total equity}}$
Debt Utilization Ratios	
Debt to equity ratio	$\dfrac{\text{Total debt}}{\text{Total equity}}$
Total debt to total assets ratio *or* Debt to total capital ratio	$\dfrac{\text{Total debt}}{\text{Total equity}}$ *or* $\dfrac{\text{Total debt}}{\text{Total debt} + \text{Total equity}}$
Times interest earned ratio	$\dfrac{\text{EBIT}}{\text{Interest expense}}$
Cash coverage ratio	$\dfrac{\text{EBIT} + \text{Depreciation}}{\text{Interest expense}}$
Market Value	
Price/earnings ratio	$\dfrac{\text{Price per share}}{\text{Earnings per share}}$
Book value per share	$\dfrac{\text{Common equity}}{\text{Shares outstanding}}$
Market/book ratio	$\dfrac{\text{Market Price per Share}}{\text{Book Value per Share}}$

EXHIBIT 6.7   Limited Ratio Analysis

$\dfrac{\text{Current assets}}{\text{Current liabilities}}$	This is simply the current ratio and shows how well a company's short-term liabilities are covered by its short-term assets.
$\dfrac{\text{Current assets} - \text{Inventory}}{\text{Current liabilities}}$	A more conservative measure of the above ratio that includes all current assets other than inventory.
$\dfrac{\text{Net income}}{\text{Average total capital}}$	Indicates what percentage of the company's capital (debt and equity) results in bottom line net profit.
$\dfrac{\text{Cash flow from operations}}{\text{Average total assets}}$	Shows what percentage of the company's total assets generate cash flows from its primary business.
$\dfrac{\text{Sales}}{\text{Average total capital}}$	Indicates how much revenue is being generated from a company's capital.
$\dfrac{\text{Cash}}{\text{Total assets}}$	Shows how much cash is on hand in proportion to the business's total assets.
$\dfrac{\text{Current assets}}{\text{Total assets}}$	Shows what percentage of a company's total assets are available for conversion to cash within one year from the date of the balance sheet.
$\dfrac{\text{Debt}}{\text{Equity}}$	Shows the proportion of all debt to equity within the capital structure of the company.
$\dfrac{\text{Net liabilities}}{\text{Total capital}}$	Net liabilities is another term for long-term debt. This ratio shows what percentage of a company's capital is long-term debt.
$\dfrac{\text{Inventory}}{\text{Current assets}}$	This ratio shows what percentage of current assets is represented by inventory.

Although it utilizes many of the same tools and techniques, financial capability analysis in the acquisition environment has a focus distinct from analysis performed by a bank or a potential investor. Typical objectives are to determine if a company has sufficient cash to support subcontractors; if it will be able to finish a long-term, high-risk project; and to improve the company working relationship through increased understanding of the company's financial philosophy and practices.

The main purpose of financial capability analysis is to use the information and model tools to identify problem areas within a company that may affect its performance on a contract (see Exhibit 6.8).

EXHIBIT 6.8   Operational Performance Measures

Measure Name	Definition
Adaptability	The ability of a product to become suitable for a specific use or situation that was not originally intended
Administrative actions	The percent of or cost of administrative actions required (e.g., reduction in the number of administrative appeals)
Communicability	The ability of a product or service to be reliably transmitted over a medium and understood by the receiver
Compliance	The ability to meet legislative or regulatory mandates
Flexibility	The ability of force structure to adapt to surge and changing mission requirements
Morale	The measure of employee attitude to work
Price	End users' satisfaction with what they are paying for the product or services as compared to their other options
Process time	The elapsed time between the commencement and completion of an activity
Quality	End users' perceived quality of the products and services delivered by the program
Response time	The elapsed time between the request for a product and when the system or component begins to process the request
Responsiveness	End users' perception that they get what they need when they need it
Reusability	Ability of the system or parts of the system to be used again
Service life	Length of time the equipment will be able to support the operation
Set-up time	The period of time during which a system or component is being prepared for a specific operation
Simplicity	An evaluation of difficulty of performing a particular operation
Speed	The amount of time necessary to respond to project requirements
Staffing structure	Changes to the structure of the project unit
System procurement	The time and difficulty of procuring the system
Turnaround time	The elapsed time between the submission of a request for a product and delivery of completed product
Understandability	The clarity of the system and its functions

Ratio analysis addresses managerial trends in asset management, operating strategies, and risk, and assists the business manager in determining a company's solvency.

Ratio analysis is extremely important to financial analysis. However, none of the ratios or models presented in this chapter should be used in isolation, that is, without considering any additional information that is available.

7

PERFORMANCE MEASURES

STRATEGIC PLAN

Strategic planning is a disciplined effort to produce fundamental decisions and actions that shape and guide what an organization is, what it does, and why it does it. It requires broad-scale information gathering, an exploration of alternatives, and an emphasis on the future implications of present decisions. Each strategic plan is to include a mission statement, general performance goals and objectives, a description of how the goals will be achieved, and an indication of how program evaluations were used in establishing or revising the goals.

The mission of an organization describes its reason for existence. Mission statements are broad and expected to remain in effect for an extended period of time. The statement should be clear and concise, summarizing what the organization does by law, and presenting the main purposes for all its major functions and operations. They are often accompanied by an overarching statement of philosophy or strategic purpose intended to convey a vision for the future and an awareness of challenges from a top-level perspective.

Performance goals are sometimes referred to as objectives by other organizations. Note that the terms may be used interchangeably. Performance goals or objectives elaborate on the mission statement and constitute a specific set of policy, programmatic, or management objectives for the programs and operations covered in the strategic plan. They must be expressed in a manner that allows a future assessment of whether a goal has been achieved.

A description of how the goals will be achieved must also be included in a strategic plan. The description should include a schedule for significant actions, a description of resources required to achieve the goals, and the identification of key external factors that might affect achievement of the goals.

Program evaluation is an analytic process used to measure program outcomes. The results of program evaluations are used to help establish and/or revise goals.

Performance Measures

Performance measures are used to measure goal attainment. They provide a basis for comparing actual program results with established performance goals. A range of measures should be developed for each program.

There are three major categories of performance measures defined by the Comptroller of the Department of Defense, Directorate for Business Management: factor of production measures, outcome measures, and work process measures. It is usually desirable for all three categories to be represented among an organization's set of measures to achieve balanced measurement across a mission.

Factor of Production Measures.   These measures typically describe the resource to output relationship. They often focus on different aspects of the resources to output relationship. There are four distinct types of factor of production measures. The four types are:

1. **Input Measures**
   These measures describe the resources, time, and staff utilized for a program. Financial resources can be identified as current dollars, or discounted, based on economic or accounting practices. Nonfinancial measures can be described in proxy measures. These measures are not described in terms of ratios. They are often used as one element of other measures, such as efficiency and effectiveness measures, described later.

   Examples: (1) Total funding
                (2) Actual number of labor hours

2. **Output Measures**
   These measures describe goods or services produced. Outputs can be characterized by a discrete definition of the service or by a proxy measure that represents the product. Highly dissimilar products can be rolled up into a metric. As with input measures, these measures are not described in terms of ratios. They are often used as one element of other measures such as efficiency and effectiveness measures, described later.

   Examples: (1) Number of line items shipped
                (2) Number of pay accounts maintained
                (3) Dollar of sales for commissary
                (4) Net operating result
                (5) Total number of transactions for the period

3. **Efficiency Measures**
   Efficiency is the measure of the relationship of outputs to inputs and is usually expressed as a ratio. These measures can be expressed in terms of actual expenditure of resources as compared to expected expenditure of resources. They can also be expressed as the expenditure of resources for a given output.

   Examples:

   (1) Unit cost per output $$\dfrac{\text{Total cost of operations}}{\text{Number of completed transactions (or units produced)}}$$

   (2) Labor productivity $$\dfrac{\text{Number of completed transactions (or units produced)}}{\text{Actual number of labor hours}}$$

(3) Cycle time

$$\frac{\text{Number of days to complete job order}}{\text{Number of job orders completed}}$$

4. Effectiveness Measures

These are measures of output that conform to specified characteristics.

Examples:

(1) Quanity

$$\frac{\text{Number of engines repaired}}{\text{Number of engines requiring repair}}$$

(2) Timeliness

$$\frac{\text{Number of transactions completed by target time}}{\text{Total number of transactions for period}}$$

(3) Quality

$$\frac{\text{Number of defect-free products received by customers}}{\text{Number of products received by customers}}$$

(4) Customer Satisfaction (a) Customer satisfaction survey results

(b) Complaint rates

Outcome Measures. Outcome measures describe the results achieved by the product being produced with given characteristics. There are two types of outcome measures. These include:

1. Direct Outcome Measures

These measures assess the effect of output against given objective standards.

Examples: (1) Material readiness rate

(2) Health status of eligible population provided with medical care

2. Impact Measures

Impact measures describe how the outcome of a program affects strategic organization or mission objectives.

Work Process Measures. Work process measures are indicators of the way work gets done in producing the output at a given level of resources, efficiency, and effectiveness. These measures are a direct by-product of the technique, but do not measure the attributes of the final product, per se. These measures are typically processes, or tools, to evaluate and help improve work processes. Some of the common measures include:

1. Cost-Effectiveness

This is an evaluation process to assess changes in the relationship of resources to: (1) an outcome; (2) an efficiency rate; or (3) an effectiveness rate.

Examples:

(1) Outcome   Is it cost effective to spend 10 percent more on resources to improve base security by 5 percent?

    (2) Efficiency   Will an investment in equipment whose depreciation increases unit cost by 5 percent reduce operating costs by more than that amount?

    (3) Effectiveness   Will a change in the process result in the same efficiency rate but at a much improved effectiveness rate as measured by quality, timeliness, and so forth?

2. Efficiency Reviews or Management Analysis

These basic industrial engineering approaches:
- Identify the essential output;
- Chart (flow chart) the existing work processes used to achieve that output;
- Identify resources associated with those processes;
- Identify and eliminate unnecessary tasks;
- Perform methods analyses to complete necessary tasks in most efficient/effective manner; and
- Estimate cost benefits of investment necessary to support alternative methods of performing tasks.

3. Flow Charting

This is a work process evaluation tool that graphically maps the activities that make up a process. It illustrates how different elements and tasks fit together. They can be used to describe a business process and the physical flow over space and time. They thus provide insight about efficiency and effectiveness opportunities.

4. Cost-Based Activity Modeling Systems

These are widely used techniques to capture the processes and structure of information in an organization. The analysis charts work processes, identifies and eliminates non–value-added tasks, identifies costs of remaining tasks, and focuses on process changes to accomplish needed tasks at reduced costs.

5. Theory of Constraints

This is a work engineering process that specifically focuses on maximizing throughput, inventory reduction, and turnaround time as key work process indicators.

6. Macro Management Analysis Reviews

These reviews typically use economic analysis techniques rather than industrial engineering approaches to assess alternative organizations or work processes. An example of this type of review includes a consolidation study of alternative work methods that consolidates organizations or work processes to achieve economies of scale.

7. Benchmarking

Benchmarking systematically compares performance measures such as efficiency, effectiveness, or outcomes of an organization against similar measures from other internal or external organizations. This analysis helps uncover best practices that can be adopted for improvement.

8. Statistical Process Control

   This is a measurement method used for assessing the performance of processes. Statistical evaluation techniques identify whether a process is in control (e.g., produces results in a predictable manner) and assess the impact of method changes on process results.

9. Status of Conditions Indicators

   These are measures such as accident rates, absenteeism, and turnover rates. They are indirect measures of the quality of work life that impact efficiency and effectiveness.

10. Organizational Assessment Tools

    These are measurement tools designed to identify organization culture and management style, workforce and management knowledge, application of quality and process improvement tools, and organizational outcomes. This form of measurement is increasingly used in leading private sector corporations to assess potential for innovation, employee empowerment, internal and external customer relations, and satisfaction.

11. Innovation

    These measures are typically qualitative indicators of the rate of introduction of managerial or technological innovations into the work process. Innovation can be used as a barometer of organizational health and openness to new methods and processes.

12. Quality

    These indicators for work processes are various methods of identifying the costs of waste due to work processes or methods that produce less than standard output. These include such indicators as defect rates, rework, and "cost of quality" such as the total resources of time, personnel, and materials engaged in inspection, rework, scrap, and more.

BUSINESS GOALS

Setting Business Goals: Guidelines for Developing a Performance Measurement Process

Good management is the key to success and good management starts with setting goals. Set goals for yourself for the accomplishment of the many tasks necessary in starting and managing your business successfully. Be specific. Write down the goals in measurable terms of performance. Break major goals down into sub-goals, showing what you expect to achieve in the next two to three months, the next six months, the next year, and the next five years. Beside each goal and sub-goal place a specific date showing when it is to be achieved. Plan the action you must take to attain the goals. While the effort required reaching each sub-goal should be great enough to challenge you, it should not be so great or unreasonable as to discourage you. Do not plan to reach too many goals at once. Establish priorities.

Plan in advance how to measure results so you can know exactly how well you are doing. This is what is meant by "measurable" goals. If you can't keep score as you go along, you are likely to lose motivation. Rework your plan of action to maneuver around or minimize obstacles that may stand in your way.

1. Develop a corporate strategy that uses the input of the leadership of the organization, the expectations of the various stakeholder groups, and best practices (e.g., maintain customer loyalty through new product development versus lowering prices).

2. Communicate the strategy and need for a new performance measurement system (e.g., one-hour company-wide meeting).

3. Develop goals (e.g., get products to the market 50 percent faster over the next two years).

4. Identify the critical processes.
   - Identify the major process of the organization. Start with the customer, with an understanding of what the customer receives from the organization, and work backwards to the organization. This distinguishes the primary, support, and management processes.
   - Identify the critical process by using the goals of the organization as criteria.

5. Design and develop output measures.
   - Identify customers.
   - Identify and understand customers' expectations of the process.
   - Filter and prioritize customers' expectations based on the goals of the organization.
   - Select output performance measures.
   - Set targets.

6. Identify key activities in the new process.
   - Define the process (e.g., where it starts and stops and the inputs to the process).
   - Document the process (e.g., process mapping).
   - Identify (critical tasks) in the process.

7. Design process performance measures for each key activity.
   - Examine the goals of the organization.
   - Use the cost, quality, and time criteria as a guide in the selection of the process performance measures.
   - Determine what and how to measure (e.g., early supplier involvement; have suppliers involved by a specific date).
   - Validate these process performance measures.
   - Determine whether the performance measures are attribute or variable. Measurement is simple with attribute measures (yes or no). Variable measures are used to continuously improve the process or to elicit the reasons for a "no" attribute measure.

8. Implement and continuously improve.
   - Gain management sign-off.
   - Present the plan to process employees or alternatively include them in aspects of this effort.
   - Start measuring and reporting.

Best Practices of a Product Realization Process

1. *Teams/Teamwork.* The ability to work with diverse, multidisciplinary team members to successfully reach a goal or objective.

2. *Design for Manufacture (DFM).* Design to maximize ease of manufacture by simplifying the design through part-count reduction, developing modular designs, minimizing part variation, and designing a part to be multifunctional. DFM is facilitated by using multidiscipline teams from the project start, including manufacturing engineering. Use DFM checklists early in the project. Not every item on the checklist must be answered yes, but have a good reason for all deviations.

3. *Computer-aided drafting (CAD) Systems.* Computer-aided drafting boards that allow a user to define a new product by (a) creating images and (b) assigning geometry, mass, kinematics, material, and other properties to the product. CAD systems vary in complexity and capability.

4. *Professional Ethics.* The ability to conform to standards of conduct determined by one's profession, in alignment with team and corporate standards. Follow the Golden Rule: Treat others as you would have them treat you.

5. *Creative Thinking.* The process of generating ideas, which frequently emphasizes making and expressing meaningful new connections, thinking of many new and unusual possibilities, and extending and elaborating on alternatives.

6. *Design for Performance.* Designed to perform to product requirements under a wide variety of manufacturing and user operating conditions.

7. *Design for Reliability.* Designing the product so it works the first time, every time, for the life of the product (decreasing cycle failure).

8. *Robust Design.* In its most general sense, robust design ensures operation in a variety of environments, throughout life. Environmental Stress Testing weeds out problems by subjecting samples to a simultaneous set of extreme operating conditions.

9. *Design for Safety.* Design so that the manufacture of and the use or abuse of the product minimize the possibility of injuries which could lead to product liability problems.

10. *Concurrent Engineering.* An approach to new product development where the product and all of its associated processes, such as manufacturing, distribution, and service, are developed in parallel.

11. *Sketching/Drawing.* The ability to clearly illustrate ideas and design by freehand sketching.

12. *Design for Cost.* Meeting customer requirements while minimizing cost of all aspects of the product, including production, assembly, distribution, and maintenance.

13. *Application of Statistics.* Methodology of effectively designing tests and analyzing test data using statistical techniques that are founded in probability theory.

14. *Reduce variability in performance of parts to achieve specific performance of an electronic system.* Example: Determine how much testing must be performed on a critical weld to achieve a specified high confidence that the weld meets specifications.

15. *Reliability.* A subset of statistical engineering methodology that predicts performance of a product over its intended life cycle and promotes understanding of the effects of various failure modes on system performance.

16. *Geometric Tolerancing.* An agreed-upon convention of symbols and terms used on engineering drawings to connote geometric characteristics and other dimensional requirements.

17. *Tolerances.* Tolerances are used to control form, profile, orientation, location, and runout. Geometric tolerancing helps ensure the most economical and effective production of parts with features that offer function and have proper relationships.

18. *Value Engineering.* A systematic approach to evaluating design alternatives that seeks to eliminate unnecessary features and functions and to achieve required functions at the lowest possible cost while optimizing manufacturability, quality, and delivery. Multidisciplined value engineering sessions conducted in a retreat mode (away from normal work distractions) can also aid team-building. Get manufacturing and purchasing to make realistic estimates in real time, calling on experts as needed.

19. *Design Reviews.* Design reviews are the scheduled checkpoints for assessing the design progress toward meeting product requirements and budget. Participants in a design review should be knowledgeable people, some from parts of the organization other than the group whose design is being reviewed, who can ask insightful questions that may expose things that have been overlooked. You want action items to come from the review.

20. *Manufacturing Processes.* Processes that are used to create or further refine work pieces, such as molding and casting, machining, extruding, stamping, forming, bonding, welding, coating, plating, painting, fabrication, and assembly. Product design engineers need to be familiar with manufacturing processes which could be used to make their products, so they can make educated trade-offs among them. The need is for familiarity, so that they know to which experts they can turn for more detailed information needed to choose among alternatives. This is strongly linked to design for manufacture.

21. *Systems Perspective.* The up-front identification of system components and their interactions for the purpose of optimizing the performance of the system

as a whole. Various methods and tools are useful. Brainstorming by cross-functional teams helps to bring various issues to the surface.

22. *Design for Assembly.* Making the product easier to assemble, thereby reducing cycle time during production.

Buying

Skillful buying is an important essential of profitable operation. This is true whether you are a wholesaler or retailer of merchandise, a manufacturer, or a service business operator. Some retailers say it is the most important single factor. Merchandise that is carefully purchased is easy to sell. Determining what to buy means finding out the type, kind, quality, brand, size, color, style—whatever applies to your particular inventory—that will sell the best. This requires close attention to salespeople, trade journals, catalogs, and especially the likes and dislikes of your regular customers. Analyze your sales records. Even the manufacturer should view the problem through the eyes of customers before deciding what materials, parts, and supplies to purchase.

A Valuable Resource

Know your regular customers, and make a good evaluation of the people you hope will become your customers. In what socioeconomic category are they? Are they homeowners or renters? Are they looking for price, style, or quality? What is the predominant age category?

The age of your customers can be a prime consideration in establishing a purchasing pattern. Young people buy more frequently than older people do. They need more, have fewer responsibilities, and spend more on themselves. They are more conscious of style trends whether in apparel, cars, or electronic equipment. If you decide to cater to the young trade because they seem dominant in your area, your buying pattern will be completely different than if the more conservative middle-aged customers appear to be in the majority.

Study trade journals, newspaper advertisements, catalogs, and window displays of businesses similar to yours. Ask advice of salespeople offering you merchandise, but buy sparingly from several suppliers rather than one, testing the water, so to speak, until you know what your best lines will be. Locating suitable merchandise sources is not easy. You may buy directly from manufacturers or producers, from wholesalers, distributors, or jobbers. Select the suppliers who sell what you need and can deliver it when you need it. Most businesspeople who rely on quick fill-ins between factory shipments use distributors and jobbers.

You may spread purchases among many suppliers to gain more favorable prices and promotional material, or you may concentrate your purchases among a small number of suppliers to simplify your credit problems. This will also help you become known as the seller of a certain brand or line of merchandise, and to maintain a fixed standard in your products, if you are buying materials for manufacturing purposes.

When to buy is important if your business will have seasonal variations in sales volume. More stock will be needed prior to the seasonal upturn in sales volume. As sales decline, less merchandise is needed. This means purchases of goods for resale and materials for processing should vary accordingly. At the outset, how much to buy is speculative. The best policy is to be frugal until you have had enough experience to judge your needs. On the other hand, you cannot sell merchandise if you do not have it.

To help solve buying problems, you should begin to keep accurate stock control records. This will help you keep the stock in balance—neither too large nor too small—with a proper proportion and adequate assortment of products, sizes, colors, styles, and qualities.

Fundamentally, there are two types of stock control—control in dollars and control in physical units. Dollar controls show the amount of money invested in each merchandise category. Unit controls indicate the number of individual items purchased by category. A good stock control system can help you determine what, from whom, when, and how much to buy.

8

PRICING POLICIES

PRICING AND PROFITABILITY

Much of your success in business will depend on how you price your services. If your prices are too low, you will not cover expenses; too high and you will lose sales volume. In both cases, you will not make a profit. Before opening your business you must decide on the general price level you expect to maintain. Will you cater to people buying in the high, medium, or low price range? Your prices, choice of location, appearance of your establishment, quality of goods handled, and services to be offered will all depend on the customers you hope to attract.

After establishing this general price level, you are ready to price individual items. In general, the price of an item must cover the cost of the item, all other costs, plus a profit. Thus, you will have to mark up the item by a certain amount to cover costs and earn a profit. In a business that sells few items, total costs can easily be allocated to each item and a markup quickly determined. With a variety of items, allocating costs and determining markup may require an accountant. In retail operations, goods are often marked up by 50 to 100 percent or more just to earn a 5 to 10 percent profit! Let us work through a markup example. Suppose your company sells one product, Product A. The supplier sells Product A to you for $5 each. You and your accountant determine the costs entailed in selling Product A are $4 per item, and you want a $1 per item profit. What is your markup? Well, the selling price is $5 plus $4 plus $1 or $10; the markup therefore is $5. As a percentage, it is 100 percent ($5 markup = $5 cost of the item). So you have to mark up Product A by 100 percent to make a 10 percent profit.

Many small companies are interested in knowing what industry markup norms are for various products. Wholesalers, distributors, trade associations, and business research companies publish a huge variety of such ratios and business statistics. They are useful as guidelines. Another ratio (in addition to the markup percentage) important to small companies is the gross margin percentage (GMP). The GMP is similar to your markup percentage but while markup refers to the percent above your cost of each item that you must set the selling price of in order to cover all other costs and earn profits, the GMP shows the relationship between sales revenues minus the cost of the item, which is your gross margin, and your sales revenues. What the GMP is telling you is that your markup bears a certain relationship to your sales revenues. The markup percentage and the GMP are essentially the same formula, with the markup referring to individual item pricing and GMP referring to the item prices times the number of items sold (volume).

Your business sells Product Z. It costs you $.70 each and you decide to sell it for $1 each to cover costs and profit. Your markup is 43 percent. Now let us say you sold 10,000 units of Product Z last month thus producing $10,000 in revenues. Your cost to purchase Product Z was $7,000; your gross margin was $3,000 (revenues minus cost of goods sold). This is also your gross markup for the month's volume. Your GMP would be 30 percent. Both of these percentages use the same basic numbers, differing only in division. Both are used to establish a pricing system. And both are published and can be used as guidelines for small start-up companies. Often, managers determine what GMP they will need to earn a profit and simply go to a published markup table to find the percentage markup that correlates with that margin requirement.

While this discussion of pricing may appear, in some respects, to be directed only to the pricing of retail merchandise, it can be applied to other types of businesses as well. For services, the markup must cover selling and administrative costs in addition to the direct cost of performing a particular service. If you are manufacturing a product, the costs of direct labor, materials and supplies, parts purchased from other concerns, special tools and equipment, plant overhead, selling, and administrative expenses must be carefully estimated. To compute a cost per unit requires an estimate of the number of units you plan to produce. Before your factory becomes too large it would be wise to consult an accountant about a cost accounting system. Not all items are marked up by the average markup. Luxury articles will take more, staples less. For instance, increased sales volume from a lower-than-average markup on a certain item—a "loss leader"—may bring a higher gross profit unless the price is lowered too much. Then the resulting increase in sales will not raise the total gross profit enough to compensate for the low price.

Sometimes you may wish to sell a certain item or service at a lower markup in order to increase store traffic with the hope of increasing sales of regularly priced merchandise or generating a large number of new service contracts. Competitors' prices will also govern your prices. You cannot sell a product if your competitor is greatly underselling you. These and other reasons may cause you to vary your markup among items and services. There is no magic formula that will work on every product or every service all of the time. But you should keep in mind the overall average markup, which you need to make a profit.

Checklist for Pricing Policies and Strategies

The following list of questions will help you select the pricing policies and strategies that will best suit your business, allowing you to remain competitive and providing you with the profit you want.

1. Do you price all items at a level that provides an adequate profit margin? If not, why?

2. Do you constantly monitor costs and make price changes to provide for continued profitability, particularly in periods of rapid inflation?

3. Do you price to cover your variable costs and fixed costs?

4. Is your goal to find the price-volume combination that will maximize profits?

5. When setting a price strategy, do you consider these factors: (a) channels of distribution? (b) competitive and legal forces? (c) annual volume and life-cycle volume? (d) opportunities for special market promotions?

6. Is your price consistent with the product image?

7. Because customers often equate the quality of unknown products with their price, do you adjust prices accordingly?

8. Do you reduce prices whenever the added volume resulting from the reduction produces sufficient sales revenue to offset the added costs of increased production?

9. When reducing prices, do you consider your competitors' probable reactions?

10. Do you want your business to be a price leader?

11. Do your initial markups cover (a) operations, particularly selling expenses? (b) profit? (c) subsequent price reductions?

12. Does your company break down costs by product to price effectively?

13. Does your company practice price lining?

14. Does your company practice odd pricing?

15. To avoid retaliation by competitors, have you tried adding extra services, providing warranties, or paying transportation costs rather than lowering prices?

16. Do you realize that facilities have certain costs whether you use them or not?

Selling

Whether you operate a factory, wholesale outlet, retail store, service shop, or are a contractor, you will have to sell. No matter how good your product is, no matter what consumers think of it, you must sell to survive. Direct selling methods are through personal sales efforts, advertising, and, for many businesses, display—including the packaging and styling of the product itself—in windows, in the establishment, or both. Establishing a good reputation with the general public through courtesy and special services is an indirect method of selling. While the latter should never be neglected, this brief discussion will be confined to direct selling methods. To establish your business requires a great deal of aggressive personal selling. You may have established competition to overcome. Or, if your idea is new with little or no competition, you have the problem of convincing people of the value of the new idea. Personal selling work is almost always necessary to accomplish this. If you are not a good salesperson, seek an employee or associate who is.

A second way to build sales is by advertising. This may be done through newspapers, shopping papers, the yellow pages section of the telephone directory, or other published periodicals; radio and television; handbills; and direct mail. The media you select, as well as the message and style of presentation, will depend on the particular customers you wish to reach. Plan and prepare advertising carefully or it will be ineffective. Most media will be able to describe the characteristics of their audience (e.g., readers, listeners). Your initial planning described the characteristics of your potential customers; now you want to match these characteristics with the media audience.

If you are selling expensive jewelry, do not advertise in high school newspapers. If you repair bicycles, you probably should advertise there, as well as in other media targeted at a young audience. Advertising can be very expensive. It is wise to place a limit on your advertising expenditures and then stay within that limit. To help you in determining how much to spend, study the operating ratios of similar businesses. Media advertising salespeople will help you plan and even prepare advertisements for you. Be sure to tell them your budget limitations.

A third method of stimulating sales is effective displays both in your place of business and outside it. If you have had no previous experience in display work, you will want to study the subject or turn the task over to someone else. Observe displays of other businesses and read books, trade magazines, and the literature supplied by equipment manufacturers. It may be wise to hire a display expert for your opening display and special events, or you may obtain the services of one on a part-time basis. Much depends on your type of business and what it requires. The proper amount and types of selling effort to use vary from business to business and from owner to owner. Some businesses prosper with low-key sales efforts. Others, such as used-car lots, thrive on aggressive, extravagant promotions. In any event, the importance of effective selling cannot be overemphasized.

On the other hand, do not lose sight of your major objective—to make a profit. Anyone can produce a large sales volume selling dollar bills for ninety cents. But that won't last long. So keep control of your costs, and price your product carefully.

Record Keeping

The keeping of adequate records cannot be stressed too much. Study after study shows that many failures can be attributed to inadequate records or the owner's failure to use what information was available. Without records, the businessperson cannot see in advance which way the business is going. Up-to-date records may forecast impending disaster, forewarning you to take steps to avoid it. While extra work is required to keep an adequate set of records, you will be more than repaid for the effort and expense.

If you are not prepared to keep adequate records—or hire someone keep them for you—you should not try to operate a small business. At a minimum, records are needed to substantiate:

- Your returns under tax laws, including income tax and Social Security laws;
- Your request for credit from equipment manufacturers or a loan from a bank; and
- Your claims about the business, should you wish to sell it.

Most importantly, you need them to run your business successfully and to increase your profits. With an adequate yet simple bookkeeping system, you can answer such questions as:

- How much business am I doing?
- What are my expenses? Which ones appear to be too high? What is my gross profit margin? My net profit?

- How much am I collecting on my charge business?
- What is the condition of my working capital?
- How much cash do I have on hand? How much is in the bank? How much do I owe my suppliers?
- What is my net worth? That is, what is the value of my ownership of the business?
- What are the trends in my receipts, expenses, profits, and net worth? Is my financial position improving or growing worse? How do my assets compare with what I owe?
- What is the percentage of return on my investment?
- How many cents out of each dollar of sales is net profit?

Answer these and other questions by preparing and studying balance sheets and profit-and-loss statements. To do this, it is important that you record information about transactions as they occur. Keep this data in a detailed and orderly fashion and you will be able to answer the previous questions. You will also have the answers to other vital questions about your business, such as:

- What products or services do my customers like best? Next best? Not at all?
- Do I carry the merchandise most often requested?
- Am I qualified to render the services they demand most?
- How many of my charge customers are slow payers?
- Shall I switch to cash only, or use a credit card charge plan?

The kind of records and how many you need depends on your particular operation. A girl selling newspapers part time each day does not need inventory records. She buys and sells her entire stock each day. But shoe store or dress shop operators will soon find they cannot keep necessary inventory information in their heads. Following is a list of records, grouped according to their use. No business will need them all. You may need only a few. As a matter of fact, you should not maintain a record without answering these three questions: (1) How will this record be used? (2) How important is the information likely to be? (3) Is the information available elsewhere in an equally accessible form? The following list may call your attention to records you can use to great advantage:

- Inventory and Purchasing Records (provide facts to help with buying and selling)
- Inventory Control Record
- Item Perpetual Inventory Record
- Model Stock Plan
- Out-of-Stock Sheet
- Open-to-Buy Record
- Purchase Order File
- Open to Purchase Order File

- Supplier File
- Returned Goods File
- Price Change Book
- Accounts Payable Ledger
- Sales Records (help determine sales trends)
- Individual Sales Transactions
- Summary of Daily Sales
- Sales Plan
- Sales Promotion Plan
- Cash Records (show what is happening to cash)
- Daily Cash Reconciliation
- Cash Receipts Journal
- Cash Disbursements Journal
- Bank Reconciliation
- Credit Records (show who owes you money and whether they are paying on time)
- Charge Account Application
- Accounts Receivable Ledger
- Accounts Receivable Aging List
- Employee Records (show legally required information and information helpful in the efficient management of personnel)
- Employee Earnings and Amounts Withheld
- Employees' Expense Allowances
- Employment Applications
- Record of Changes in Rate of Pay
- Record of Reasons for Termination of Employment Employee Benefits Record
- Job Descriptions
- Crucial Incidents Record
- Fixtures and Property Records (list facts needed for taking depreciation allowances and for insurance coverage and claims)
- Equipment Record
- Insurance Register
- Bookkeeping Records (needed if you use a double-entry bookkeeping system)
- General Journal
- General Ledger

For efficient business operation, use information from records to keep inventory stock in line with sales, to watch trends, and for tax purposes. Use records to plan. A well-thought-out business plan will strengthen your chances for success.

A record showing the data for your business plan is the budget. Work up a budget to help you determine just how much increase in profit is reasonably within your reach. The budget will answer such questions as: What sales will be needed to achieve my desired profit? What fixed expenses will be necessary to support these sales? What variable expenses will be incurred? A budget enables you to set a goal and determine what to do in order to reach it. Compare your budget periodically with actual operations figures. Then where there are discrepancies, you can take corrective action before it is too late. The right decisions for the right corrective action will depend on your knowledge of management techniques in buying, pricing, selling, selecting, and training personnel, and handling other management problems.

You probably are thinking you can hire a bookkeeper or an accountant to handle the record keeping for you. Yes, you can. But remember two very important facts:

1. *Provide the accountant with accurate input.* If you buy something and don't record the amount in your business checkbook, the accountant cannot enter it. If you sell something for cash and don't record it, the accountant will not know about it. The records the accountant prepares will be no better than the information you provide.

2. *Use the records to make decisions.* If you went to a physician and he told you you were ill and needed certain medicine to get well, you would follow his advice. If you pay an accountant and he tells you your sales are down this year, do not hide your head in the sand and pretend the problem will go away. It won't.

Financial Profitability Tools

Basic Cash Flow Management.   Managing cash must carry equal weight with net income. In financial management, "cash is king" is a frequent motto. Your first step in managing cash is to elevate the importance of cash. The basic process for managing cash is straightforward. Try to maintain an adequate level of cash to meet current obligations and invest idle cash into earning assets. Earning assets must have high liquidity; that is, you must be able to convert investments back into cash quickly. Additionally, you want to protect your cash balance by paying obligations only as they come due.

Managing cash also involves aggressive conversion of current assets into cash. Inventory levels must be converted into accounts receivables and accounts receivables must be converted into cash. Ratios should be used to monitor the conversion of cash, such as number of days in inventory and number of days in receivables. Cash balances are the result of a combination of cycles: inventory, purchasing, receivables, and payables. The key is to properly manage these cycles for conversion into cash.

Once conversion cycles are identified, cash forecasts can be prepared for managing cash. Weekly cash reports are used to monitor balances. Because everything ultimately passes through your cash account, a strong internal control system is required. This involves the separation of duties in handling cash, reconciling cash accounts, adequate support for cash disbursements, and other control procedures. The overall objective is to protect cash just like any other asset through a system of internal controls.

Improving Cash Flow

The first step for improving your cash flow is to understand the history of your cash flow. This requires scheduling cash inflows and outflows. Once you understand the history, you can take steps to cut cash outflows and increase collections.

One of the biggest cash outflows is payroll. Payroll should be managed with flexibility in mind. You need a workforce that works when needed as opposed to 5 days a week, 8 hours a day. Consider diversifying your workforce into a mix of temporary workers, part-time workers, and outsourcing of non–value-added activities. Also, do not forget that you can extend your payroll float by distributing payroll checks after 2 o'clock on Fridays.

Your purchasing practices should also consider a mixed approach. For example, why do you have to buy everything new? Purchasing used items or renting can save a lot of cash flow. You may want to purchase in minimum quantities, especially if your cash flow is tight. In addition, do not hold inventory that is not moving—get rid of it!

Other cash traps include insurance. Do not use insurance to cover all risks. Make sure you retain some risks, especially if the risk is not materially significant and not likely to occur very often. One of the fastest rising insurance outflows is health care costs. Make sure you have a preventive program for your employees. This can include things like annual cholesterol screenings, reimbursement for smoking cessation programs, and company participation in outdoor activities. Finally, aggressively monitor your outstanding receivables and begin to act at the first sign of trouble. If you have doubts about a customer's ability to pay, require an advance deposit.

Cash Support for Sales Growth

As sales grow, cash needs will grow. Planning for future sales must include planning for additional requirements for cash. A basic formula can be used to help determine the amount of additional cash needed for new sales. The formula is calculated as follows:

Additional Cash = New Sales − Gross Profit + Additional Overhead/Sales Growth Duration in Days × Average number of days to collect Receivables + Safety Factor

Example: We expect $10,000 of additional sales during the year (365 days) with a corresponding increase of $3,000 in overhead. All payables are paid on time, we do not expect any changes in our collection periods, and we expect a continued gross profit margin of 25 percent. The average period to collect receivables is 40 days and we will build a safety factor of 20 percent into our estimate. Thus:

($10,000 − $2,500) + $3,000/365 = $28.77 × (40 × 1.20) = $1,381 of additional cash is needed to support the $10,000 of additional sales.

The above formula is a quick and rough estimate for estimating how much cash is needed to carry additional sales. Changes in collections and payment cycles need to be considered when using this formula.

Effective Interest Rate

The effective interest rates you pay are a function of how much money you have available and how much money you give up for the use of these funds. In the simplest form of borrowing, a 1-year loan of $10,000 at 12 percent interest will cost $1,200. The effective interest rate is $1,200/$10,000 or 12 percent. As we change the costs and/or amount of funds available, the effective interest rate will change.

> *Example:* You borrow $10,000 at 12 percent, which is discounted by the bank at 10 percent, thereby reducing the amount of funds you have available. The effective interest rate is: $1,200/$9,000 or 13.3 percent.

Compensating balances also decrease the proceeds of the loan. As proceeds decline, the effective interest rate rises.

> *Example:* You borrow $30,000 at 12 percent. The bank requires that you maintain a 10 percent compensating balance. The effective interest rate is: $3,600/($30,000 − $3,000) = 13.3 percent.

Financing Inventories

Inventory financing can be used where inventories are highly marketable and no threat of obsolescence exists. The inventory serves as collateral within the financing arrangement. Financing can occur in up to 70 percent of inventory values provided that inventory prices are relatively stable. The costs of financing inventory can be very high (such as 6 percent over the prime lending rate).

Three types of financing arrangements for inventory are available. They are floating liens, warehouse receipts, and trust receipts. Floating liens place a lien on the overall inventory stock. Warehouse receipts give the lender an interest in your inventory. And trust receipts represent a loan that is released as you sell your inventory. The costs of financing inventory is illustrated in the following example:

> *Example:* You would like to finance $100,000 of your inventory. You need the funds for 3 months. You will use a warehouse receipt arrangement. This arrangement requires that you set up a separate area for the lender's inventory. You estimate an additional $2,000 in costs for storing and maintaining the inventory. The lender will advance you 80 percent at 16 percent.
>
> The costs of financing inventory is $5,200 as calculated below:

$$.16 \times .80 \times \$100,000 \times \tfrac{3}{12} = \$3,200 + \$2,000 \text{ or } \$5,200$$

Operating Leverage

The use of fixed assets in generating earnings is referred to as operating leverage. Operating leverage is measured by comparing the change in profits to the change in sales. Higher levels of operating leverage tend to result in wider variations in profits given a change in sales. This variation is called operating risks. Therefore, higher levels of fixed costs are often associated with high levels of operating risks, which in turn leads to fluctuations of earnings given a change in sales.

Breakeven analysis is often used in conjunction with operating leverage. As we increase sales beyond the breakeven point, the effects of operating leverage diminish because the sales base we are using has increased. We can use breakeven analysis to calculate operating leverage.

Degree of Operating Leverage (DOL) = % Change in Earnings before Interest and Taxes (EBIT)/% Change in Sales

Example: Price of Product = $10.00, Variable Cost per unit = $6.00, Fixed Cost = $12,000 and 5,000 units are sold.

DOL = $10.00 − $6.00 × 5,000/$10.00 − $6.00 × 5,000 − $12,000 = 2.5

What we can conclude from our calculation is that when sales increase by say 10 percent, we can expect a 25 percent increase in earnings, as we have an operating leverage of 2.5. Thus, operating leverage gives us some measure of variations in earnings from changes to sales.

Percentage of Sales Financial Forecasting

Financial forecasting often begins with a forecast of future sales. The sales forecast serves as the basis for estimating future expenses, assets, and liabilities. Many of these accounts vary with changes in sales. Therefore, using a percent of sales can be very useful for forecasting a balance sheet.

The following steps can be used to prepare a forecasted *(pro forma)* balance sheet based on the percent of sales method:

1. Determine which balance sheet accounts vary with sales (such as accounts receivable). Calculate the percent of sales for each account that varies with sales.

2. Multiply the percent from Step 1 by the forecasted sales amount to determine the projected balance sheet account.

3. For accounts that do not vary with sales (such as long-term debt and equity), simply list the current balances from the last balance sheet.

4. Calculate the future retained earnings balance by adding projected net income and subtracting any future dividends from the beginning balance for retained earnings. Don't forget to calculate a percent of sales for net income and dividends.

5. Add up your assets to determine total projected assets. Now add up your liabilities and equity to determine the financing of assets. If total assets is greater than total liabilities and equity, then you will need to raise additional capital.

Please note that the percent of sales method is based on the assumption that you are operating at full capacity. Also, you will need to prepare a cash budget for a more accurate estimate of financing requirements.

BUDGETING

The Budgeting Process

One of the most non–value-added activities within financial management is budgeting. Budgets are prepared to allocate and control how resources will be used in the future. Unfortunately, the future is hard to predict and upper-level management does not always communicate with people who prepare budgets. Because of poor communication, budgeting becomes an exercise in futility. Some of the main problems associated with budgeting are:

- Poor communication from decision makers;
- Too many people involved in the process;
- Budgets do not help manage business;
- Budgets are outdated by external events; and
- Budgets are difficult to revise.

Because upper-level management often circumvents the budgeting process, the first thing to do when budgeting is to find out what management expects from the budgeting process. Next, make sure management decision making is linked to the budgets. You can accomplish this by creating budgets within the strategic planning process. Do not forget to include external factors when preparing budgets. Outside events and issues can impact your budget estimates.

Budgets should be easy to revise. When new planning data pops up, your budgeting process should adopt and accept this new data. Hold your cost centers responsible for meeting their budgets. This can force feedback from end-users for improvements in the budgeting process. If you find yourself always revising a budget, consider preparing several budgets or set up a contingency budget if you expect changes. Prepare the basic outline or summary of a budget and get approval before you spend a lot of time preparing detailed budgets. Or better yet, try to reduce the detail in your budgets to streamline the entire process.

Budgeting should be a dynamic process within strategic planning. The more your budgets can react to change, the closer budgeting will be to a value-added activity. If your budgets do not add value to decision making, then it is time to improve the process.

There are many turns and twists when it comes to forecasting cash flows and other amounts. The last thing you need in your analysis is statistical errors that distort your estimates. The problem is: What amount do I use? Do I use the average amount? Do I use the most likely amount? Do I use the expected value?

Use expected value to come up with a realistic estimate of what amount will occur in the future. Expected value is not the same as average value or most likely value. Expected value is derived by looking at all possibilities and taking into account the probability of occurrence. Using expected value has statistical merit over other approaches as you are forced to give consideration to all possible outcomes. Also, the difference you get in estimates can be extremely significant.

Say you need to estimate the cash inflows for next month. You have three customers who have outstanding receivable balances. Based on past histories, you can assign probabilities to receiving payment next month.

Customer A owes $10,000; there is a 60 percent probability of receiving payment next month.

Customer B owes $20,000; there is a 30 percent probability of receiving payment next month.

Customer C owes $30,000; there is a 10 percent probability of receiving payment next month.

$$\text{Total Expected Value next month} = (\$10,000 \times .60) + (\$20,000 \times .30) + (\$30,000 \times .10)$$
$$= \$15,000. \text{ Total Average Value}$$
$$= (\$10,000 + \$20,000 + \$30,000)/3 = \$20,000.$$
$$\text{Total Most Likely Value} = \$10,000 + \$0 + \$0 = \$10,000.$$

As you can see, it makes a difference which approach you take in coming up with your estimate. We can use an expected value of $15,000, an average value of $20,000, or a most likely value of $10,000. Therefore, it is very useful to go through a decision-based approach to estimation, which is accomplished by calculating expected values.

Capital Budget Leasing

Planning for capital assets involves a process of calculating the net present value of the investment. Net present value is calculated by discounting the future changes in cash inflows and cash outflows using the weighted average cost of capital. The resulting present value of cash flows is compared to the net investment for the capital asset. The result is called net present value. It should be noted that net investment includes all costs to place the capital asset into service plus any working capital requirements. If the capital asset has above average risks, then we would increase the weighted average cost of capital.

If the net present value is positive, this indicates that value is added by making the investment. If the net present value is negative, this indicates value destroyed. The objective is to have a total asset portfolio where the total net present values are above zero. Besides net present value, we can use internal rate of return and discounted payback period to evaluate capital projects.

Internal rate of return is the rate of return that the project earns. It is calculated by finding the discount rate whereby the total present value of cash inflows equals the total present value of cash outflows. Modified internal rate of return can be used to remove the assumption that funds are reinvested each year at the internal rate of return. We can also calculate the number of years it takes to recoup our net investment. Simply calculate a running total of the discounted cash inflows to determine the discounted payback period.

Net present value, internal rate of return, and discounted payback period are three popular economic criteria for evaluating whether or not to invest in a capital asset. All three concepts give consideration to the time value of money. Estimating incremental cash flows is one of the most difficult steps in the overall evaluation process.

Internal Rate of Return

The actual rate of return earned on a project is called internal rate of return (IRR). The IRR is the discount rate where the total present value of cash outflows equals the total present value of cash inflows. For projects with equal cash flows, a payback calculation can be used to find the IRR. If projects have varying cash flows over the life of the project, a trial and error approach must be used. However, most spreadsheet programs include an IRR formula, which makes the calculation very simple.

> *Example:* We have a project with an initial cash outlay of $40,000 and cash inflows each year are $10,000 over the next five years.
>
> $40,000/$10,000 = 4.0 factor, look up the 4.0 factor under Present Value of Annuity Table, across for periods = 5, we find 3.993 under 8 percent. The internal rate of return is approximately 8 percent.

It should be noted that IRR is probably the most popular economic criteria for evaluating capital projects. IRR is best used in conjunction with other economic criteria, such as net present value and discounted payback.

Discounted Payback

Perhaps one of the most popular economic criteria for evaluating capital projects is the payback period. Payback period is the time required for cumulative cash inflows to recover the cash outflows of the project. For example, a $30,000 cash outlay for a project with annual cash inflows of $6,000 would have a payback of 5 years ($30,000/$6,000). The problem with the payback period is that it ignores the time value of money. In order to correct this, we can use discounted cash flows in calculating the payback period. Referring back to our example, if we discount the cash inflows at 15 percent required rate of return we have:

Year 1 – $6,000 × .870 = $5,220   Year 6 – $6,000 × .432 = $2,592
Year 2 – $6,000 × .765 = $4,536   Year 7 – $6,000 × .376 = $2,256
Year 3 – $6,000 × .658 = $3,948   Year 8 – $6,000 × .327 = $1,962
Year 4 – $6,000 × .572 = $3,432   Year 9 – $6,000 × .284 = $1,704
Year 5 – $6,000 × .497 = $2,982   Year 10 – $6,000 × .247 = $1,482

The cumulative total of discounted cash flows after 10 years is $30,114. Therefore, our discounted payback is approximately 10 years as opposed to 5 years under simple payback. As the required rate of return increases, the distortion between simple pay-back and discounted payback grows. Discounted payback is a more appropriate way of measuring the payback period because it considers the time value of money.

Too often financial managers rush into a capital project by simply analyzing the cash flows. Because high levels of uncertainty are associated with most capital proj-ects, the first place to start is with an analysis of the decision itself. Decision trees are extremely useful for mapping out a decision so that all alternatives are considered in relation to probabilities. Decision trees walk you through the different stages and events within the project. Expected values are calculated and a logical outcome is pre-sented for making the right selection.

Cost of Capital

There is a cost of doing business that must serve as your benchmark for how you invest in long-term assets. This cost is called "cost of capital." Cost of capital is the rate you pay to those who lend or invest money into your business. You can think of cost of cap-ital as the rate of return investors require for incurring risk whenever they give you money. Cost of capital applies to long-term funding of assets as opposed to short-term funding of working capital.

Why is cost of capital so important? Well, you have to earn an overall rate of return on your assets that is higher than your cost of capital. If not, you end-up destroying value. So how do you calculate cost of capital? The most popular approach is called the capital asset pricing model or CAPM. CAPM estimates your cost of equity by taking a risk-free rate and adjusting it by risks that are unique to your company or industry. Long-term government bonds are often used to estimate risk-free rates while overall market premiums run around 6 percent.

CAPM is not perfect, as it has many unrealistic assumptions and variations in esti-mates. For example, sources (such as Bloomberg and S&P) for reporting market risks of specific companies provide very different estimates. Additionally, you might find simple estimates are just as accurate as CAPM. For example, simply adding 3 percent to your cost of debt may provide a reasonably accurate estimate of your cost of capital. You can also look at companies that are very similar to your company. In any event, you need to calculate your cost of capital as it is an extremely important component in financial management decision making.

Weighted average cost of capital (WACC) is the overall costs of capital. WACC is based on your current capital structure. Market values are used to assign weights to different components of capital. It should be noted that market weights are preferred over book value weights because market values more closely reflect how you raise your capital. Market weights are calculated by simply dividing the market value for each component by the sum of market values for all components. The following exam-ple illustrates how you calculate WACC.

Current capital structure consists of three components: Long-term debt (10-year A bonds) with a book value of $400,000 and a cost of capital of 6 percent. Common stock with a book value of $200,000 and a cost of capital of 18 percent. Retained earnings with a book value of $50,000 and a cost of capital of 16 percent.

1. *Determine market values for capital components.* Ten-year grade A bonds are selling for $1,150 per bond and the common stock is selling for $40.00 per share. Assume we have 500 bonds outstanding and 15,000 shares of stock outstanding. Market value for debt is $575,000 ($1,150 × 500) and market value for stock is $600,000 ($40.00 × 15,000).

2. *Allocate the equity market value between common stock and retained earnings based on book values.* Common stock = $480,000 ($200,000/$250,000 × $600,000). Retained earnings = $120,000 ($50,000/$250,000 × $600,000).

3. *Calculate the WACC using market weights:*
The debt (bonds) has a market weight of .49 ($575,000/$1,175,000) × .06 cost of capital = .029. Stock has a market weight of .41 ($480,000/$1,175,000) × .18 cost of capital = .074. Finally, retained earnings has a market weight of .10 ($120,000/$1,175,000) × .16 cost of capital = .016. This gives us a WACC of .119 or 11.9 percent (.029 + .074 + .016).

Capital Structure

The theory behind capital structure is to find the right mix of long-term funds that minimizes the costs of capital and maximizes the value of the organization. This ideal mix is called the optimal capital structure. It can be argued that an optimal capital structure really does not exist, because changing the mix of capital will not change values.

However, four approaches can be used to find the optimal capital structure. They are: Net Operating Income (NOI), Net Income (NI), Traditional, and Modigliani-Miller. It should be noted that all of these approaches assume no income taxes exist, all residual earnings are distributed as dividends, and operating risks remain consistent.

The NOI approach holds that costs of capital are relatively the same regardless of the degree of leverage. The NI approach takes the opposite view; costs of capital and market values of companies are affected by the use of leverage. The Traditional approach is a mix of both the NOI approach and the NI approach. Finally, the Modigliani-Miller view is that costs of capital and market values are independent of your capital structure. In practice, there are many factors that influence capital structure. They include growth in sales, asset composition, risk attitudes within the organization, and so on. The best approach seems to be to focus on a range of capital structures in managing the organization.

One way of determining the right mix of capital is to measure the impacts of different financing plans on earnings per share (EPS). The objective is to find the level of EBIT (Earnings before Interest and Taxes) where EPS does not change; that is, the EBIT breakeven. At the EBIT breakeven, EPS will be the same under each financing plan we have under consideration. As a general rule, using financial leverage will generate more EPS where EBIT is greater than the EBIT breakeven. Using less leverage will generate more EPS where EBIT is less than EBIT breakeven.

EBIT breakeven is calculated by finding the point where alternative financing plans are equal according to the following formula:

(EBIT − I) × (1.0 − TR)/Equity number of shares after implementing financing plan
I: Interest Expense TR: Tax Rate formula assumes no preferred stock

The formula is calculated for each financing plan. For example, you may be considering issuing more stock under Plan A and incurring more debt under Plan B. Each of these plans will have different impacts on EPS. You want to find the right plan that helps maximize EPS, but still manage risks within an acceptable range. EBIT-EPS analysis can help find the right capital mix for high returns and low costs of capital.

For publicly traded companies, capital is raised by issuing debt or equity which in turn is invested into assets. Hopefully these capital investments will earn a rate of return higher than your cost of capital. Capital assets are reported on the balance sheet. As the world becomes more and more competitive, the returns generated by assets not reported on the balance sheet becomes much more important. And for some organizations, this may represent the single biggest source of value creation.

One of these hidden assets for creating value is so-called intellectual capital. Intellectual capital (IC) is the intangible stuff that provides your organization with knowledge, strategy, and customer service. Internal sources of IC include your people who possess the knowledge and expertise to make your organization work. Internal IC also includes your management information systems, brand names, and copyrights. External IC would represent your loyal customers and suppliers.

Finally, how do you measure IC? Well it is not easy because IC is such a new concept. Measurement of IC can include things such as employee qualifications, customer retention rates, and registered copyrights. For now, most companies are focused on measuring the traditional sources of capital. However, in the future intellectual capital may become one of the most important components of value creation.

RATIOS AND ANALYSIS

Cash Flow Ratios

Although not widely used, cash flow ratios can be useful in determining the adequacy of cash and cash equivalents. Cash flow ratios are used depending on the critical needs of cash. For example, if cash is critical to servicing long-term debt, then cash flow to long-term debt would be a good ratio. If liquid assets are critical to meeting current liabilities, then cash + marketable securities to current liabilities would be useful. Some of the variations for cash flow ratios include:

> Cash Flow/Total Debt, Cash Flow/Long-Term Debt, Cash
> + Marketable Securities/Working Capital, Cash
> + Marketable Securities/Current Liabilities.

Another good cash flow ratio is operating cash flow to net income. This ratio shows the extent to which net income is supported by operating cash flows. Cash flow from operations is calculated by adjusting net income for noncash items, such as depreciation.

Cash flow is reported on the statement of cash flows and cash flow ratios can be calculated from a complete set of financial statements.

Accounts Receivable Ratios

Ratio analysis can be used to tell how well you are managing your accounts receivable. The two most common ratios for accounts receivable are turnover and number of days in receivables. These ratios are calculated as:

Accounts Receivable Turnover = Credit Sales/Average Receivable Balance.

Example: Annual credit sales were $400,000, beginning balance for accounts receivable was $55,000, and the year-end balance was $45,000. The turnover rate is 8, calculated as follows: Average receivable balance is $50,000 ($55,000 + $45,000)/2. The turnover ratio is $400,000/$50,000. This indicates that receivables were converted over into cash eight times during the year.

Number of days in receivables = 365 Days in the Year/Turnover Ratio. Using the same information from the previous example gives us 46 days on average to collect our accounts receivable for the year.

Two other ratios that can be used are receivables to sales and receivables to assets. Referring back to our first example, we would have a receivable to sales ratio of 12.5 percent ($50,000/$400,000). Remember, ratios are only effective when used in comparison to other benchmarks, trends, or industry standards. A turnover ratio well below the industry average would indicate much slower conversion of receivables than other companies. A much lower receivables to sales ratio than the industry average might indicate much better policies in getting sales converted into cash.

Asset Ratio Analysis

The ability to generate revenues and earn profits on assets can be measured through ratio analysis. Several types of ratios can be calculated regarding the utilization of assets.

Example: Asset turnover gives an indication of how often assets are converted into sales. The asset turnover ratio is calculated as follows: Sales/Average Assets. If annual sales were $200,000 and the average asset balance for the year was $160,000, the asset turnover rate would be 1.25. A higher turnover rate implies effective use of assets to generate sales.

Receivable and inventory ratios are part of asset ratio analysis. Inventory turnover gives an indication of how much inventory is held during the reporting period.

Example: Cost of goods sold for the year was $270,000 and the average inventory balance during the year was $90,000. This results in an inventory turnover rate of 3 ($270,000/$90,000). The average number of days inventory is held is calculated as: 365 Days in the Reporting Period/Inventory Turnover Rate. In our example, this would be 122 days.

Finally, you can look at the use of capital for generating revenues. Two common ratios are total capital turnover and investment rate. Total capital turnover is calculated as: Sales/Average Total Capital. Average total capital consists of both debt and equity. The investment rate is the rate of change in capital. The investment rate is calculated by simply dividing the amount of change in capital/total beginning capital. A high investment rate would imply an aggressive program for generating future sales.

Accounts Receivable Ratio Analysis

Ratio analysis can be used to determine the time required to pay accounts payable invoices. This ratio is calculated as follows: Accounts Payables/Purchases per day.

Example: Assume we have total accounts payables of $20,000 and our annual purchases on account total $400,000. Our purchases per day are $400,000/365 days in the annual reporting period or $1,096. The average number of days to pay accounts payable is $20,000/1,096 or 18 days. The result of this ratio should be compared to the average terms available from creditors.

If the average number of days is close to the average credit terms, this may indicate aggressive working capital management; that is, using spontaneous sources of financing. However, if the number of days is well beyond the average credit terms, this could indicate difficulty in making payments to creditors.

Another ratio that can be used in managing accounts payable is sales to accounts payable. This ratio gives an indication of a company's ability to obtain interest-free funds.

Example: If we had sales of $600,000 and accounts payables of $20,000, this gives us a ratio of 30. As this ratio increases, it becomes more difficult to obtain trade credit.

Return on Equity

For publicly traded companies, one of the most watched financial measurements is return on equity. Return on equity is calculated by dividing net income over average shareholder's equity. Financial managers break this ratio down into three components for managing the organization. The three components of return on equity are return on sales, asset turnover, and financial leverage. Therefore, we can breakdown return on equity as: (net income/sales) × (sales/assets) × (assets/equity).

Example: Net income is $100,000, equity is $400,000, sales were $500,000, and assets are $600,000.

Return on equity = ($100,000/$500,000) × ($500,000/$600,000) × ($600,000/$400,000)
= .20 × .8333 × 1.50 = .25 or 25 percent.

The trick is to manage these three components in such a way that you maximize return on equity. Remember, if you increase one ratio, it will decrease a corresponding component. For example, if you were to increase assets, this would increase your leverage (assets/equity), but would decrease your turnover (sales/assets). Additionally, you can further break down the three component ratios into more detailed ratios. For example, the first component ratio is return on sales. This can be broken down into operating margin on sales. The point is to start at the top (return on equity), move to the middle layer (3 component ratios), and then move to the bottom layer (detail ratios).

Profitability Ratios

Profitability ratios are used to evaluate management's ability to create earnings from revenue-generating bases within the organization. Profitability ratios measure the earnings by dividing the earnings by a base, such as assets, sales, or equity. Four common profitability ratios are:

Profit Margin on Sales = Net Income/Sales

Operating Margin on Sales = Earnings before Interest and Taxes/Sales

Return on Assets = Net Income/Average Assets

Return on Equity = Net Income/Average Common Equity

Example: Net sales (gross sales less allowances) are $500,000.

Earnings before interest and taxes are $50,000 and net income is $25,000. Asset balances are: beginning $190,000 and ending $210,000.

Common stock balances: beginning $325,000 and ending $325,000

Retained earnings balances: beginning $100,000 and ending $150,000

Profit margin = $25,000/$500,000 = .05 or 5 percent

Operating margin = $50,000/$500,000 = .10 or 10 percent

Return on assets = $25,000/($190,000 + $210,000)/2 = .125 or 12.5 percent

Return on equity = $25,000/($425,000 + $475,000)/2 = .055 or 5.5 percent

Profitability ratios are widely used by creditors, investors, and others who are interested in finding out how management generates its earnings.

Operating Cost Ratios

Ratios can be used to help measure the effectiveness over cost control. Operating costs can be monitored with the use of direct and indirect operating ratios. Examples of direct operating ratios are:

Direct Labor to Sales = Direct Labor Costs/Sales

Direct Materials to Sales = Direct Materials/Sales

Factory Overhead to Sales = Factory Overhead/Sales

Indirect operating ratios can be computed for almost any itemized expense. Two examples are:

Computer Expenses to Sales = Computer Expenses/Sales

Travel Expenses to Sales = Travel Expenses/Sales

Example: Direct labor costs are $100,000, factory overhead is $200,000, computer expenses are $15,000, and sales were $500,000.

Direct Labor to Sales = $100,000/$500,000 = .20 or 20 percent

Factory Overhead to Sales = $200,000/$500,000 = .40 or 40 percent

Computer Expenses to Sales = $15,000/$500,000 = .03 or 3 percent

Operating cost ratios are often used by production managers to monitor trends and identify problems. If a significant change occurs, the problem must be identified as either internal (such as operations) or external (such as economic conditions). Because investors and other outsiders do not have access to operating information, operating ratios are rarely used outside the organization.

Sustainable Growth

Is there such a thing as too much growth? In financial management, we try to balance the management of growth with our asset base. For example, if sales were to grow too fast, then we would deplete our financial assets, resulting in extreme risks to the organization. If sales grow too slow, then we run the risk of destroying value by holding assets that earn a rate below the cost of capital. The objective in financial management is to manage a sustainable rate of growth that creates value year after year.

The growth rate in sales is limited by the growth we can obtain from the equity side of the balance sheet. Therefore, sustainability is a function of equity growth rates, not sales growth rates. The formula for calculating a sustainable growth rate (G) is:

G = Margin × Turnover × Leverage × Retention

Margin = Net Income/Sales

Turnover = Sales/Assets

Leverage = Assets/Equity

Retention = % of Earnings Retained

Consequently, if we want to maintain a consistent level in profit margins, asset turnover, leverage, and retained earnings, then we should grow our sales by G (sustainable growth rate). Changing the sustainable growth rate is a function of the four components of sustainable growth. For example, eliminating marginal products can increase the margin component or paying out less dividends will increase the retention component. The trick is to manage the four components so that sales growth follows the sustainable growth rate.

The Z Score to Assess Bankruptcies

Financial insolvency or bankruptcy can be forecasted using the Z score. The Z score combines several ratios with a statistical application called MDA—multiple discriminant analysis. The Z score is highly accurate in predicting bankruptcies. The Z score is about 90 percent accurate in forecasting business failures the first year and about 80 percent accurate the second year.

The Z score is calculated by adding five ratios with applicable MDA weights:

$$Z = 1.2\,(A) + 1.4\,(B) + 3.3\,(C) + .6\,(D) + .999\,(E)$$

A: working capital/total assets
B: retained earnings/total assets
C: earnings before interest taxes/total assets
D: market value of equities/book value of debt
E: sales/total assets

The following guideline is used to score an organization:

If the Z score is 1.8 or less, very high probability of bankruptcy.

If the Z score is 1.81 to 2.99, not sure about bankruptcy.

If the Z score is 3.0 or higher, bankruptcy is unlikely.

Example: Total assets = $1,000, retained earnings = $400, earnings before interest and taxes = $50, sales = $1,500, market value of stock = $600, book value of debt = $700, and working capital = $100.

$$1.2 \times (\$100/\$1,000) = .120$$
$$1.4 \times (\$400/\$1,000) = .560$$
$$3.3 \times (\$50/\$1,000) = .165$$
$$.6 \times (\$600/\$700) = .514$$
$$.999 \times (\$1,500/\$1,000) = 1.499$$

Total Z score = 2.86 not sure

9

OPERATIONS

EFFICIENCY MEASURES

Almost every discussion of competitiveness revolves around the concept of productivity improvement. How to measure that concept, unfortunately, remains a matter of controversy. In today's relatively unforgiving business environment, a company that enjoys a clear productivity advantage usually finds that fact reflected in a comparatively high *Net Profit to Net Sales,* a relatively high *Net Profit to Net Worth,* and a list of satisfied customers. Likewise, most companies with low productivity already understand the consequences. There is, however, no universal measure of company productivity, although this concept is often defined *as the number of units of output produced per unit of input.*

Some economist attempt to use financial ratios as substitutes for actual physical measures in productivity analysis. All evidence suggests that the conclusions drawn from such studies are, at best, confusing and, at worst, utterly misleading. *Net Sales to Fixed Assets* is, for example, not a good productivity measure, since the book value of fixed assets is greatly affected by the depreciation period allowed and by the age of the assets. *Net Sales of Fixed Assets* is an important causal ratio with respect to a company's operating results and its fundamental financial structure, but it is not intended to measure the productivity of physical facilities.

As a compromise between broad generalities and unreasonably detailed approaches, a simple ratio, *Units per Man-Hour* (person-hours), would seem to be a basic measure of employee productivity and is often employed. As a company acquires new technology, there is often a shift in the balance between direct-labor employees (who work directly on the product) and indirect-labor employees (who are involved in estimating, software support, supervision/coordination, and maintenance). With increased automation, indirect labor tends to rise rapidly, leading to an artificially great increase in reported productivity if management continues to use direct-labor man-hours as the denominator for this ratio. Should *Units per Man-Hour* be based on the hours of all employees, including sales, general, and administrative personnel? The answer depends on the purpose of the analysis.

A somewhat more narrowly focused ratio, designed to measure labor productivity, is *Value Added per Man-Hour,* which involves subtracting all outside purchases (such as utilities, supplies, and services), as well as direct material, from net sales before dividing by total man-hours for the year. If, for example, the company had purchased

111

$200,000 of such utilities, supplies, and services during the year, its value added would be $600,000: net sales of $1 million minus total outside purchases of $400,000 (direct material of $200,000 plus other outside purchases of $200,000). Value added of $600,000 divided by 20,000 man-hours yields *Value Added per Man-Hour* of $30.

In any process in which work must flow from one operation to another, from one workstation to another, the capacities of each workstation must match. Just as the chain is only as strong as its weakest link, so too is the work output as great as the smallest capacity. In an examination of more than 500 operations, in which workflow depended on matched capacities, it has been found that, in the majority of cases, mismatches were the order of the day.

Myths and Realities

Tough competition worldwide is forcing service center executives to reconsider their conceptions about productivity. As we look closely at these beliefs, we find that many of them are simply myths. Companies that base productivity programs on such myths may actually achieve gains, but these gains will fall far short of their potential and come at too high a cost.

Everyone's view of productivity is different. To one, it is making labor work faster. To another, it is the development of systems. To another, it is the use of capital. To others, it is new equipment, a new organization, a computer system, only to name a few. Companies tend to deal with each of these elements in isolation, assuming that, by upgrading each separately, they will gain a full measure of improvement. That is a myth. This piecemeal approach fails, because it ignores the fact that all of these elements are interconnected and affect each other in a myriad of ways. The real productivity payoff comes from dealing with all of the related elements at the same time so that everything is made to happen as planned, in the right quantity and quality, with the right work effort, in the right amount of time, and in the right place.

At first glance, most service center operations appear to have this kind of synchronization, with an incredible number of things happening with amazing precision. This synchronization seems very impressive, until you look behind it. Then you discover that it actually involves the calculated use of a large amount of waste. Companies, for instance, meet their schedules by building excess time and a certain number of rejects into them. This kind of waste, in terms of manpower, material, inventory, equipment, and facilities, riddles virtually every facet of every kind of organization.

The total amount of waste, once identified, can be dismaying. Yet, identifying such waste is the first step toward eliminating it. The resultant gains in productivity can be enormous, and the savings are almost pure profit, dropping straight to the bottom line.

Myths about Middle Management.   When management attacks waste across the board, it obtains far greater gains in a far shorter time than expected. It also uncovers several more myths about productivity. A major myth is the belief that someone with the title "manager" or "supervisor" actually knows how to manage or supervise. Middle managers, in fact, are generally named to their positions without their having a clear understanding of their new responsibilities or adequate training in how to carry them out. Studies show that the training of middle management is almost universally neglected. This neglect can be enormously wasteful, since it is the middle manager who has the mission of implementing senior management's directives and accomplishing its goals.

Diagnostic attitude and perception studies show that senior and middle management are often pursuing different, even conflicting, goals. While senior management's goal may be to improve profits, middle management may be directing its main efforts toward keeping the workforce happy, or the equipment running. Diagnosing each individual manager's attitudes, perceptions, and goals can be a first step toward building an effective management team—one that knows where it is going and how to get there.

When things go wrong, the blame generally falls not on the managers, but on the workers. The typical complaint is that workers do not really want to work or improve, or that they take no pride in their jobs or their companies. Attitude studies, however, refute these charges. They show that the vast majority of workers want to work much closer to their capabilities, but are kept from doing so by inadequate and uninspired management and supervision.

Myths about Systems.   In recent years companies have tried to manage their operations more effectively through the use of systems such as production control, strategic planning, human resources, billing control, and management by objectives. Here the myth is that, by simply imposing a new system and giving it an impressive-sounding name, you are actually going to get improved results. The reality is that such systems are no better than the people running them. If those people lack the proper skills and supervision, they will simply degrade the system. Too often the system is never properly implemented in the first place. What is needed is someone who understands the system, with all its potential imperfections, who can put it in place, adjust it, and, as conditions change, continue to upgrade it. The goal must be to make the system work as planned, with everyone involved knowing their function and carrying it out correctly. Only then does the system truly work and repay the company with increased productivity.

Myths about Computers.   Another increasingly prevalent myth is the idea that computers in themselves are the answer to all problems. The reality is that computers can represent a huge uncontrolled cost, with results that fall far short of expectations. An analysis of a typical computer system uncovers a large amount of incompatibility and redundancy, a dearth of software for operational or training functions, a lack of adequate training and communications, and an inadequate measurement of costs and results. Costs are generally understated, ignoring the user cost, while results are often unknown.

In most companies, senior management has effectively abdicated its control over the computer area, by leaving key decisions to the data-processing experts. Left to set their own goals, most data-processing experts design a system that may be technically correct, but which, as a practical matter, may not help management in achieving its goals and objectives.

To regain control over its computer systems, management must first begin communicating its needs to the data-processing experts and, perhaps, even retraining those experts so that they can better understand and support management's objectives. Once management succeeds in harnessing its computers to its objectives, it is well on its way to creating a more manageable, more productive, and more profitable operation.

The failure of computers to live up to expectations should not be surprising. Business has developed a great many ingenious systems for improving productivity, all of which, in practice, have been disappointments. The fault, though, is not with the computers or the systems, but with the people running, supervising, and managing them. Computers and systems are just tools. The human beings using those tools must be skilled in their use and capable of applying them to the proper objectives. Accomplishing this is not easy, nor does it lend itself to a piecemeal approach.

The Myth That "We Can Do It Ourselves."   With regard to installing productivity-improvement programs, one fundamental myth stands out time and again: Company managements believe they can make the necessary changes themselves. What these managers fail to realize is the incredible resistance to change that exists in every type of business.

Experience shows that, by far, the greatest difficulty encountered in trying to improve productivity is not in finding large areas of waste, or even developing prescriptions and solutions to break down the barriers to productivity and allow people to achieve their full potential. By far, the greatest difficulty is overcoming resistance to change, in order to get the process started. It requires dedication and tenacity to overcome such resistance.

Summary

The most effective approach, as stated earlier, is to seek productivity improvements, on a simultaneous basis, throughout the entire organization. In this way, as management upgrades systems and equipment, it also upgrades the people who make those systems and equipment work, thus making everything more responsive to management's goals.

When implemented properly by management that truly wants to increase productivity, such changes can create a synergistic effect—an operation where the total productive result really does exceed the sum of the separate parts.

Exhibits 9.1 through 9.4 provide an experienced-based review of how to meet nonuniform production demands that will help contradict productivity improvement myths. Exhibit 9.5 provides you with an analysis form for the purpose of analyzing your own operational improvement methods.

After review of the analysis results, go back and review Exhibits 9.1 through 9.4 and pick which operational planning strategy is right for you.

**EXHIBIT 9.1   Operational Planning and Control Strategies
for Meeting Nonuniform Demands**

Methods	Costs	Remarks
Strategy: Absorb demand fluctuation by shifting manpower capacity.		
Move employees from one position to another, where the demand is higher	No additional cost is involved, except perhaps the cost of additional training of employees	The motivation level of some employees may decrease as a result of a frequent shifting to different positions
Strategy: Use part-time employees.		
Hire part-time employees, when the demand increases	Additional cost of searching for and compensating part-time employees	Part-time employees may not perform effectively enough if they do not get sufficient training
Strategy: Use existing employees for overtime.		
Work overtime to accommodate peak demands	Additional cost of overtime	Additional compensation may enhance motivation of employees
Strategy: Reschedule the vacation period of employees.		
Reschedule the vacation period to accommodate peak demands	No additional cost, except perhaps an "appreciation" bonus	Occasionally employees may get dissatisfied for not having vacations when they want them
Strategy: Use variable work shifts.		
Assign employees to various work shifts to meet specific operational goals	No additional costs, except perhaps increased pay rate for night shifts	Sometimes employees may be discouraged from the lack of constant work schedules
Strategy: Stabilize demand pattern for services.		
Offer special price reductions or discounts during a period of low demand	Cost of discounts only	Stabilizing demand pattern may create a more uniform operational procedure
Strategy: Use an appointment procedure.		
Develop and maintain an appointment schedule for specialized services	No additional cost	Stabilizing the equipment and human resource capacity utilization
Strategy: Use a priority procedure.		
Develop and maintain a priority procedure to accommodate the operational demands	No additional cost	Stabilizing the equipment and human resource capacity utilization
Strategy: Use a delayed delivery procedure.		
Develop and maintain a delayed delivery schedule to meet operational requirements	No additional cost	Stabilizing the equipment and human resource capacity utilization
Strategy: Maintain a fixed operational schedule.		
Develop and maintain a fixed operational schedule for standard service	Cost per unit service is reduced to a minimum	This is one of the most popular methods of rendering a standard service

EXHIBIT 9.2 Production Planning Strategies for Meeting Nonuniform Demands

Methods	Costs	Remarks
Strategy: Absorb demand fluctuations by varying inventory level, back-ordering, or shifting demand.		
Produce in earlier period and hold until product is demanded	Cost of holding inventory	Service operations cannot hold service inventory. They must staff for peak levels or shift demand
Offer to deliver the product or service later when capacity is available	Causes a delay in the receipt of revenue at the minimum. May result in lost customers	Manufacturing companies with perishable products often are restrained in the use of this method
Special marketing efforts to shift the demand to slack periods	Costs of advertising, discounts, or promotional programs	This is another example of the interrelationship between functions within a business
Strategy: Change only the production rate in accordance with the nonuniform demand pattern.		
Work additional hours without changing the work-force size	Requires overtime premium pay	Reduces the time available for maintenance work without interrupting production
Staff for high production levels, so that overtime is not required	Excess personnel wages during periods of slack demand	Sometimes workforce can be utilized for deferred maintenance during periods of low demand
Subcontract work to other firms	The company must still pay its own overhead plus the overhead and profit for the subcontractors	Utilizes the capacity of other firms, but provides less control of schedules and quality levels
Revise make-or-buy decisions to purchase items when capacity is fully loaded	The company must have skills, tooling, and equipment that will be unutilized in slack periods	All of these methods require capital investments sufficient for the peak production rate, which will be underutilized in slack periods
Strategy: Change the size of the workforce to vary the production level in accordance with demand.		
Hire additional personnel as demand increases	Employment costs for advertising, travel, interviewing, training, etc. Shift premium costs if an additional shift is added.	Skilled workers might not be available when needed, since they are more likely to be employed elsewhere

116

EXHIBIT 9.2 *(Continued)*

Methods	Costs	Remarks
Lay off personnel as demand subsides	Cost of severance pay and increases in unemployment insurance costs. Loss of efficiency because of decreased moral and higher-seniority workers being moved into jobs for which they are inexperienced as they move into ("bump") jobs of workers with less seniority	The company must have adequate capital investment in equipment for peak workforce level

EXHIBIT 9.3   Classification of Operational Activities

Manufacturing Activities		
Job Shop Production	**Batch Production**	**Flow Production**
Custom-designed products	Bakery	Appliances
Special purpose machinery	Clothing	Brewery
Tool-making manufacturing	Electrical products	Brick and tile
General engineering shop	Fasteners	Cable and wire
Model manufacturing	Footwear	Chemicals
Handmade products	Furniture	Cement
	Jewelry	Cosmetics
	Machinery	Food
	Metal products	Glass
	Plastic products	Newspapers
	Printing	Paint
	Sheet metal products	Paper mill
		Pharmaceutical
		Refinery
		Soft drinks
		Textile mill
		Tobacco products
		Vehicles

**EXHIBIT 9.4 Comparative Evaluation
of Manufacturing Methods**

Description	Manufacturing Methods		
	Job Shop	**Batch Production**	**Flow Production**
Manufacturing	To customer's orders only	To customer's orders only	To stock and sometimes to order
Type of order	Most orders are unique and nonrepetitive	Most orders are not unique and repetitive	All orders are standard and repetitive
Product range	There is no standard range of products	There is a broad range of standard and non-standard products	There is a limited range of standard products
Product unit cost	Very high	Average	Very low
Production volume	Very low, usually one or few items	Average, in batches of tens, hundreds, or even thousands	Very high
Production method	Very diversified and sometimes repetitive	Diversified, but usually repetitive	Standardized and repetitive (e.g., conveyor line)
Equipment application	Very general application to various manufacturing processes	General and semispecialized; approximately 1 week in manufacturing processes	Very specialized application to a limited number of tasks
Operational capacity planning	Can be scheduled at short notice only	Can be planned and scheduled approximately 1 week in advance	Must be planned and scheduled well in advance
Raw material inventory	Should be purchased for every order on an individual basis	Should be purchased in advance in optimal quantities	Must be repurchased in advance in optimal quantities
Work-in-process and components inventory	No need	Buffer stocks should be kept in optimal quantities for selected products	Buffer stocks should be kept in optimal quantities for all products
Finished-goods inventory	No need	Optimal quantities should be kept for selected products	Optimal quantities should be kept for all finished goods
Subcontracting services	Should be used on an individual order basis	Should be preplanned and used on an individual batch basis	Must be planned well in advance for every production run
Personnel skills, requirements	Very high level for a general application	Average level for semi-standardized application	Average level for a highly standardized application

EXHIBIT 9.5   Job Sequence Outline

Date: _____

Staff: _____

Area: _____

Reviewed by: _____

1. *Organization Chart:* (See Attachment A*)
   a. Prepare organizational chart for areas in similar manner as shown on Attachment A.

2. *Department Functions:*
   a. Brief description of department's function: _____
   _____
   _____

   b. Supervisors and foremen's names and their normal working hours:

Name	Position	Hours

   c. Prepare the 'Employee Flexibility and Training Needs Status' data:

   (See Attachment B)

   d. Identify normal working hours of department, shifts, breaks, and lunch times.

Name	Position	Hours

   e. How are vacations and absenteeism covered in the department? Are employees borrowed from other areas to cover these situations? Which departments are people drawn from normally? Can and do they shift people out of the area due to major breakdowns? How is this time reported? What is the absentee percentage in department in last 12 months?
   _____
   _____
   _____
   _____

*Attachments are not included.

(continued)

EXHIBIT 9.5 *(Continued)*

f. What is the relationship of this department to others?

g. Are there any repetitive problems in such relationships that need attention, in order to make interfacing of workflow more effective? What are they?

3. *Department Scheduling:*
   a. Where do production schedules originate?

   How soon does the department receive the schedules? Are they timely?

   When do the people involved in the flow, line supervisors, actually get the schedules?

   Does the supervisor think the schedules are adequate?

   b. Does the schedule tie in materials and personnel requirements effectively? If not, who determines this date and when?

   c. How is production stated on schedules and reports? In terms of units per hour, shift, day, week, etc?

   Are due dates or completion times reflected on these schedules?

   Who establishes times of completion? Are they realistic?

EXHIBIT 9.5 *(Continued)*

d. What is the frequency of schedule changes?

Is this a formal (written) or a verbal change?

e. Do any schedules exist for support personnel functions?

Who prepares these schedules?

How are major clean-ups handled?

What type of checklist/reports are used for supporting functions?

(1) In any given area of the department, how are work assignments made? Verbal, Written?

(2) How is work laid out in the department? Is it planned a day ahead, 1 week prior? How?

(3) Does a line supervisor shift personnel on need-priority during the day? How is this done? How is different work tracked?

(4) What happens, particularly in production areas, when product mix changes? How is this handled? By whom? What types of schedules or controls are used for making changes and reporting changes?

(5) How is nonscheduled work, e.g., cleaning (minor), or other small tasks, requiring shift of employees, handled? How is this work scheduled? If not scheduled, how does supervisor plan these support functions?

(6) Does the supervisor experience problems due to inadequate planning? What does he feel would prevent these situations from recurring?

(continued)

EXHIBIT 9.5   *(Continued)*

f. Do backlogs exist in the department?
   How are the backlogs expressed in hours, units, work orders, etc.?

   What is the normal backlog in the department?

g. In *maintenance-type areas,* where does work input originate?

   Who receives input and what is done with it?

   Does a work order system exist in the department? How does it function?

   How are work schedules prepared? By whom?

   Are schedules prepared in terms of person-hours per job? If not, how is it done?

   Are only actual person-hours reported for work after work is completed? Why?

   How are these hours reported? By whom?

   How are work priorities established for the department? By whom?

   Does this system of setting priorities work?

h. Describe peak workload periods experienced by the department. When do they occur? Hourly, daily, weekly, monthly?

   What are the reasons for these peaks and valleys in the department workload?

   Does the supervisor think this fluctuation is necessary? Could it be reduced? How?

EXHIBIT 9.5 *(Continued)*

    i. In clerical areas, list *key* documents processed. Describe purpose, where documents originate, how often received, what is done with them, who handles them, and where they go when they are completed:

Document	Purpose	Originator	Frequency Received	What Is Done to Them?	By Whom?	Where Are They Sent?

    j. What types/categories of historical data are maintained in the department?

_____

_____

Are these records/logs updated on a routine basis? By whom?

_____

What is the purpose of maintaining data/logs?

_____

Note: Obtain live samples of each type volume log/record maintained in department or sketch of column heading for each type identifying data covered and purpose of each.

    k. What standards are used in the department?

_____

Are these standards used for scheduling purposes? If not, why not?

_____

_____

Are supervisors' estimates used for scheduling work?

_____

List estimates used in the department and units of measure, work-to-time relationships:

_____   _____

_____   _____

_____   _____

_____   _____

4. *Physical Layout:*
   a. Draw physical layout of area. Indicate area designations, major pieces of equipment, furniture, etc. Denote names of areas surrounding this department as they exist.

5. *Personnel Roster:*
   a. Complete personnel roster, indicating employees names, hire dates, shifts, job classifications, and positions, as well as appropriate pay rates and vacations, in weeks, for total department. Employees' names should be arranged in alphabetical order.

6. *Flexibility Chart:*
   a. Flexibility charts are used to identify employee's skills. How could they be used in the department where he/she now works?

(continued)

EXHIBIT 9.5 *(Continued)*

7. *Equipment List and Location within the Department:*
   a. List all major machines and equipment located in the department. Their limitations and normal operating output speeds in units/hour:

   (Production Areas Only)

Quanity	Name of Equipment of Machine	Limitations Maximum Output/Hour	Normal Operating Speed-Output/ Hour
_____	_____	_____	_____
_____	_____	_____	_____
_____	_____	_____	_____
_____	_____	_____	_____
_____	_____	_____	_____
_____	_____	_____	_____

   b. Draw equipment layout as shown on Attachment G. (Sample)

8. *Current System:*
   a. Prepare paper/workflow of existing system in force as per sample. Break system down from input (planning) to execution (implementation of plan) to reporting stage (what was accomplished and when).
   b. Obtain live copies of all controls/documents used in area and write purpose of each on reverse side of controls and number each control to identify position in flow cycle of existing system.

9. *Product Flow:*
   a. Indicate flow of finished product/materials through area, starting with first stage of activity, moving through area, routing movement through department through final output from area.

10. *Major Operating Problems:*
    a. What are the major *operating* problems existing in the department as described by the supervisor?

	Problems	Reasons
1.	_____	_____
2.	_____	_____
3.	_____	_____
4.	_____	_____
5.	_____	_____
6.	_____	_____
7.	_____	_____
8.	_____	_____
9.	_____	_____
10.	_____	_____

11. *Method Changes Anticipated in the Future:*
    a. What changes are contemplated for the department? When will they take place? What effect will they have on the department's functions/workload.

Definition of Change	Time Table	Effect of Change
_____	_____	_____
_____	_____	_____
_____	_____	_____
_____	_____	_____

EXHIBIT 9.5 *(Continued)*

b. What is the relationship of these plans/changes to the planned installation of the pending system?

_____

_____

_____

12. *Supervisory Points:*
   a. What is the supervisor looking to us to provide, to assist him in better control and scheduling of his/her department?

   _____

   _____

   _____

   _____

13. *Training:*
   a. Do you have any formal or special training for your people?

   _____

   _____

   _____

   b. If no, how do you train your people?

   _____

   _____

   _____

   c. Do you feel this is adequate?

   _____

   _____

   _____

   d. What do you feel are its shortcomings?

   _____

   _____

   _____

   e. How much time during a month do you spend on training?

   _____

   f. How do you know when a person needs training? (By new person to job, by error rates, by performance, etc.)

   _____

   _____

   _____

   g. What type of historical data are maintained on training needs and results?

   _____

   _____

   _____

ANALYSIS AND EVALUATION

Productivity Defined

Productivity, in its simplest form, is a ratio of the products and services of an organization to the inputs consumed to generate them. Looked at a little differently, it is a measure of the efficient use of a company's resources. For the mathematically oriented:

$$\text{Productivity} = \frac{\text{Total outputs of the firm}}{\text{Total inputs used by the firm}}$$

Thus, if a company generates the same output with less input, the ratio gets larger, and it can be said that the organization has been more productive. This increase, then, is at the heart of productivity-improvement efforts. It is insufficient to measure the ratio of output to input, unless something is done to increase that ratio overtime. To do this, management and the organization, as a whole, have only five options to making the ratio bigger.

1. Make the output larger for the same input;
2. Make the input smaller for the same output;
3. Increase the output while decreasing the input;
4. Increase output faster than the input increases; and
5. Decrease the output less than the inputs decrease.

Story of the Pipeline

Many years ago, it is told, a farmer in a Midwest community decided to pipe water from a stream on his property to a corner of his farm, which was given over to grazing his cows. He bought one-hundred feet of three-inch-diameter pipe and, when he had it all laid out and connected, he found he was about twelve feet short of the trough to which the water was to be piped. When he went to the store for additional pipe he found that they were out of three-inch pipe, so he bought two reducers and twelve feet of one-inch pipe, and got his twelve additional feet. The output of water to the trough was insufficient to keep the cows supplied with water. Explaining the problem to a neighbor, he expressed perplexity at his problem and showed him how well the water pumped into the beginning of the line at maximum pressure; but at the delivery end, he had hardly a trickle. The neighbor explained to him that the output at the end of the pipe was controlled by the capacity of the twelve-foot length of one-inch pipe. No more water could pass through the line in a given period than could pass through the smaller diameter pipe.

This story may seem exaggerated, but, in many service center flows, the mismatching of capacities is a very serious situation.

Aspects of Financial Statements Most Critical to Management

Although the statement of income (Exhibit 9.6) and statement of financial position (Exhibit 9.7) reflect the financial health of the entire business, certain portions of both statements pertain directly to the manager's area of direct control.

Cost of goods sold represents the cost of manufacturing the company's products, and consists of direct materials, direct labor, and manufacturing overhead, which are covered in the following section.

The cost of materials used directly in the company's products, will be: (1) raw material and (2) purchased parts.

Direct labor costs are those associated with processing. Machine operators and assemblers, who work directly on the product itself, are classified as direct labor, as opposed to such people as inspectors, material handlers, and maintenance people (called indirect labor), who provide essential services, but who do not work on or change the configuration themselves.

The final cost (costs included in overhead) consists of all other costs not considered direct materials or direct labor costs. Overhead includes such costs as indirect labor; taxes and insurance; heat, light, and power; depreciation; and indirect materials and supplies (tooling, janitorial supplies, lubricating oils, paperwork expenses).

EXHIBIT 9.6   Statement of Income

Statement of Income
For Year Ended Dec. 31, 20XX

Gross sales		$45,750,525
Less: Returns and allowances	$ 732,561	
Cash discounts	683,228	
		1,415,789
Net sales		$44,334,736
Cost of goods sold		25,110,706
Gross Margins		$19,224,134
Sales administration	700,335	
Sales commissions	652,079	
General and administrative	1,632,994	
Total		$ 2,895,408
Operating Profit		$16,238,726
Gain on assets sold	950	
Rental and interest income	25,245	
Total		$ 26,195
Net income before taxes		$16,264,921
Federal income tax		7,807,162
Net Income		$ 8,457,759

EXHIBIT 9.7   Statement of Financial Position

Statement of Financial Position
December 31, 20XX

Current assets		
Cash		$ 658,007
Securities (at cost)		525,362
Accounts receivable	$ 7,894,210	
Minus reserve for bad debts	24,000	
Net accounts receivable		7,870,210
Inventories		
Houston	12,003,865	
Pittsburgh	2,833,529	
Los Angeles	1,702,058	
Total inventories		$16,539,452
Prepaid expenses		9,406
Total Current Assets		$25,602,437
Plant and equipment	25,876,254	
Less depreciation	12,325,976	
Total plant and equipment		13,550,278
Total Assets		$39,152,715
Current liabilities		
Accounts payable		$ 1,823,151
Accrued liabilities		1,602,252
Payroll deductions		87,155
Total Current Liabilities		$ 3,512,558
Equity		
Corporate clearing account		$ 8,592,891
Divisional control		17,335,627
Retained earnings		9,711,639
Total equity		$35,640,157
Total Liabilities and Equity		$39,152,715

Gross margins, then, reflect profits before other company costs such as sales and administrative expenses are subtracted from gross margins. When they are subtracted, net income is the final result.

Those accounts concerning the manager directly are inventories and plant and equipment. The inventories account represents the different stages of processing: (1) raw materials and purchased parts; (2) work-in-process, which denotes the former raw materials and purchased parts somewhere in the process of being manufactured; and (3) finished-goods inventory—the stock of completely processed products ready for sale.

Plant and equipment includes buildings, machinery, and equipment. This subject will be discussed in more detail later. For the moment, just remember that plant and equipment represents an investment that must be made to yield attractive profits for the business. When a manager seeks to add new plants and equipment, profitability must be carefully determined and actual results monitored to assure that the investments are paying off.

Calculating Return on Assets.   If you, as a person, invest money, your very first concern is "How much will I earn?" A business asks exactly the same question when it invests its money. Return on assets (ROA) is the measurement of success ("How much did I earn in relation to my investment?") that corporate management burdens its divisions with. Return on assets is the ratio of net income to sales, multiplied by asset turnover, as seen here:

$$\text{ROA} = \frac{\text{Income before taxes}}{\text{Net sales}} \times \frac{\text{Net sales}}{\text{Total assets}}$$

By canceling out the net sales (in true arithmetical form), ROA then becomes:

$$\text{ROA} = \frac{\text{Income before taxes}}{\text{Total assets}}$$

Return on assets is the prime measurement of how well each division performs financially. It is the best way of answering the question, "How well did this division perform in relation to the assets it had at its disposal?"

Below are the steps involved in calculating ROA:

1. Add total assets. These numbers are taken directly from the balance sheet (Statement of Financial Position). They are added together to form the total assets shown to the immediate right of the left-hand column.

2. Divide net sales by total assets, to show asset turnover, that is, how many sales dollars were generated with the assets.

3. Determine net income before taxes, by subtracting sales administration expenses, sales commissions, and general (administrative) expenses from gross margins. Then, add miscellaneous income to gross margins.

4. Divide net income before taxes by net sales, to derive return on sales.

5. Multiply asset turnover by return on sales to get ROA.

Capacity Utilization Calculation

Exhibit 9.8 displays a 9-month summary showing a total of 21,424.5 tons processed, using *.69* hours, or *1.44* hours per ton.

At a rate of *.69* tons per hour, from the number of hours worked for that entire period, it can be determined that the department functioned at only *88* percent of its capacity (see Exhibit 9.9).

Regardless of the service center, most companies keep records of production in an identifiable unit of measure. They also keep records of hours worked. *What few companies do is to actually compare the units and hours to determine the consistency or variances in the output.*

The higher the variances, the more indication of the lack of good operational tools to control costs and, therefore, the greater potential for improvement.

EXHIBIT 9.8 Utilization Analysis Report

Month	Jan.	Feb.	Mar.	Apr.	May	June	July	Aug.	Sep.	Oct.	Nov.	Dec.	Total
Number of work days													
Gross hours—eight people													
Vacation, absent hours													
Actual hours worked	3895.75	3855.5	4619.75	3310.25	4439.2	3651.25	3336.25	4202.25	3511.50				
Tons processed	2424	2457	2608	2297	2808	2428	1946	2304.5	2152				
Tons per hour	0.62	0.63	0.56	0.69	0.63	0.66	0.58	0.54	0.61				
Hours per ton	1.61	1.56	1.77	1.44	1.58	1.50	1.71	1.82	1.63				
Variance low to high				1.44				1.82					
Percent utilization	.895	.917	.812	.999	.910	.957	.839	.789	.882				

Hours .38 = 26%

EXHIBIT 9.9 Capacity Utilization Calculation

$$\text{Percent capacity} = \frac{\text{Hours per ton} \times \text{Tons processed}}{\text{Actual hours worked}} \times 100$$

$$\text{Percent capacity} = \frac{1.44 \times 21424.5}{34821.75} = \frac{30851.28}{34821.75} = 88\%$$

(The best hours per ton (1.44) becomes the standard for the calculation in the other months.)

The best performance was in the month of April, when production reached 99% of its capacity.

$$\text{Percent capacity for April} = \frac{1.44 \times 2297}{3310.25} = 99\%$$

The worst month was August, at 78.9% of its capacity.

There is a variance of 25% of its capacity. These figures go straight to the bottom line: (.26 × Total labor costs = Savings)

Operating Performance Ratios

Operating performance ratios are listed below:

- Percent productivity is the percentage indicator that measures the output (earned hours) versus input (available hours).

$$\text{Percent productivity} = \frac{\text{Earned hours*}}{\text{Available hours}} \times 100$$

- Percent performance is the *output* of measured work in relationship to total hours worked. It also measures how *productive* the area is.

$$\text{Percent performance} = \frac{\text{Earned hours}}{\text{Total hours worked}^\dagger} \times 100$$

- Percent efficiency represents how *well* an employee has *performed* on measured work.

$$\text{Percent efficiency} = \frac{\text{Earned hours}}{\text{Hours on measured work}^\ddagger \text{ (actual hours)}} \times 100$$

*Earned hours are the output of measured hours of work produced (real work accomplished) in the department.
†Hours on measured work represent those hours actually spent by employees on measured or estimated work.
‡Total hours worked are the total clock hours for which an employee works in the department.

- Percent utilization represents the percentage of time employees are working against measured activities and is determined by:

$$\text{Percent utilization} = \frac{\text{Measured hours worked}}{\text{Total hours worked}} \times 100$$

- Percent scheduled attainment is the successful completion of planned volume, at a controlled reasonable cost, and on schedule (this is the goal of the service center).

$$\text{Percent scheduled attainment} = \frac{\text{Operations completed}}{\text{Total operations}} \times 100$$

Other Direct Labor Control Measures

Many other measurements of direct labor can be made to control and correct costs. Some of the more prevalent are as follows:

Utilization

$$\text{Utilization} = \frac{\text{Time on standards}}{\text{Total time available}} \times 100$$

Example: A processing department with 20 direct-labor employees shows the following statistics for one 8-hour production:

$$\text{Total time available} = 20 \times 8 = 160 \text{ Person-hours}$$

$$\text{Time on standards} = 120 \text{ Person-hours}$$

$$\text{Time off standards} = 40 \text{ Person-hours}$$

$$\text{Utilization} = \frac{120}{160} \times 100\% = 75\%$$

Direct-Labor Productivity

$$\text{Productivity} = \text{Performance} \times \text{Utilization} \times 100\%$$

Example: In the same department cited in the example on utilization, performance (percent efficiency of direct labor) was 95 percent for that shift:

$$\text{Productivity} = 95.0\% \times 75.0\% \times 100\% = 71.3\%$$

Labor productivity is a more encompassing index than separate measures of performance and utilization. It provides a ready measurement of direct-labor productivity in a single ratio.

Direct-Labor Cost per Unit

$$\text{Direct-labor cost per unit} = \frac{\text{Total direct-labor costs}}{\text{Number of units produced}}$$

Example: If the 20 direct-labor employees each were paid $10 per hour, then

$$\text{Direct-labor cost per unit} = \frac{20 \times \$10 \times 8 \text{ Hours}}{1,000} = \frac{\$1,600}{1,000} = \$1.60$$

Average Earnings.   Average earnings is defined as those earnings derived from operations not on standard. In most union shops, average earnings is a negotiable issue, and payment resulting from average earnings is based on what each individual operator averaged on incentive for the past week. If a sheer operator, for example, ran several jobs not yet measured on incentive (usually new jobs), his incentive pay for those jobs would be the average incentive pay he earned during the previous week.

Average earnings is payment of something for nothing. Since unmeasured work is looked on as a fault of management, unions are generally successful in their demands for average earnings. In that case, the measurement of average earnings becomes a significant ratio for management.

$$\text{Average earnings} = \frac{\text{Average earnings}}{\text{Total incentive earnings}} \times 100\%$$

The service center had the following average earnings for one calendar year:

$$\text{Average earnings} = \frac{\$241,632}{\$1,550,750} \times 100 = 15.6\%$$

No matter how you look at it, either 15.6 percent, or $241,632 is too much. Most average earnings are better held to maximums of 5 to 7 percent.

Percent Performance to Standard.   This ratio is the most significant one in measuring the results of incentive coverage. It shows increases in performance that can be directly related to increases in production. The service center, before incentives, had the following annual performance:

$$\text{Performance} = \frac{\text{Earned hours}}{\text{Standard hours}} \times 100$$

$$\text{Performance} = \frac{398,140}{563,178} = 100 = 70.7\%$$

After installation of the incentive system for 1 year, their performance had improved 25 percent (despite their average earnings), as seen here:

$$\text{Performance} = \frac{506,442}{571,280} \times 100 = 88.7\%$$

In terms of actual improvement in performance:

$$\text{Percent improvement} = \frac{88.7\% - 70.7\%}{70.7\%} \times 100 = 25.5\%$$

The 25.5 percent improvement in performance represented a real gain of equal amount in production output.

Exhibit 9.10 charts a report on efficiency, utilization, and productivity.

EXHIBIT 9.10 Efficiency, Utilization, and Productivity Report

Week No.	Dept.	(1) Actual Hours	(2) Quantity Processed	(3) Earned Hours	(4) Available Hours [(1)(8)]	(5) Percent Efficiency [(3)/(1)]	(6) Percent Utilization [(1)/(4)]	(7) Percent Productivity [(3)/(4)]	(8) Total	Indirect Hours Training	Meetings	Down Time	Waiting Parts	Medical	Other
1	64122	854.50	155347	1391.49	913.70	162.84	93.52	152.29	59.20	2.00	1.70	0.00	0.00	0.00	55.50
2	64122	1258.00	79326	921.50	1316.50	73.25	95.56	70.00	58.50	3.20	7.60	0.00	4.80	0.00	42.90
3	64122	1211.60	160031	1562.86	1306.00	128.99	92.77	119.67	94.40	20.00	4.90	3.40	0.00	0.00	66.10
4	64122	1064.90	110948	1132.24	1139.60	106.32	93.45	99.35	74.70	7.00	0.00	5.70	0.00	4.00	58.00
Monthly Totals		4389.00	503652	5008.09	4675.80	114.11	93.87	107.11	286.80	32.20	14.20	9.10	4.80	4.00	222.50
1	64126	396.00	337	502.83	409.20	126.98	96.77	122.88	13.20	0.00	0.00	0.00	13.20	0.00	0.00
2	64126	445.80	282	503.33	466.90	112.90	95.48	107.80	21.10	0.00	2.20	6.00	7.90	0.00	5.00
3	64126	434.30	271	469.42	469.50	108.09	92.50	99.98	35.20	0.00	1.82	2.10	22.30	0.00	9.00
4	64126	447.90	401	572.33	464.00	127.78	96.53	123.35	16.10	0.00	0.00	2.50	10.60	0.00	3.00
Monthly Totals		1724.00	1291	2047.91	1809.60	118.79	95.27	113.17	85.60	0.00	4.00	10.60	54.00	0.00	17.00
1	64134	383.70	298	234.00	429.00	60.99	89.44	54.55	45.30	0.00	10.70	0.40	2.00	0.00	32.20
2	64134	474.30	761	628.50	522.50	132.51	90.78	120.29	48.20	0.00	13.80	0.10	6.10	0.00	28.20
3	64134	515.10	586	478.67	580.00	92.93	80.81	82.53	64.90	0.00	3.50	2.60	7.70	0.00	51.10
4	64134	573.50	650	528.58	623.90	92.17	91.92	84.72	50.40	1.50	0.00	4.00	7.60	0.00	37.30
Monthly Totals		1946.60	2295	1869.75	2155.40	96.05	90.31	86.75	208.80	1.50	28.00	7.10	23.40	0.00	148.80
Weekly Plant Composite															
1	All	1634.20	153982	2128.32	1751.90	130.24	93.28	121.49	117.70	2.00	12.40	0.40	15.20	0.00	87.70
2	All	2178.10	80369	2053.33	2305.90	94.27	94.46	89.05	127.80	3.20	23.60	6.10	18.80	0.00	76.10
3	All	2161.00	160888	2510.95	2355.50	116.19	91.74	106.60	194.50	20.00	10.20	8.10	30.00	0.00	126.20
4	All	2086.30	111999	2233.15	2227.50	107.04	93.66	100.25	141.20	8.50	0.00	12.20	18.20	4.00	98.30
Monthly Totals		8059.60	507238	8925.75	8640.80	110.75	93.27	103.30	581.20	33.70	46.20	26.80	82.20	4.00	388.30

134

EXHIBIT 9.11 Operations to Return on Assets

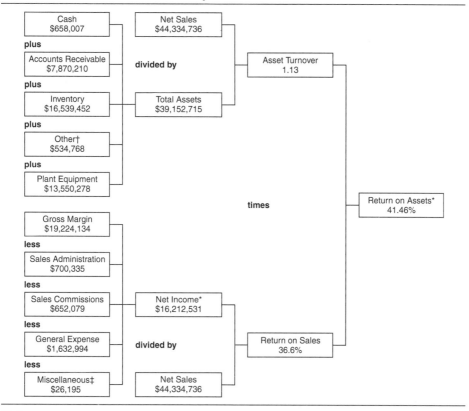

*Before taxes.
†Securities plus prepaid expenses.
‡Gain on assets sold plus rental and interest income.

Return on Assets. While ROA is a picture of overall divisional performance (see Exhibit 9.11), the chief contributor to results, either good or bad, is the operations function.

Control of ROA, therefore, is *the paramount concern* for the manager.

Cost of Goods Sold Analysis. Return on assets, while being the yardstick of divisional financial status, is only one of the several measures used by corporate management to control divisional performance. There are several additional measures that you should know to help monitor progress to achievement of ROA goals. A description of the more popular of these follows.

Analyzing Gross Margins. Gross margins reflect that portion of money left over after operations cost of goods sold is subtracted from net sales. Gross margins, as a percentage of net sales, is a basic indicator of how good a job is being done to control operating costs.

(Thousands Omitted)

	20X0	19X9	19X8	19X7	19X6
Net sales	$44,334	$42,105	$39,634	$30,912	$30,027
Cost of goods sold	25,110	25,263	28,536	22,878	23,727
Gross margins	$19,224	$16,842	$11,098	$ 8,034	$ 6,300
$\dfrac{\text{Gross margins}}{\text{Net sales}} \times 100 =$	43.4%	40.0%	28.0%	25.9%	20.9%

Note: Gross margins divided by net sales, as shown above, is multiplied by 100 to obtain a percentage. All three can be analyzed by breaking down cost of goods sold for the 5-year period under study:

(Thousands Omitted)

	20X0	19X9	19X8	19X7	19X6
Net sales	$44,334	$42,105	$39,634	$30,912	$30,027
Cost of goods sold					
Material	$10,322	$ 9,004	$ 8,225	$ 7,195	$ 7,248
Direct labor	4,379	4,980	5,163	5,632	5,465
Overhead	10,409	11,079	15,148	10,051	11,014
Total Costs	$25,110	$25,163	$28,536	$22,878	$23,727

To break down those costs, we will take each of the cost categories (material, direct labor, overhead) individually, and divide them by net sales for the year, and multiply the result by 100 to obtain the percentage of costs to sales:

	199X	*198X*
Material	23.3%	23.3%
Direct labor	9.9%	18.2%
Overhead	23.5%	35.6%

Example: Material costs for 199X were $10,332, and sales were $44,334. Then, dividing material costs by sales, and multiplying the result by 100 provides the 23.3%.

$$\frac{\$10,332}{\$44,334} \times 100 = 23.3\%$$

Material costs as a percentage of net sales have held steady over the last 5 years.

Inventory Turnover

Inventory turnover is an indication of how efficiently an organization is using materials that comprise the products. A low inventory turnover rate could indicate excessively high levels of usable inventory, or high levels of obsolete inventory.

Too high an inventory turnover rate, conversely, could indicate that not enough inventory is on hand to satisfy customer demands—a condition that results almost invariably in lost sales. This same condition can also be an indication of short machine run times, with its consequent higher costs resulting from excessive machine set-ups and higher material handling costs.

How to Calculate Inventory Turnover. Inventory turnover is computed as follows:

$$\frac{\text{Manufacturing cost of goods sold}}{\text{Average inventory levels during the year}} = \text{Inventory turnover}$$

Inventory turnover, however, is not a measure that stands alone. It must be analyzed in relation to company objectives. If you will recall the ROA formula, it is just as important to determine how much profit is being generated per turnover.

Overhead as a Yardstick of Performance

As explained earlier, overhead is composed of all operating costs other than direct material and direct labor.

Example: $10,655,000 for 1 million machine hours:

	Budget	Actual
Manufacturing overhead	$10,655,000	$10,051,000
Machine hours	1,000,000	800,000
Overhead rate	$ 10.65	$ 12.56

Computing Fixed and Variable Costs

While direct material and direct-labor dollars are relatively accessible for purposes of measurement and control, overhead costs are not. Overhead is composed of a variety of costs, both fixed and variable, which need to be separated and measured to control overhead performance.

Fixed costs are those costs that do not change in response to a change in product volume. Typical fixed costs are depreciation, management salaries and benefits, taxes, rent, heat, light, and some power costs. From the viewpoint of the manufacturing manager, costs should *never* be considered fixed.

Variable costs are those costs that move, more or less, proportionately with product volume. Direct materials and direct labor are the prime examples. Others include indirect supplies, most power costs, and maintenance costs.

How Overhead Is Measured and Controlled

It is necessary to define the ways in which manufacturing overhead is measured and controlled. Variances for overhead are classically divided into three categories: *spending, efficiency,* and *capacity.*

Calculating Spending Variance. This is found by comparing overhead costs of budgeted machine hours to overhead costs of actual machine hours. It is a measure of efficiency of machine hours used.

Budget at 800,000 machine hours	$10,003,000
Actual at 700,000 machine hours	− 9,676,000
Unfavorable efficiency variance	$ 327,000

Calculating Capacity Variance. This measures the variance derived from performance attributable to operating the plants at below-normal capacity. Normal capacity can be defined as *average* use of facilities over the past several years.

Normal capacity	1,000,000	Machine hours
Actual hours used	− 800,000	Machine hours
Underabsorbed capacity	200,000	Machine hours

Now that machine hours have been determined in the capacity variance calculation, costs must be applied. Since capacity variance measures the overabsorption or underabsorption of *fixed* overhead, variable costs are not considered (because they change with changes in product volume, while fixed costs do not). Using the fixed overhead rate shown, $7.39 per machine hour, the capacity variance is calculated:

$$\text{Fixed overhead rate} \times \text{Underabsorbed machine hours}$$

$$\$7.39 \times 200,000 = \text{Capacity variance } \$1,478,000$$

Combining Variances. Exhibit 9.12 allows the pulling together of all three variances to observe their cumulative impact on costs. The chart that follows summarizes this impact.

Actual overhead	$10,051,000		
		Spending variance $48,000	
Flexible budget for 800,000 hours actually used	$10,003,000		Controllable variance $375,000
		Efficiency variance $327,000	
Flexible budget for 700,000 hours required	$ 9,676,000		

The $375,000 represents that portion of the overhead that could have been avoided, had manufacturing management done a better job. It is an unfavorable variance that is strictly controllable.

Capacity variance, on the other hand, is related to product volume attributable to sales, and, as such, is beyond the control of the manufacturing manager.

EXHIBIT 9.12   Flexible Budget

					20XX Actual Results
Number of parts produced	5,000,000	4,500,000	4,000,000	3,500,000	3,500,000
Machine hours of operation	1,000,000	900,000	800,000	700,000	800,000
Variable overhead:					
Indirect materials and supplies	$ 1,116,000	$ 1,004,000	$ 893,000	$ 781,000	$ 946,000
Maintenance	810,000	729,000	648,000	567,000	648,000
Power	1,277,000	1,149,000	1,022,000	894,000	1,022,000
Other	60,000	54,000	48,000	42,000	50,000
Total Variable Costs	$ 3,263,000	$ 2,936,000	$ 2,611,000	$2,284,000	$ 2,666,000
Fixed Overhead:					
Supervision	$ 3,003,000	$ 3,003,000	$ 3,003,000	$3,003,000	$ 3,003,000
Taxes and insurance	2,370,000	2,370,000	2,370,000	2,370,000	2,349,000
Heat and light	792,000	792,000	792,000	792,000	805,000
Depreciation	1,177,000	1,177,000	1,177,000	1,177,000	1,177,000
Other	50,000	50,000	50,000	50,000	51,000
Total Fixed Costs	7,392,000	7,392,000	7,392,000	7,392,000	7,385,000
Total Overhead	$10,655,000	$10,328,000	$10,003,000	$9,676,000	$10,051,000

Note: Variable overhead rate per machine hour $ 3.26
Fixed overhead rate per machine hour   7.39
Total overhead rate per machine hour $10.65

Both controllable and uncontrollable variances, when put together, look like this:

Unfavorable spending and efficiency variances	$ 375,000
Capacity variance	1,478,000
Total variances	$1,853,000

Overhead costs are important to the manager. Through use of a flexible budget and monthly reports of the variances indicated, you can keep the manufacturing overhead rate in line and hold costs to a minimum.

10

OPERATIONS EFFICIENCY MEASURES

CAPACITY ANALYSIS

Every manager needs to be aware of what the capacity of his plants is. Having this knowledge assures that realistic workloads are scheduled. Too heavy a workload in relation to capacity leads to missed customer promises and high in-process inventory levels. Too light a workload causes high capacity variances.

Capacity is the amount of product the facilities are capable of producing within a given time period. Capacity is generally expressed in terms of standard direct-labor hours. Normal capacity refers to *average* use of the facilities over a number of years, while manufacturing capacity, as discussed here, signifies capability of the facilities to manufacture the most product possible or the most product schedules.

Generally, capacity is calculated, by product line, for each production machine in the plant.

Determination of capacity is basically a three-step process:

1. *Determination of weekly raw capacity.* This assumes that all machines run 7 days per week on three shifts, at 8 hours per shift, with no allowances for downtime. It is a starting point only, and the purpose is to make management aware of

EXHIBIT 10.1   Determination of Weekly Raw Capacity

Department	Available Machines	Crew Size	Total Crew	× Days Available	× Shifts per Day	× Hours per Shift	= Raw Capacity Standard Direct-Labor Hours
Chuckers	14	.5	7	7	3	8	1,176
Grinders	12	.5	6	7	3	8	1,008
Millers	12	1	12	7	3	8	2,016
Drills	12	1	12	7	3	8	2,016
Heat treat	4	.5	2	7	3	8	336
Plating line	4	1	4	7	3	8	672
Paint booths	5	1	5	7	3	8	840
Assembly lines	3	4	12	7	3	8	2,018
Total Plant			60				10,082

EXHIBIT 10.2   Determination of Weekly Planned Capacity

Department	Available Machines	Planned Machines	Total Crew	×	Days Planned	×	Shifts Planned	Hours per Shift	=	Planned Capacity Standard Direct-Labor Hours
Chuckers	14	12	7		5		1	10		350
Grinders	12	10	6		5		1	10		300
Millers	12	12	8		5		1	10		400
Drills	12	10	8		5		1	10		400
Heat treat	4	4	2		5		1	10		100
Plating line	4	2	2		5		1	10		100
Paint booths	5	4	4		5		1	10		200
Assembly lines	3	3	3		5		1	10		150
Total Plant			40							2,000

the full capability of equipment, were it to be employed in its most productive state. (See Exhibit 10.1.)

2. *Determination of weekly planned capacity.* This calculation is based on the number of days per week the machinery is scheduled to operate, along with the number of shifts and the number of hours per shift. (See Exhibit 10.2.)

3. *Determination of weekly available capacity.* Using planned capacity as a base figure, available capacity realistically subtracts standard hours lost because of downtime and yields. Yields include direct-labor hours for producing both avoidable and unavoidable scrap. Unavoidable scrap examples are chips and shavings removed during machining operations, skeleton scrap from stamping operations, and gates and risers out from castings. (See Exhibit 10.3.)

EXHIBIT 10.3   Determination of Weekly Available Capacity

Department	Planned Standard Hours	×	Uptime Objective Percent	×	Yield Percent	=	Available Capacity Standard Direct-Labor Hours
Chuckers	350		80		90		252
Grinders	300		75		85		191
Millers	400		80		90		288
Drills	400		90		94		338
Heat treat	100		80		90		72
Plating line	100		80		95		76
Paint booths	200		95		97		184
Assembly lines	150		75		85		96
Total Plant	2,000						1,497

EXHIBIT 10.4   Capacity Analysis Summary

| Department | Standard Direct-Labor Hours—Weekly | | |
	Raw Capacity	Planned Capacity	Available Capacity
Chuckers	1,008	250	158
Grinders	840	250	180
Millers	1,680	400	288
Drills	1,680	400	285
Heat treat	168	50	44
Plating line	336	100	87
Paint booths	504	150	138
Assembly lines	1,344	400	304
Total Plant	7,560	2,000	1,484

Note: Planned capacity is based on one shift, 5 days per week, 10 hours per day.

Capacity Summary

It is helpful at this stage to put raw capacity, planned capacity, and available capacity together and to compare them. The first, and most obvious, conclusion (see Exhibit 10.4) is that available capacity of 1,484 standard hours is but a small percentage of the 7,560 standard hours of raw capacity. That is true, but it must be remembered that Los Angeles is a new plant, and that available capacity will expand to more closely approximate raw capacity, given time. Shifts will be added to increase available capacity. Additionally, as time progresses and the learning curve extends, uptime and yields will improve as management and operators refine production operations.

Division: Capacity Analysis Summary

Capacity planning allows management to marry production forecasts with available capacity. Through knowledge of what plant capacity is, management can more effectively make plans for future workloads. As sales levels grow, management will have a base upon which to ask for additional facilities.

EMPLOYEE TURNOVER ANALYSIS

Exhibit 10.5 depicts a turnover analysis. If the manager knows what to expect in the way of employee turnover, he can better control his staffing and on-the-job training, either formal or informal, and will know much better what to expect from a standpoint of permanency of the employees. An examination of the attitudes of long-term and new employees is shown in Exhibit 10.6.

Another service that can help the manager in his analysis of his workforce is a listing, or marked map, of locations of employees' residence areas. This enables him to better judge possibilities of absenteeism due to weather disturbances or problems with traffic.

EXHIBIT 10.5 Turnover Analysis

	Month	YTD	Prior YTD	Prior Year Total
Job Group				
Hours				
Travel too far			2	2
Better job	2	2	1	11
Dissatisfied with job				3
Family	2	3	2	8
Other	1	3	1	2
Not qualified (term)			2	3
Not dependable				4
Permanent force reduction			1	1
Violation of rules	1	1		
Other		1		
Organization				
Production	5	9	9	39
Materials	2	3	3	9
Engineering	1	1		2
Management		1	1	1
Average Years of Service	2.2	2.0	1.5	2.2
Percent Turnover	3.7	6.6	5.8	23.3
Job Group				
Managers		1	1	1
Supervisors				
Buyers				1
Engineers				1
Technicians	3	5	1	10
Clerks	1	1	1	1
Secretaries				
Analysts				1
Group leaders		1	1	1
Assemblers	3	5	8	27
Material handlers				5
Machine operators				
Custodial workers				1
Schedulers	1	1		2
Total	8	14	12	51
Reasons				
Wages (Quit)				
School				4
Leaving locality	2	4	4	12
Health				1

EXHIBIT 10.6   Long-Service Interviews: Then and Now Comparisons

No.	Statement	Long-Term Then	Long-Term Now	New Employees Now
1.	People were (are) important.	9.0	5.6	8.3
2.	Experience was (is) respected.	7.2	5.6	7.2
3.	The company was (is) a nice place to work.	9.4	7.3	8.2
4.	Employees had (have) an opportunity to get ahead.	7.4	6.3	7.4
5.	The benefit package was (is) good.	8.6	8.6	8.4
6.	Salary was (is) fair.	7.5	6.3	6.4
7.	The work environment was (is) pleasant.	8.7	7.1	7.6
8.	There was (is) too much red tape.	2.0	3.6	3.7
9.	The company was (is) responsive to employees' needs.	8.4	6.1	8.1
10.	Employee questions were (are) answered quickly.	7.6	6.1	7.0
11.	People were (are) proud of their work.	9.2	6.0	7.2
12.	Employees were (are) competent.	9.0	7.0	7.5
13.	Solutions to problems made (make) sense.	7.5	7.1	7.2
14.	Employees had (have) job security.	8.6	6.5	7.7
15.	Pay was (is) related directly to performance.	4.2	3.4	4.7
16.	Top managers talked (talk) to employees.	9.5	4.6	7.9
17.	The company was (is) better than other companies.	8.8	8.1	7.5
18.	Employees helped (help) run the business.	7.8	6.6	6.4
19.	We had (have) a team spirit.	9.4	5.4	8.0
20.	Supervisors listened (listen) to their employees.	7.6	6.7	7.0
21.	The company had (has) a bright future.	9.3	7.7	8.5

1 = Strongly disagree; 10 = Strongly agree.

DOWNTIME ANALYSIS

One of the very useful by-products of both direct and indirect-labor control is the realization that downtime must be quantified and categorized so that it can be reduced. Exhibit 10.7 is an example of a downtime summary by company division. Exhibit 10.8 analyzes by operation. The report is presented in two sections: (a) Summary, and (b) Detail Analysis. The summary describes, by total division and individual plant, the number of direct-labor hours used on production, and the number of direct-labor hours wasted on downtime.

In Exhibit 10.7, under "Detail Analysis," general categories of downtime are listed. Notice the relatively large amount of direct-labor hours Los Angeles lost on machine repairs. In fact, the amount of time Los Angeles lost for set-up, machine adjustments, and tooling repairs are very high in comparison to its sister plants, when you consider that Los Angeles' total number of direct-labor hours worked are smaller.

Tooling repairs for the three plants, for example, when considered as a percentage of their direct-labor hours worked, looks like this:

$$\text{Houston} = \frac{153 \text{ Hours}}{8{,}163 \text{ Hours}} \times 100 = 1.9\%$$

$$\text{Pittsburgh} = \frac{116 \text{ Hours}}{4{,}015 \text{ Hours}} \times 100 = 2.9\%$$

$$\text{Los Angeles} = \frac{312 \text{ Hours}}{2{,}725 \text{ Hours}} \times 100 = 5.0\%$$

Los Angeles, most obviously, is experiencing more than its share of machine repair downtime. Now let's look at machine repairs:

$$\text{Houston} = \frac{253 \text{ Hours}}{8{,}163 \text{ Hours}} \times 100 = 3.1\%$$

$$\text{Pittsburgh} = \frac{285 \text{ Hours}}{4{,}015 \text{ Hours}} \times 100 = 7.1\%$$

$$\text{Los Angeles} = \frac{312 \text{ Hours}}{2{,}725 \text{ Hours}} \times 100 = 11.4\%$$

Here again, Los Angeles is in far worse shape than Houston and Pittsburgh.

Total machine repair hours, for example, constitute almost 27 percent of all downtime experienced (850 Hours/3,199 Hours $\times$ 100 = 26.5%). To the practiced eye, that is quite a bit: Machine repair in most manufacturing operations will probably be among the highest of downtime categories, but it should not amount to 27 percent. In like fashion, rework is a hefty 746 hours. To a large extent, rework can always be reduced and, as a guide, should not exceed 10 to 15 percent of downtime hours. In this case it is 23.3 percent (746 Hours/3,199 Hours $\times$ 100 = 23.3%), and can readily be reduced.

EXHIBIT 10.7   Downtime Analysis Summary

	Houston	Pittsburgh	Los Angeles	Total Plants
A. Summary				
Total direct-labor hours worked	8,163	4,015	2,725	14,903
Direct-labor hours on production	7,018	2,996	1,690	11,704
Direct-labor hours on downtime	1,145	1,019	1,035	3,199
Downtime (percent)	14.0	25.4	38.0	21.5
B. Detail Analysis (in Direct-Labor Person-Hours)				
Set-up	215	139	181	535
Machine adjustments	190	112	131	433
Rework	306	265	175	746
Wait time—materials	28	94	60	182
Machine repairs	253	285	312	850
Tooling repairs	153	116	136	405
Training	0	8	40	48
Totals	1,145	1,019	1,035	3,199

EXHIBIT 10.8 Downtime Analysis

A. Summary

	Person-Hours	Percent
Direct-Labor Hours on Production	1,690	62.0
Direct-Labor Hours on Downtime	1,035	38.0
Total Direct-Labor Hours Worked	2,725	100.0

B. Detail Analysis

	Direct-Labor Person-Hours								
	Chuckers	Grinders	Milling	Drilling	Heat Treat	Plate	Paint	Assembly	Total
Set-up	42	20	28	46	23	0	5	17	181
Machine adjustments	25	17	11	33	0	9	11	25	131
Rework	56	22	8	27	33	8	21	0	175
Wait time—materials	0	0	15	0	0	0	0	45	60
Machine repairs	64	38	41	109	18	29	0	13	312
Tooling repairs	27	43	26	20	0	0	0	20	136
Training	0	0	0	0	0	0	0	40	40
Totals	214	140	129	235	74	46	37	160	1,035
Percent of Total	20.7	13.5	12.5	22.7	7.1	4.4	3.6	15.5	100.0

The Pareto Principle

After carefully analyzing the downtime percentages, the manager is then able more effectively to focus the organization's attention on problem correction. Inherent in that statement is the assumption that just a few of the many problems that confront a manufacturing business at any given time generate the lion's share of lost dollars.

If, for example, the manufacturing manager were able to dissect the 850 machine-repair labor hours lost during the week, he might find this distribution:

Machine Repair Category	Direct-Labor Hours Lost
Electrical repairs	574
Mechanical repairs	105
Hydraulic repairs	93
Air system repairs	78
Total	850

Electrical repairs are the main problem. If the manager had not made this subsequent breakdown, that fact might never have emerged. Having done so, he is in a much better position to take corrective action.

In similar fashion, had he asked *where* the electrical problems were located, these facts might have surfaced:

Plant	Department	Hours Lost
Houston	Equipment	160
Pittsburgh	Equipment	94
Los Angeles	Equipment	256
Total		510

Therefore, 510 of the 574 direct-labor hours lost to electrical repairs were attributable to problems found in equipment in all three plants.

At this stage, the manager is in an excellent position to focus corrective actions where they will do the most good. The type of analysis this represents is referred to as the "Pareto Principle." Pareto was an Italian economist who discovered, early in the twentieth century, that a relatively large amount of money was concentrated in a relatively small proportion of the problems that make up the population. The application of the Pareto Principle to manufacturing problems remains a viable tool in the resolution of those problems.

COST REDUCTION/PRODUCTIVITY IMPROVEMENT ANALYSIS

The program for cost reduction/productivity improvement will be most successful if all areas are subjected to an analysis that will define the potential, and enable a schedule to be made and goals to be set. The analysis will be similar to a physician's examination of a patient. It will be designed to assess those systems that indicate the need for remedial action. The methodology will basically be a threefold approach, as follows:

1. Interviews with those people closest to each operation;
2. Review of historical records; and
3. Observations of current activities.

From these three simple steps, it is possible to develop enough symptomatic data upon which to base decisions relative to developing the program.

It is best to begin analysis in those areas that are labor intensive. An examination of the organizational structure and payroll records can usually reveal which areas incur the highest costs. Once these are defined in terms of size, the analysis can be started.

Interviews with Department
Managers and Supervisors

The interview technique (see Exhibits 10.9 and 10.10) is designed to determine just how much information the manager and the supervisor have at their command, which enables them to manage the resources for which they are responsible. It will further develop how they use the data in the day-by-day function of control. The results will go a long way toward revealing the potential degree of improvement that is available through the development of productivity-improvement techniques. The interview will also develop information on the managers' or supervisors' attitudes, how they perceive their problems, and, indeed, what some of the problems are that detract from the department's ability to produce.

Interview the Manager

An overall picture of a department, that has supervisor between management and the workforce, should be obtained from the manager. The following information should be sought:

- An overview of the department and its functions;
- How the department is organized to accomplish the function (full details on the structure of the department, down to the last person in it);
- Knowledge of the work input, flow-through, and output of the department and subsections; and
- Deadline requirements for work output.

The key to the management interview, as it relates to the potential for cost savings, is how much knowledge the manager has of the volume of work and how well he has related to it the workforce, equipment, and other necessary resources. Are records of input available? Records of output? Records of hours worked? Are the volume records

EXHIBIT 10.9   Management Interview Summary

	Yes	No
Does manager have accurate records of:		
Work input?	_____	_____
Work output?	_____	_____
Hours worked?	_____	_____
Backlog?	_____	_____
Does manager have established goals to accomplish		
Weekly?	_____	_____
Daily?	_____	_____
Hourly?	_____	_____
Does manager relate hours worked to units produced?	_____	_____
Does manager know how the number of people in his department was established?	_____	_____
Does manager receive reports from his supervisors		
Weekly?	_____	_____
Daily?	_____	_____
Does manager know his schedule status at all times?	_____	_____
Does manager have objective criteria by which to rate his supervisors?	_____	_____

Each yes answer has a point value of 1

Rating

Excellent	Good	Fair	Poor
12–14	9–11	7–10	under 7

compared to the hours worked? Is there a goal(s) of accomplishments based on some kind of unit of work production? How well are the goals met? How were they established? Are the goals monthly, weekly, daily? Are records kept? Pick up samples of available records.

How was the staffing in the department established? Are there *specific* yardsticks by which to relate the number of people to the work volume? What are they? Again, pick up samples of any records.

Does the manager receive reports directly from the supervisors on work output, backlogs, schedule conditions, problems? Are these formal reports with documentation? How often are they received? Are they kept in a file? Ask for copies of reports for at least the past several weeks.

How does the manager rate the supervisors? Does he have clear-cut, objective yardsticks related to the performance that is measurable? Are these ongoing? How are they used to improve supervisory performance? Ask for a specific example and copies of any documentation.

EXHIBIT 10.10   Supervisor's Interview Summary

	Yes	No
Does supervisor know how many people are in the department?	_____	_____
Does supervisor know how many people are actually at work on the day interview?	_____	_____
Could supervisor locate each person in his department?	_____	_____
Did supervisor know each person's specific assignment?	_____	_____
Did supervisor know when each person's current assignment		
Started?	_____	_____
Would be completed?	_____	_____
Did supervisor have each one's next assignment planned?	_____	_____
Did supervisor have a departmental work plan?	_____	_____
Does supervisor know if the plan is on schedule?	_____	_____
Does supervisor assign work directly to each person or work group?	_____	_____
Does supervisor relate each person or group assignment to a time requirement?	_____	_____
Does supervisor inform the person or group of the time requirement?	_____	_____
Does supervisor maintain ongoing records of:		
Work input?	_____	_____
Work output?	_____	_____
Backlog?	_____	_____
Productivity?	_____	_____
Does supervisor adjust the workforce to fluctuating volumes?	_____	_____
Does supervisor formally document operational problems?	_____	_____
Does supervisor follow-up on work assignments		
Daily?	_____	_____
Hourly?	_____	_____

Each yes answer has a point value of 1

Rating

Excellent	Good	Fair	Poor
17–19	14–16	10–13	under 10

Interview the Supervisor

The supervisor should have the most intimate knowledge of the workings of his or her department or section. The line of questioning involved is designed to determine just how much knowledge he or she has of the productive output of the people, and how well their time is utilized on a day-to-day or even hour-to-hour basis. The less knowledge demonstrated by the supervisor, the higher the probability that there is room for increasing the productivity of the work area.

When the answers to these questions are positive, the interviewer must follow up and request further data, or, with the supervisor, verify the accuracy of the information. For example:

1. *How many people are at work today?* Get an actual head count, verify that the answer is correct or not, and mark the chart accordingly.

2. *Do you know if your department is on schedule as of now?* Determine what the schedule is and how the actual schedule is measured against the planned schedule. Is there a true means of determining the schedule position, or is the supervisor just making an assumption?

3. *Do you have a method of measuring the productivity of the department?* What is the method? Does it measure output in terms of units per hour? Per day? Get copies of productivity records.

Evaluating the Interview Results

With both the manager's and supervisor's interview forms, the evaluation is one of summing-up positives and negatives. Each negative answer demonstrates a decided weakness. Each positive answer demonstrates a strength.

It will be found that the majority of supervisors will not have positive answers to many of the questions. For those that do, the examination of the facts will reveal that the answers have no real basis in fact. The reason that this is true is not a reflection on the supervisor, but the result of a lack of training and a lack of management tools that might enable the supervisor properly to manage the time of the people and the other resources under his or her control.

Review of Historical Records

The purpose of a review of historical records will primarily be to investigate the consistency, or, more likely, the inconsistency of performance. The company may or may not have the information available in the format that this portion of the analysis requires. If it does not, it will be necessary to go to several different sources to get it. Charting this information is the best way to demonstrate the impact of actual practices and to reveal the potential for improvement. On the basis of the information given in Exhibit 10.11, and a cost of $7.00 per hour, the order-processing labor cost in October was $2,448 higher than in August (2,690 × .13 × $7.00). This is a considerable cost variance and strongly indicates a cost-reduction potential.

EXHIBIT 10.11   Example of Performance Record

Month	June	July	Aug.	Sept.	Oct.
Number of work days	22	22	21	21	22
Gross hours—eight people	1,320	1,260	1,260	1,320	1,320
Vacation, absent hours	150	165	255	90	105
Actual hours worked	1,170	1,155	1,005	1,170	1,215
Orders processed	3,461	2,640	3,192	2,859	2,690
Orders per hour	2.96	2.28	3.17	2.44	2.21
Hours per order	.34	.44	.32	.41	.45
Variance low to high	.13 Hours = 40%				

Hours versus Production Units

The example seen in Exhibit 10.10 can be developed in various forms. The elements required are simple; units of work produced and the hours required to produce them. In the exhibit, we find a monthly record, and monthly records tend to have a flattening effect. Though they reveal a strong variance, this variance will become more dramatic as the time span is shortened. For example, in Exhibit 10.11, an actual case, the month of June was broken down into 22 working days. On a day-by-day basis, variances as high as 230 percent became evident.

Regardless of the type of business, most companies keep records of production in an identifiable *unit of measure*. They also have records of hours worked. What few do is to actually compare the units and hours to determine the consistency or variances in the output. The higher the variances, the more indication of lack of good operational tools to control costs, and, therefore, greater potential for improvement.

In-Process Time versus Time in Process

Another technique of analysis is to compare in-process time to the time in process. In any company or department within a company, two elements of information are required.

1. How long it takes, from start to finish, to produce an item in process time; and

2. The *actual* time applied to the item at each stage of production time in process.

Standard versus Actual Performance Records

In any organization that works with engineered time standards, records are available to show actual performance against the standard. These reports normally will reveal worker productivity on a weekly basis, or actual versus standard performance on each job completed or some combination of the two. Careful analysis is required, particularly when performance is rated close to 100 percent and the reports create the impression that everything is close to or on schedule.

Observations as the Key to Analysis

Interviews with management and supervision and looking for variances and problems within company records are usually very revealing, and will alert the analyst to the degree of improvement potential from a probability standpoint. Actual observations of the people at work are even more revealing. This portion of the chapter will explain the types of observations that should be made, how to make them, and how to chart results. (See Exhibits 10.12 and 10.13.)

Near–Far Observations. The near–far observation is perhaps the simplest one to make and can be done in several different ways. It can be applied to a variety of work activities. Basically it involves observing a worker or workers performing their normal activities at close range, with full knowledge on their part that they are being observed. Count the result of their effort. The observation time can be relatively short, say, 15 minutes to a half-hour.

Move away from the workstation to a point where the worker believes that he or she is no longer being observed and continue the observation. Again, count the number of "pieces" produced. For simplicity, use the same length of time for the *far* observation.

Convert both observations into pieces per hour. The results will often be very startling.

Another method of the same theme would be to take several *near* observations of the same activity at different times, even on different days. There will probably be slight variances in units per hour from one observation to the other. Then, secure the actual production and the actual time spent by the person observed on that particular activity, for a complete day or week. Again, the contrast will be quite startling.

EXHIBIT 10.12   Near–Far Observation—Invoice Processing

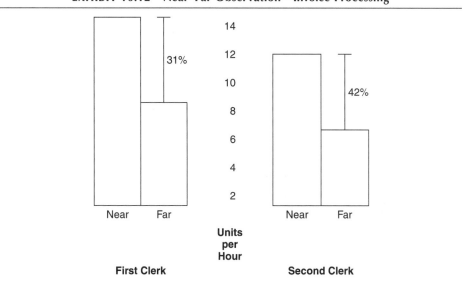

EXHIBIT 10.13   Near–Far Observation—Filling Number 3 Size Tubes

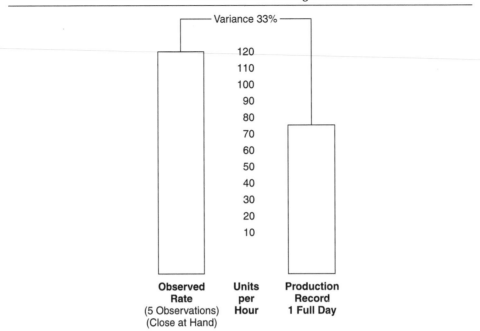

Ratio Delay Studies.   A ratio delay study can best be applied to groups of workers. It is designed to determine what percentage of the time at work is actually productive and what percentage represents delay or lost time. A number of observations are required. (See Exhibit 10.14.)

The observer records the date, department, and name of the supervisor on a worksheet. The observer must know, in advance, the number of people that are at work in the area. This can be the number of people in an office, on a shipping platform, in a manufacturing department, and so forth.

The observer goes into the area and quickly counts the number of people actually present in the department, noting how many people are actively working and how many people are not. It is like taking a flash picture, quick and simple. Some people will be found busily at work, some will be idle, and others will not be in evidence.

Record each observation on a ratio delay format. A line will be filled out for each observation, noting the time that the observation was made, how many people were supposed to be in the department (crew size), how many were observed working, and the number that were idle. These are recorded under **W** (working) and **I** (idle). The difference between the sum of W and I and the crew size is recorded under **A** (away). For each observation, then, we know that, out of a group of a given number of people, a certain number were actually working, others were idle, and some were not at their workstations.

EXHIBIT 10.14   Ratio Delay Study

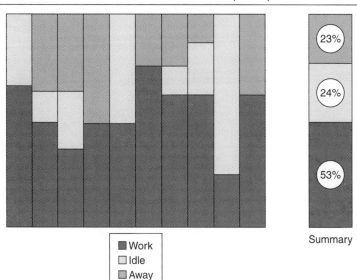

Work
Idle
Away

Summary

It is important to note on the form the shift (if applicable), start time, break times, lunch times, and stop time. Any observations taken within five minutes of start and stop times or during break periods should be discounted, because of the normal delays and inaccuracies that could exist.

It is rare that the observer will find *less than 20 percent* outright lost time. Very often it will exceed *30 percent.*

Time Diaries.   A time diary (see Exhibits 10.15 and 10.16) is the result of a continuing observation of a person, or group of people, for a specified period of time. Observations of 20 minutes to several hours in duration can be made. The observer must be in a position to distinguish actual work being done from idle time that exists. The record is kept in blocks of time, distinguishing between the two. The observations can then be charted as observed and can be charted in summary. These observations are usually very revealing and reflect direct lost time, much of which can be captured and put back to work.

Performance versus Ability to Perform.   A 5-month summary showed a total of 14,842 orders processed, using 5,715 hours or 2.6 hours per order. Observations were taken on several different occasions, which showed an ability on the part of the department to produce at a rate of 3.5 orders per hour. From the number of hours worked for that entire period, it can be determined that the department functioned at only 74 percent of its capacity.

$$14,842 / (5,715 \times 3.5)$$

EXHIBIT 10.15   Time Diary—Repair of Solar Gear Box

Assignment: Repair Solar Gear Box   Maintenance
Crew–2 Contract Workers   Platform 41-B
–3 Company Workers

Time Diary

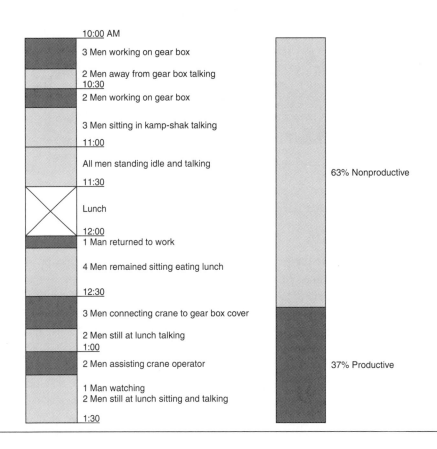

The best performance was in the month of August, when production reached 91 percent of capacity.

$$3192 / (1,005 \times 3.5)$$

The worst was the month of October, with a performance of 63 percent. This type of performance is not unusual. Though it may take considerable time and effort to research and make the observations, the results, most often, will be quite startling. This type of analysis can be applied to any operation where a defined unit for measuring productive output is available.

EXHIBIT 10.16   Time Diary—Replace Valve on Heater #2

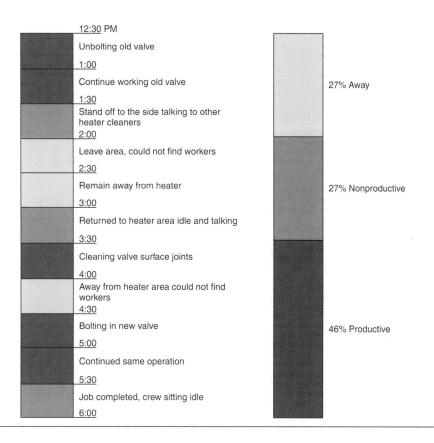

Calculating the Dollar Improvement Potential.   In order to determine the priority of a department's position in the program, the real potential for dollar improvement should be determined. Recognize that, at this point, it is not necessary to determine *how* this improvement will be brought about. That will be determined in the actual program development. Exhibit 10.17 demonstrates the potential for dollar recovery.

Once the analysis reveals that enough symptoms exist to indicate a strong potential for improvement, the degree of that potential can be figured out and a goal established—a 53.6 percent lost-time factor for a crew of 27 people with an annual wage of $16,250 each. It has been determined that 46.4 percent of their time is productive and has a value of $203,580. The remaining 53.6 percent represents lost time of $235,170. Consideration has been given that 25 percent of the lost time is, most likely, not recoverable. This gives a recoverable factor of $175,500, representing 40 percent of the total payroll.

EXHIBIT 10.17   Dollar Improvement Potential

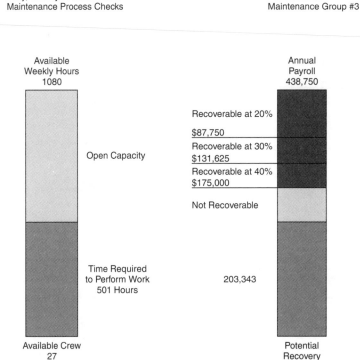

Daily, Weekly Production and
Maintenance Process Checks

Production and
Maintenance Group #3

Targets can be set lower than the 40 percent, and a judicious application of common sense may dictate that a target of 20 or 30 percent would be more practical and achievable. It is better to set a lower target and achieve more than to set one too high and fall short. During the application of the program, the objective will be to achieve the highest practical figure.

In assuring that all departments receive their proper priority, the recovery percentage should be uniform throughout. The target, though established on the basis of the payroll, does not necessarily mean that payroll will be reduced by the target amount. It means that the cost of doing business in a given department will be reduced when measured against the department output. This could mean an increase in production, reduction of rework, better quality, or any combination of measurable factors. The payroll approach is usually the simplest to apply in arriving at a potential, and is normally quite accurate, regardless of the way the final results are measured.

11

REDUCING OPERATING COSTS

Once action plans have been established, and once the organization is in place to achieve those action plans, some method of measurement and control is needed, to assure the plans are being completed according to established timetables. Controls are the proven method of accomplishing that goal.

USING PROCESSING CONTROLS TO REDUCE COSTS

Effective controls are superb tools for reducing costs and holding them down at lower levels. But they must first possess certain attributes in order to make them successful. They need these three characteristics:

1. *Controls must be simple.* A control measurement must be both easily applied and understood.
2. *Controls must be expressed quantitatively.* An old management expression is "if you can't reduce it to numbers, it ain't worth a darn." Controls that are not measurable in numbers are too easily misinterpreted. Subjective judgments and opinions substitute for objective measurements. Progress, or lack of it, cannot be readily determined.
3. *Controls must be timely.* What happened last quarter is of historical interest only. It is too late to do anything about it. If it is too late to take effective corrective action, then reporting is not timely. Measurements of operations need to be geared to the events being measured. Such important events as production and direct labor, for example, need to be measured *at least* daily, if not every few hours. The short interval of time between the event and its feedback to management permits corrective action to bring the plan back into schedule before it is too late. In operations, almost all events need to be reported weekly or daily, seldom at longer intervals.

CUTTING DIRECT-LABOR COSTS

Daily Labor Report

The first control tool installed was the direct-labor control report. (See Exhibit 11.1.) The left-hand column of Exhibit 11.1 lists each of the plant's operating departments.

EXHIBIT 11.1   Daily Labor Report—8/16/XX

	Direct-Labor Measurements				
Department	Standard Hours	Earned Hours	Percent Efficiency	Time Off-Standard	Percent Off-Standard
Pre-heat	260.0	260.0	100.0	20.0	7.1
Hot roll	232.4	216.6	93.2	63.6	21.5
Pre-heat	248.0	258.4	104.2	0	0
Cold roll	231.5	217.6	94.0	48.5	17.3
Slitters	574.7	471.6	82.1	201.3	25.9
Anneal	148.0	148.0	100.0	0	0
Packing	470.0	456.4	97.1	50.0	9.6
Totals	2164.6	2028.6	93.7	383.4	15.0

The next column to the right displays Standard Hours. These numbers reflect the total standard hours for the work performed in each department for the time period being measured, in this case, 1 day.

Earned Hours, the next column, shows actual performance measured in labor hours. This example explains how earned hours are derived:

Operation	Standard Hours
Slit 6″ Coils	.5 Per Coil

In the plant, the operator would be required to slit 16 six-inch coils in an 8-hour shift to meet standard. Following are earned hours an operator will be awarded for different production levels of six-inch coils.

No. of 6″ Coils Slit	Percent Efficiency	Earned Hours
4	25.0%	2.0
8	50.0	4.0
12	75.0	6.0
16	100.0	8.0
20	125.0	10.0
24	150.0	12.0

Earned hours for the day are accumulated for all direct-labor operations for each department and posted to the report shown. For the day in question, the plant averaged 95.2 Percent Efficiency.

Percent Off-Standard displays the total time that direct-labor employees are performing jobs not measured by standard hours. These hours can be caused either by time spent on direct-labor jobs, which have not yet been measured, or by downtime. In the case above, the percent of time off-standard for the day amounted to 18.6 percent.

Daily Downtime Analysis

This report, shown in Exhibit 11.2, also issued daily, expands information taken from the "Percent Off-Standard" section of the Direct-Labor Control Report. It describes reasons for the occurrences of off-standard time. In essence, it is a downtime report.

The first column in Exhibit 11.2 lists the same production departments found in the Daily Labor Report. The second column shows the Percentage of Off-Standard Time also contained in the former report. The following column shows year-to-date results (YTD), and the next column displays last year's averages. The final column, Downtime Reasons, describes reasons for the current day's downtime.

Notice that downtime for the plant has been reduced from 9.8 percent in 20X1 to the current year's average of 7.2 percent through August 16.

The Daily Downtime Analysis is a useful tool for analysis of downtime, where it occurred, how extensive it is, and reasons for the downtime.

Monthly Direct-Labor Control Report

The final report used by the aluminum plant to reduce costs is historical in nature but useful, nevertheless, to compare direct-labor performance over a period of time. (See Exhibit 11.3.)

The columns in Exhibit 11.3 are arranged the same as for the Daily Downtime Report, but the results for the current period are monthly, not the daily period of the Daily Downtime Report.

Notice in Exhibit 11.3 that, while results for the current month and year exceed levels of the previous year, the slitter department's performance is depressed, and the reason given is electrical problems. A careful analysis of both daily performance and downtime reports by plant management should yield clues about reasons for the lackluster performance. Corrective action can then occur.

EXHIBIT 11.2   Daily Downtime Report—8/16/X2

Department	Percent Time Off-Standard			Downtime Reasons
	Today	YTD	20X1	
Pre-heat	7.1	4.5	6.4	Thermostat Failure
Hot roll	21.5	6.8	9.5	Roll Crack 3
Pre-heat	0	3.1	2.9	—
Cold roll	17.3	10.7	8.9	Electrical Failure
Slitters	25.9	8.5	10.3	Electrical Failure
Anneal	0	3.1	16.4	—
Packing	9.6	1.8	2.1	Interleave Quality Problem
Totals	15.0	7.2	9.8	

EXHIBIT 11.3   Monthly Labor Report—8/X2

	Percent Efficiency			
Department	**This Month**	**YTD**	**20X1**	
Pre-heat	95.2	93.8	85.4	—
Hot roll	90.7	91.4	82.8	—
Pre-heat	98.5	97.0	95.3	—
Cold roll	97.3	98.1	104.1	—
Slitters	80.1	82.5	93.2	Electrical Problems
Anneal	102.1	100.8	70.1	—
Packing	93.2	90.6	93.4	—
Totals	96.0	96.8	89.2	

Calculating Savings by Monitoring Direct-Labor Costs

A plant that does not have direct-labor control reports can generally realize a savings of 10 to 20 percent when the reports are published and used for corrective action. The savings are generated basically through reduced downtime, but some increases in direct-labor performance can be anticipated. In the case of the plant that employed 320 direct-labor people, the equivalent of 35 employees was eliminated over a period of 18 months, through implementation of direct-labor controls. The breakdown is seen in Exhibit 11.4.

Four Ways to Measure Direct-Labor Control

Many other measurements of direct labor can be made to control and correct costs. Some of the more prevalent are as follows:

1. *Calculate Labor Utilization*

$$\text{Utilization} = \frac{\text{Time off standards}}{\text{Total time available}} \times 100\%$$

Example: A production department with 20 direct-labor employees shows the following statistics for one 8-hour day.

$$\text{Total time available} = 20 \times 8 = 160 \text{ Labor hours}$$

$$\text{Time on standards} = 120 \text{ Labor hours}$$

$$\text{Time off standards} = 40 \text{ Labor hours}$$

$$\text{Utilization} = \frac{40}{160} \times 100\% = 25\%$$

2. *Calculate Direct-Labor Productivity*

$$\text{Productivity} = \text{Performance} \times \text{Utilization} \times 100\%$$

Example: In the same department cited in the example on utilization, performance (percent efficiency of direct labor) was 95 percent for that shift.

$$\text{Productivity} = 95.0\% \times 75.0\% \times 100\% = 71.3\%$$

Labor productivity is a more encompassing index than separate measures of performance and utilization. It provides a ready measurement of direct-labor productivity in a single ratio.

EXHIBIT 11.4   Savings through Monitoring of Direct-Labor Costs

Downtime Savings

Department	Hours/Years Saved	Dollars per Year Saved at $10/Hour*
Pre-heat	4,150	$ 41,500
Hot roll	6,670	66,700
Pre-heat	6,830	68,300
Cold roll	4,060	40,600
Slitters	14,190	141,900
Anneal	5,350	53,500
Packing	8,170	81,700
TOTALS	49,420	$494,200

Performance Savings

Department	Hours/Years Saved	Dollars per Year Saved at $10/Hour*
Pre-heat	8,990	$ 89,900
Hot roll	6,350	63,500
Pre-heat	2,280	22,800
Cold roll	(1,672)	(16,720)
Slitters	(3,830)	(38,300)
Anneal	10,150	101,500
Packing	Even	Even
TOTAL	22,268	$222,680

Total Direct-Labor Savings

	Dollars	Percent
Downtime savings	$494,200	68.9
Performance savings	222,680	31.1
Total	$716,880	100.0%

*The $10 per hour is based on an average hourly rate of $8, and a fringe level of $2 per hour (25 percent).

Notice that downtime savings are approximately double performance savings, and that performance savings are somewhat erratic with both the cold roll and slitter departments showing decreases in performance. Nevertheless, total direct-labor savings amounted to over $700,000 for the entire plant.

3. *Measure Units per Employee*

$$\text{Units per employee} = \frac{\text{No. of units produced (output)}}{\text{No. of direct-labor employees}}$$

Example: Continuing with the same department example, if 20 workers had produced 1,000 valves during their shift, then:

$$\text{Units per employee} = \frac{1,000}{20} = 50$$

This ratio is used only when high production volumes of discrete units are produced. If the same 20 workers assembled two tractors during one shift, use of the "units per employee" ratio would be meaningless.

4. *Calculate Direct-Labor Costs Per Unit*

$$\text{Direct-labor cost per unit} = \frac{\text{Total direct-labor costs}}{\text{No. of units produced}}$$

Example: If the 20 direct-labor employees each were paid $10 per hour, then:

$$\text{Direct-labor cost per unit} = \frac{20 \times \$10 \times 8 \text{ hrs.}}{1,000} = \frac{\$1,600}{1,000} = \$1.60$$

Incentive Coverage to Increase Production

Every organization must decide on whether or not it wants to use incentive systems to stimulate production output. Generally, incentive coverage yields more results in proportion to the amount of manual work involved. One hundred percent manual work, such as hand assembly of small components, is a natural for incentive coverage; a numerically controlled (NC) machine tool, where the machine controls the cycle, is at the other end of the spectrum. Also, short-cycle, highly repetitive work is amenable to incentive coverage, while long-cycle, highly technical, nonrepetitive work, such as missile assembly, is not.

Measuring Incentive Coverage

The first control tool when measuring incentive operations is the degree of coverage. This measurement is made in two parts:

1. Percent employees covered; and
2. Percent operations on incentive.

In the first case, it is relatively simple to measure the number of direct-labor employees on incentive. Here, 550 employees were classified as direct labor. Of these, 490 were on incentive. Therefore:

$$\text{Percent employees covered} = \frac{490}{550} \times 100\% = 89.1\%$$

For most operations, it is not necessary to have all direct-labor employees on incentive. There are always instances when to do so would not be practical. A good example is a small section of direct-labor employees doing all nonrepetitive miscellaneous operations. Standards here would be difficult to establish.

The latter measurement, "Percent Operations on Incentive," is an index that is somewhat better than "Percent Employees Covered," simply because *all* employees could be on incentive, but have only 25 percent of their work on incentive.

$$\text{Percentage operations on incentive} = \frac{\text{Operations on incentive}}{\text{Total plant operations}} \times 100\%$$

Total plant operations, of course, refers only to direct-labor work. The company had 312 operations (counting all variations as measured by production routings), and 249 of those were on incentive. Therefore,

$$\text{Percentage operations on incentive} = \frac{249}{312} \times 100 = 79.8\%$$

Generally speaking, incentive coverage of 80 percent to 90 percent is considered acceptable, but each company must make its own determination, and that is usually done by measuring production increases generated by the incentive system.

Calculating Average Earnings

Average earnings is defined as those earnings derived from operations not on standard. In most union shops, average earnings is a negotiable issue, and payment resulting from average earnings is based on what each individual operator averaged on incentive for the past week. If an operator, for example, ran several jobs not yet measured on incentive (usually new jobs), his *incentive* pay for those jobs would be the average incentive pay he earned during the previous week.

Average earnings is payment of something for nothing. Since unmeasured work is looked upon as a fault of management, unions are generally successful in their demands for average earnings. In that case, the measurement of average earnings becomes a significant ratio for management.

$$\text{Average earnings} = \frac{\text{Average earnings}}{\text{Total incentive earnings}} \times 100\%$$

A company had the following average earnings for one calendar year:

$$\text{Average earnings} = \frac{\$241,632}{\$1,550,750} \times 100 = 15.6\%$$

No matter how you look at it, either 15.6 percent or $241,632 is too much. Most average earnings are better held to maximums of 5 percent to 7 percent.

Measuring the Results of Incentive Coverage: Percent Performance to Standard

This ratio is the most significant one in measuring the results of incentive coverage. It shows increases in performance that can be directly related to increases in production. The company, before incentives, had the following annual performance.

$$\text{Performance} = \frac{\text{Earned hours}}{\text{Standard hours}} \times 100$$

$$\text{Performance} = \frac{398,140}{563,178} \times 100 = 70.7\%$$

After installation of the incentive system for 1 year, their performance had improved 25 percent (despite their large average earnings) as seen here:

$$\text{Performance} = \frac{506,442}{571,280} \times 100 = 88.7\%$$

In terms of actual improvement in performance,

$$\text{Percent improvement} = \frac{88.7\% - 70.7\%}{70.7\%} \times 100 = 25.5\%$$

The 25.5 percent improvement in performance represented a real gain of equal amount in production output.

Reducing Indirect-Labor Costs

Indirect-labor costs constitute a significant portion of overhead, and overhead is that type of cost that must be constantly pruned to keep it from growing. An operation that ignores those costs will soon find its costs escalating beyond control. Typical indirect-labor costs are:

Material handlers	Warehouse personnel
Truckers	Inspectors
Pipefitters	Machinists
Electricians	Tool grinders
Tool crib attendants	Sweepers
Janitors	Clerks
Supervisors	Managers

Comparing Direct to Indirect Labor

Section "A" of Exhibit 11.5 displays the total number of direct and indirect employees on the books for 20X0, 20X1, and the first 4 months of 20X2.

A ratio of direct labor divided by indirect labor is then developed. Notice that this ratio was 3.90 in 20X0 and 4.92 to 4.95 for the first 4 months of 20X2. This represents an improvement of 26.4 percent, as seen here:

$$\frac{4.93\% - 3.90\%}{3.90\%} \times 100 = 26.4\%$$

Section "B" of Exhibit 11.5 shows the actual number of indirect employees by classification, and reveals reductions made in each classification of indirect labor.

Measuring Indirect Labor as a Percentage of Cost of Sales

The second measurement used by the company was the ratio of indirect-labor costs to cost of sales. Use of that ratio permitted an unbiased and objective look at progress—or lack of it—in controlling indirect-labor costs. The ratio is:

$$\text{Indirect-labor costs ratio} = \frac{\text{Indirect-labor costs}}{\text{Total cost of sales}}$$

For the company being studied, his 20X0 and January–April 20X2 ratios are seen here:

$$\text{20X0 Indirect-labor costs} = \frac{\$1,963,520}{62,073,985} \times 100 = 3.16\%$$

$$\text{Jan.–April 20X2 Indirect-labor costs} = \frac{\$478,515}{21,173,228} \times 100 = 2.26\%$$

Change

$$3.16\% - 2.26\% \times 100 = 28.5\% \text{ Improvement}$$

The 28.5 percent represents real-dollar improvement adjusted for inflation, in terms of today's dollars.

EXHIBIT 11.5   Indirect-Labor Control—4/X2

	20X0	20X1	1/X2	2/X2	3/X2	4/X2
A. *Direct to Indirect*						
Direct	460	495	483	485	485	482
Indirect	118	118	98	98	98	98
Direct/Indirect	3.90	4.19	4.93	4.95	4.95	4.92
B. *Indirect Classification*						
Inspectors	29	29	22	22	22	22
Attendants	4	4	2	2	2	2
Sweepers	6	6	3	3	3	3
Maintenance	28	28	24	24	24	24
Warehouse	30	30	29	29	29	29
Truck drivers	21	21	18	18	18	18
Totals	118	118	98	98	98	98

Reducing Operating Overhead

Overhead costs are composed of the following types of accounts in operations:

- Salaries;
- Travel and entertainment expenses;
- Overtime;
- Dues and subscriptions;
- Heat, light, and power;
- Rent;
- Insurance;
- Supplies;
- Training;
- Rework and scrap;
- Depreciation;
- Downtime; and
- Recruiting expenses.

The spending variance is the difference between the actual overhead and budgeted overhead for actual standard hours of operation. The company had forecast a monthly rate of 70,000 standard hours at a total overhead cost of $280,000, as shown here:

Budgeted overhead costs:	$280,000
Actual overhead costs:	255,000
Favorable spending variance:	$ 25,000

Since actual costs were $25,000 less than anticipated, a favorable spending variance occurred. An annual rate of savings was then $300,000 ($25,000 per month × 12 months), as actually happened during the course of the year.

The company had been forecast to produce 1,200 tons during the year, and to consume 70,000 standard hours per month, or an annual rate of 840,000 standard hours (70,000 standard hours × 12 months). Instead, 760,000 standard hours were used to process those same 1,200 tons. A favorable efficiency variance resulted:

Budget for 840,000 std. hrs:	$3,360,000
Actual for 760,000 std. hrs:	3,040,000
Favorable efficiency variance:	$ 320,000
Total savings:	
Favorable spending variance:	$ 300,000
Favorable efficiency variance:	320,000
Total favorable variances:	$ 620,000

The very nature of budgeting overhead costs to departments, then measuring and reporting them by area of responsibility, soon produces cost savings. Supervisors and

EXHIBIT 11.6   Material Burden Analysis—1/X3

Price Variances	This Month		Year-to-Date	
	Standard	Actual	Standard	Actual
Soluble materials	$20,500	$18,550	$20,500	$18,550
Dry materials	16,800	17,200	16,800	17,200
Liquids	2,500	2,400	2,500	2,400
Packaging	18,900	17,500	18,900	17,500
Totals	$58,700	$55,650	$58,700	$55,650
Quality Variances	**Standard**	**Actual**	**Standard**	**Actual**
Weigh, screen, mix	12,500	10,660	12,500	10,660
Absorption and mixing	13,100	12,770	13,100	12,770
Packaging	10,000	10,000	10,000	10,000
Boxing	3,000	3,200	3,000	3,200
Totals	38,600	36,630	38,600	36,630

Quantity variances in material burden reflect the difference between specified and actual usage.

managers, when aware of *where* costs are, and *how much* they are, are then in a position to apply their skills in cost reduction. The company was successful in reducing overhead because they intelligently applied those principles.

Reducing Material Burden

Materials, in this sense, means materials used in the sold product. It does not include supplies, tools, gauges, fixtures, or any other expense classified as overhead.

There are two measurable variances connected with material burden: price and quantity. This is seen in Exhibit 11.6. That amounted to a rather large savings since material costs are usually the largest single category of cost in a service center company.

Price variances in material burden measure the difference between actual purchased prices and standard costs.

Reducing Inventory

A company reduced inventory by $1 million through use of control measurements of its inventory turnover rate, as well as the size of its inventory during different stages of manufacture. (See Exhibit 11.7.)

Measuring Inventory Turnover

Inventory turnover is the annual number of times that a plant ships products equivalent in value to the average monthly costs of its inventory. A company, for example, reported the following turnover for 2000:

$$\text{Turnover} = \frac{\text{Cost of sales}}{\text{Average monthly inventory}}$$

$$\text{Turnover} = \frac{9,350,000}{3,230,000}$$

$$\text{Turnover} = 2.89 \text{ Times per year}$$

Actual inventory turnover results are published monthly by the company and compared to the plan. (See Exhibit 11.8.)

Tracking Your Inventory Carrying Costs Carefully

In today's economy, inventory carrying costs of 30 percent of the value of the inventory are not uncommon. Therefore, the importance of keeping inventories to an absolute minimum to support delivery schedules is paramount. This annual cost includes such major segments as:

Space Costs

- Building and equipment depreciation;
- Heat, light, and power;
- Building equipment maintenance;
- Insurance;
- Fire systems; and
- Plant protection.

Inventory Costs

- Interest on capital invested (about 20 percent);
- Transportation and handling;
- Clerical costs;
- Physical inventory costs;

EXHIBIT 11.7   Inventory Turnover Rate

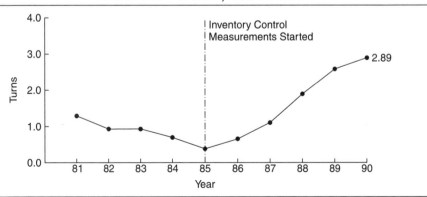

EXHIBIT 11.8   Inventory Turnover Plan—20XX

		Inventory			
	Cost-of-Sales	Raw Material	W.I.P.	Finished	Turnover
January	700,000	300,000	800,000	1,000,000	3.0
February	700,000	300,000	800,000	1,000,000	3.0
March	700,000	300,000	800,000	1,000,000	3.0
April	700,000	300,000	800,000	1,000,000	3.0
May	700,000	300,000	800,000	1,000,000	3.0
June	700,000	300,000	800,000	1,000,000	3.0
July	700,000	300,000	800,000	1,000,000	3.0
August	1,000,000	700,000	1,000,000	1,500,000	3.2
September	1,000,000	700,000	1,000,000	1,500,000	3.2
October	1,500,000	700,000	1,000,000	1,500,000	3.2
November	2,000,000	2,200,000	1,800,000	3,000,000	3.5
December	1,000,000	0	800,000	2,500,000	3.3
Total	10,700,000				

- Damage to inventory;
- Obsolescence; and
- Theft.

Maintaining Accurate Inventory Records

Accurate inventory records are of prime importance, because if they are not maintained properly, variances in purchasing materials and usage of materials in production can be expected. Shrink is caused by many different things, among them:

- Clerical errors;
- Failure to process paperwork quickly;
- Unreported scrap and rework;
- Misplaced inventory;
- Theft;
- Unauthorized material substitutions; and
- Inaccurate bills of material (see Method 8).

MONITORING SHRINKAGE THROUGH CYCLE COUNTING

A metal-working company in the South countered this problem through cycle counting. Cycle counting is a system of perpetual physical inventory-taking, conducted on selected inventory parts every day, normally after business hours. It emphasizes the

EXHIBIT 11.9   Cycle Count Report—Week of 9/7/20XX

	Part Nos. Checked	No. of Pieces
Number of Counts		
Cycle counter "A"	306	30,143
Cycle counter "B"	294	32,650
Total Counts	600	62,793
Number of Errors Found		
Cycle counter "A"	3.1%	
Cycle counter "B"	2.5%	
Total Errors	5.6%	
Errors in Dollars		

$$\frac{\text{No. of pieces wrong}}{\text{Total inventory counted}} = \frac{1,633}{62,793} = 2.6\%$$

$$\frac{\text{Pieces wrong}}{\text{Inventory counted}} = \frac{\$21,528}{1,040,697} = 2.1\%$$

review of high-value inventory parts. In cycle counting, employees physically count and check location accuracy as well. Mistakes are reconciled to perpetual inventory records.

This report, displayed in Exhibit 11.9, provides the following information:

- The actual number of different numbers checked and the total number of counts;
- The number and percentage of errors found in actual pieces counted; and
- A dollar amount on the errors found as well as a dollar and percentage figure based on the sample derived.

Use of this report (along with bills of material accuracy) enables managers to spot errors and take effective corrective action. It also gives a reliable picture of the estimated percentage of errors to be found in the inventory.

BILLS OF MATERIAL

A key function of product engineering is the creation of bills of material that accurately reflect the type and number of parts to be used in the product. Inaccurate or incomplete BOM (Bills of Material) directly affect the level of inventory accuracy. If a BOM is wrong, unauthorized parts may need to be substituted, and this generates additional costs if the substituted parts are of higher value. It then also creates quantity variances in the parts being substituted because of unplanned issues.

Typical BOM. The bill of material seen in Exhibit 11.10 is typical of bills originating in engineering departments. Listed in the body of the bill are all of the components that make up the part described on the top of the bill, in this case a tension bracket. The bill of material is used by all relevant departments—manufacturing, engineering, and accounting—to extract the information they need to do their jobs.

Engineering. Uses BOM to list and specify all components, materials, and parts in the product.

Manufacturing. Structures the bill according to sequence of manufacture (called a production routing), and specifies work methods and standards for each operation.

Accounting. Uses BOM to cost the product and obtain variances from standards.

BOM accuracy is then essentially a function of how well manufacturing and engineering have done their jobs. It is an audit of the correct parts to be used in manufacturing. In the typical BOM accuracy audit, literally hundreds of bills, such as those seen in Exhibit 11.10, are examined for errors, and a BOM accuracy rate is derived.

EXHIBIT 11.10   Bill of Material (BOM)

Part: Tension Bracket
Part Number: 136-72A

Parts Description	Part Number	Quantity Used
Bracket frame	136-72A1	1
Sprocket	136-72A2	1
Spring	136-72A3	2
Set screen	136-72A4	1
Holding screen	136-72A5	3

BOM Audit
Week of Sept. 7, 20XX
Count

Parts Audited	Specified	Actual	Comments
136-72A1	1	1	
136-72A2	1	1	Wrong part no. (should be 136-72AC)
136-72A3	2	2	
136-72A4	1	1	
136-72A5	3	2	Should be two parts

Summary of Results

$$\frac{\text{No. of parts incorrect}}{\text{No. of parts audited}} = \frac{4}{354} = 1.0\% \text{ error}$$

Summary of Errors

2	Excess parts specified
1	Insufficient parts specified
1	Wrong parts specified
4	

Exhibit 11.10 is a typical report on BOM accuracy. Both counts and correct part numbers are examined, as can be seen in the top half of the form. The bottom half lists the summary of results, along with the type of errors found.

CONTROLLING QUALITY COSTS

A plant in South Carolina was experiencing severe quality problems and high associated quality costs. In 1987 its COQ (Cost of Quality) was running about 8 percent with much of its costs deriving from warranty. Because of poor quality in customers' hands, it was beginning to lose repeat sales.

Computing Quality Costs. A new quality manager was hired and installed a quality cost report. The quality cost report, shown in Exhibit 11.11, lists the following items:

- *Warranty*—Contractual costs arising from product failures in customers' hands;
- *Rework*—Product rejected by inspectors and salvaged in the plant;
- *Scrap*—Products rejected by inspectors and scrapped;
- *Inspection*—Cost in inspectors' salaries; and
- *Support*—All other overhead expenses of the quality control department.

The bottom of the report compares total quality costs to total sales, with the derived ratio indicating that percentage of the sales dollar needed to support a quality effort. Notice that, from a high of 8 percent in 1987, COQ during 1990 is at 3 percent, a 63 percent improvement. The change from 8 to 3 percent generated a savings of over half a million dollars, based on January through October results:

$$5.0\% \times \$10,750,000 = \$537,500$$

The calculation of quality costs, along with its attendant pressure to closely examine its components, soon enabled the textile mill to achieve the significant savings shown in Exhibit 11.11.

EXHIBIT 11.11   Quality Costs—10/X0

	20X0 Oct.	20X0 YTD	19X9 Total
Warranty	$ 5,000	$ 62,000	$ 78,000
Rework	3,000	26,000	29,000
Scrap	1,000	7,000	16,000
Inspection	19,000	188,000	225,000
Support	7,000	39,000	41,000
Total	$35,000	$322,000	$389,000
Sales	1,110,000	10,750,000	8,061,000
Cost of Quality	3.2%	3.0%	4.8%

EXHIBIT 11.12   Cost-Reduction Results

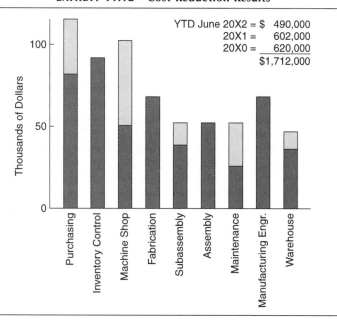

COST-REDUCTION MEASURES

Through assignment of cost-reduction goals to each segment of the organization, and with the agreement of key managers in each of those functional areas, a company was able to eliminate $1.7 million in costs from its operating budget. Each year, commitments were made and forecast, based on specific plans to reduce costs. A large board with posted results was hung outside of the plant cafeteria for everyone to see. This can be seen in Exhibit 11.12.

Typical areas of attack for cost reduction, as used by a distributor, are listed as follows:

- Opening up engineering tolerances;
- Low-cost designs;
- Increasing feeds and speeds;
- Cheaper materials;
- Standardized production methods;
- Reduction of paperwork;
- Improved materials handling;
- Replacement of slow and obsolete equipment;
- Scrap and rework reduction;
- Reducing downtime;
- Selling scrap;

- Elimination of production operations;
- Mechanizing manual operations;
- Curtailing utilities usage (fuel, etc.);
- Damage and corrosion protection;
- Traffic rate reductions;
- Implementing work standards;
- Improved material flow;
- Employee training;
- Quality cost reduction;
- Reduction of indirect labor;
- Combining salaried jobs;
- Reducing overtime;
- Reducing supply usage;
- Reducing inventory balances;
- Shrinking lead times;
- Using economic lot sizes;
- Renegotiate vendor prices; and
- Control over obsolete blueprints.

MAINTENANCE COSTS

Maintenance costs are easily forgotten in operations. There is a tendency to bury them in the overhead account and focus instead on direct-labor costs for cost reduction.

The targeting of maintenance costs for reduction, however, is an imperative for a well-run company; otherwise, those costs will grow unimpeded year after year and could damage even the most productive program for reducing direct-labor costs in two ways. First, an ever-increasing maintenance budget is a cost that offsets any gain made in other areas. Second, out-of-control maintenance costs reflect an out-of-control maintenance department. That hinders the cost-reduction efforts of production departments due to machine downtime.

There are six major ways to measure the effectiveness of the maintenance department. These are:

1. $\text{Maintenance labor ratio} = \dfrac{\text{No. of maintenance workers}}{\text{Total direct labor}} \times 100$

This demonstrates the control of the number of maintenance workers as a portion of all direct-labor workers. It is a key indicator.

2. $\text{Maintenance dollars} = \dfrac{\text{Total maintenance expenditures}}{\text{Cost of sales}} \times 100$

This is the same type of indicator as the first one, but uses dollars as the yardstick instead of number of people. It is a better reflection of the effectiveness of maintenance, because it takes into account the higher cost of maintenance workers as opposed to direct-labor workers.

3. Perishable tools $= \dfrac{\text{Perishable tool expense}}{\text{Cost of sales}} \times 100$

This ratio shows how efficiently maintenance workers are using expendable tools in their everyday jobs. Perishable tools are expensive and must be controlled or else their costs can zoom out of sight.

4. Machine uptime $= \dfrac{\text{Machine operating time}}{\text{Total operating time available}} \times 100$

This measurement comes from the production department. It is a key indication of how maintenance is doing its job. What better indicator than the percentage of time production machines are actually being used? This ratio must be interpreted with some discretion. Obviously, it is possible that factors other than maintainability, factors such as high absenteeism or low production orders, may be affecting this ratio.

5. Machine maintenance $= \dfrac{\text{Maintenance costs of machines}}{\text{Machine hours available}} \times 100$

In this case, unit maintenance costs are based on machine hours available. This method is preferred over #2 or #4 only when delays other than maintenance have been subtracted from machine hours.

6. Maintenance overtime $= \dfrac{\text{Maintenance overtime dollars}}{\text{Total maintenance labor costs}} = 100$

Maintenance departments in most plants have worse records than other departments when it comes to overtime. Nowhere is it easier to lose control because of the normally nonrepetitive type of work maintenance does—work that is hard to measure. So nowhere is it more important to measure and control overtime than in maintenance. This ratio helps accomplish that.

CAPITAL EXPENDITURES

Although capital expenditures occur less frequently than other categories of plant costs, they must be controlled as closely as other costs, because each capital expenditure is generally high. There are two ratios in common use for that purpose:

1. Capital intensity $= \dfrac{\text{Capital equipment costs}}{\text{No. of direct-labor workers}} \times 100$

This ratio is an indication of the relative expenditure made per worker. As such, its value is comparative. That is, there are no absolute good or bad ratios. Companies can observe whether or not capital expenditures are increasing proportionately from one financial period to another.

2. $\text{Capital replacement costs} = \dfrac{\text{Capital equipment costs}}{\text{Depreciation}} \times 100$

Here, the purpose is to determine how many times depreciation costs are covered by new capital expenditures. When the ratio is less than 100 percent, machinery productivity is lagging and is a sure sign that the company does not have an adequate capital expenditure program. A ratio greater than 100 percent indicates the company is investing in new equipment to keep machine productivity advancing.

EMPLOYEE CONCERNS

Keep Grievances and Disciplines to a Minimum

Grievances and workforce discipline, like other areas of concern in a plant, need to be adequately measured and controlled. In this area, particularly, trends can be discerned that will allow management to prevent serious labor problems before they occur. Four ratios are used. All of these ratios are self-explanatory and are best used as comparative measurements:

1. $\text{Grievances} = \dfrac{\text{Number of grievances}}{\text{Month}}$

2. $\text{Grievances} = \dfrac{\text{Number of grievances}}{\text{Employee}}$

3. $\text{Discipline} = \dfrac{\text{Number of disciplinary actions}}{\text{Month}}$

4. $\text{Discipline} = \dfrac{\text{Number of disciplinary actions}}{\text{Employee}}$

Control Absenteeism

Like grievances and discipline, absenteeism is a reflection of trouble brewing. Therefore, absenteeism trends need to be monitored carefully to avoid gradually slipping into a condition where absent employees disrupt the production schedule. There are three monitors in widespread use.

1. $\text{Absenteeism} = \dfrac{\text{No. of labor days lost}}{\text{Month}}$

2. $\text{Absenteeism cost} = \dfrac{\text{Cost of labor days lost}}{\text{Total labor costs}}$

3. *Reasons for labor days lost:* sickness, death in family, jury duty, other explained absences, or unexplained absences. Reasons for labor days lost must always accompany the two ratios provided.

Lower Accident Frequency

Accident frequency needs to be monitored carefully at all times. A rash of small accidents is often an indication of safety rules being ignored, which usually results in a catastrophic accident where a worker is seriously maimed. Managers and safety professionals watch these trends closely; as soon as a series of accidents is evident, you should quickly conduct a safety investigation of all the recent accidents and review whether safety rules are adhered to throughout the plant. This must be done periodically, since it is all too easy for supervisors and workers alike to gradually ignore safety precautions. There are two basic methods to monitor accident frequency. First, and foremost, is

$$\text{Accident frequency} = \frac{\text{Number of lost time accidents}}{\text{Total labor hours worked}}$$

This is the key monitor. The other way is to track workers' compensation costs. Although too far after the fact, it is a good way for financial managers to prevent their compensation rates from going through the roof.

To offset operational expenses and boost operational efficiency, Exhibit 11.13 provides a model by which you can summarize, gauge, and compare operational expense trends and operational efficiency patterns. The three key measurements for a well-run operation are percent efficiency, percent utilization, and percent productivity. The higher the percentages, the more effective the operation will be.

COST-CUTTING IDEAS FOR THE PLANT

The following is a list of ideas to spur the imagination of its salaried employees and to suggest productive areas of investigation for cost reduction. This list can be used by just about any operation to help stimulate ideas. Exhibits 11.14 through 11.18 demonstrate cost-cutting controls and reports.

Cut Costs in Product Engineering

1. Make tolerances more flexible.
2. Reduce surface finish requirements.
3. Eliminate need for a specific part.
4. Substitute a cheaper material.
5. Reduce the number of parts needed.
6. Combine part functions.

EXHIBIT 11.13 Sample Production Evaluation Report

	Attendance Hours	Standard Hours Reported	Percent on Standard	Reported Hours	Nonstandard Hours Reported	Standard Hours Earned	Downtime	Exception Hours	Efficiency Percent	Utilization Percent	Productivity Percent
Henry Smith											
Johnson	357.80	237.14	66%	349.26	112.11	72.65	0.00	0.01	52.9%	97.6%	51.6%
Jones	369.00	252.36	68	367.53	58.57	203.93	56.60	0.00	84.4	84.3	71.1
White	598.00	523.20	87	591.43	36.89	586.69	28.29	3.05	111.3	9.37	104.3
Banks	1,022.70	865.81	85	1,012.92	105.81	745.78	38.04	3.25	87.6	95.0	83.3
Carmody	433.50	314.58	73	430.56	108.70	280.30	7.27	0.00	91.9	97.6	89.7
Snover	1,152.80	948.25	82	1,144.97	170.55	1,066.68	26.12	0.04	110.6	97.1	107.3
Total	3,933.80	3,141.34	80	3,896.67	592.63	2,956.03	156.32	6.35	95.0	94.9	90.2
Jim Maliet											
Menke	515.20	451.49	88	568.50	49.26	419.79	59.80	7.95	93.7	97.2	91.0
Clemons	658.20	444.98	68	645.15	136.30	365.56	63.37	0.50	86.3	88.3	76.2
Chamberlain	650.30	431.79	66	623.56	91.41	387.31	81.53	18.83	91.5	80.5	73.6
Conrad	402.10	296.78	74	364.52	40.71	352.01	26.00	1.02	116.4	83.9	97.7
Cox	964.10	761.48	79	978.05	89.54	721.53	102.78	24.25	95.3	88.3	84.1
Total	3,189.90	2,386.52	75	3,179.78	407.22	2,246.20	333.48	52.55	95.0	87.6	83.2
Ernest Cooper											
Swift	289.40	235.49	81	345.62	50.10	211.45	55.37	4.66	91.6	98.7	90.4
Stoffa	1,002.40	431.23	43	920.78	167.06	170.69	191.96	130.53	56.5	59.7	33.7
Total	1,291.80	666.72	52	1,266.40	217.16	382.14	247.33	135.19	67.8	68.4	46.4
John Taggart											
Templer	56.00	7.27	13	55.73	11.76	2.25	36.70	0.00	73.6	34.0	25.0
Total	56.00	7.27	13	55.73	11.76	2.25	36.70	0.00	73.6	34.0	25.0
Total Workforce	8,471.50	6,201.85	73	8,398.58	1,228.77	5,586.62	778.83	194.09	91.7	87.7	80.5

EXHIBIT 11.14   Manpower Requirement Summary

Department: _____

Manager: _____

Number of people on payroll	10
Potential hours available for work 10 people @ 40 hours	400
Less absenteeism and vacation 2% (MGMT-HISTORICAL)	8
Hours available for work	392
Less lost time hours 25% (unnecessary hours)	98
Current output level	294
Person-hours required at planned performance 85% 294/.85	51.9
Fixed hour allowance (added on, if necessary)	
Total hours required	345.9
Absentee allowance & vacation 2%	6.9
Total adjusted hours required	352.8
Total equivalent people required @ 40 hours	8.8
People variance	1

EXHIBIT 11.15   Person–Load Fabrication for Master Schedule

1. Take total estimated hours.
2. Times % factor (from management history).
3. Equals required hours to perform job.
4. Hours required to do job times % absentee—vacation, etc.
   Equals additional hours required to do job.
5. Take number working days in month times 8.0 hours per day.
   Equals number of hours required for each person.
6. Take total hours required divide by 1 person–load for month.
   Equals number people required for month.
7. Subtract total people available equals + / − crew required.

Sample:

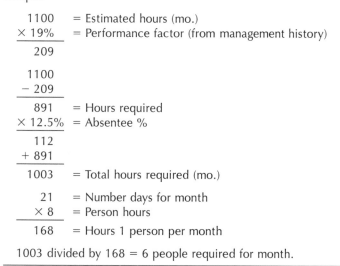

```
   1100     = Estimated hours (mo.)
 × 19%      = Performance factor (from management history)
   ─────
    209

   1100
 − 209
   ─────
    891     = Hours required
 × 12.5%    = Absentee %
   ─────
    112
 + 891
   ─────
   1003     = Total hours required (mo.)

     21     = Number days for month
  × 8       = Person hours
   ─────
    168     = Hours 1 person per month
```

1003 divided by 168 = 6 people required for month.

Note: + / − People (crew) required—available.

EXHIBIT 11.16 Production Scheduling

Action Focus	N/A	Strong	Satisfactory	Needs Some Improvement	Weak: Needs Major Improvement	Action Plan, Responsibility
Improve accuracy of production forecasts						
Enhance delivery of small quantities of raw materials frequently						
Assure vendor compliance of wrapping in exact quantities						
Check conformity to raw material quantity specifications						
Encourage proximity of suppliers to plant						
Provide for quick, easy detection of defective products						
Be willing to make engineering changes when required						
Increase inventory control system's responsiveness to JIT (just-in-time)						
Assure production equipment is operating at maximum capacity						
Verify that equipment is running at rated speed						
Provide breakdown analysis of machines to isolate "losers"						
Do maintenance in advance of peak periods						
Have planned replacement program of automated manual equipment						
Intensify use of numerical control programs						
Use computer-aided design/manufacturing (CAD/CAM)						
Examine overall plant size versus "scaled down" installation						
Review tools, jigs, etc.						
Use standard parts for different types of equipment						
Employ air pressure, gravity feed, and other natural aids						

Use automatic feed mechanisms rather than manual						
Check accuracy of gauges and other measuring instruments						
Use advanced power tools (drills, hammers, etc.)						
Review degree of cross-training and flexibility to meet changing situations						
Evaluate quality of oral instructions by supervisors						
Evaluate quality of reference manuals for job procedures						
Monitor operators' current productivity, overall trend, and quality						
Determine whether operators are meeting prescribed schedules						
Examine job setups: Operator versus setup specialist						
Analyze strength of safety inspections (better morale, cost avoidance)						
Encourage production employee cost-reduction suggestions						
Use Quality Circles to address specific production problems						
Pinpoint exact production stations causing high number of rejects						
Determine precise reasons for parts breakdowns						
Ensure that customer returns can be traced to their production source						
Use CAD to maximize product performance						
Employ robots for moving materials along prescribed paths						
Consider numerically controlled (NC) machines for specific manufacturing functions						
Combine robots and NC machines to move and operate on materials						
Integrate design, manufacturing, information management (CIM)						

EXHIBIT 11.17 Production Engineering Survey

Action Focus	N/A	Strong	Satisfactory	Needs Some Improvement	Weak: Needs Major Improvement	Action Plan, Responsibility
Intensify long-range planning for new product development						
Improve short-term planning for product improvement						
Participate in setting quality standards						
Develop more accurate product unit costs						
Evaluate customer inquiries for clues to product failures						
Review appropriations for research and development						
Investigate budget versus actual variances for new product development						
Report on projects with schedule overruns						
Coordinate with cost-accounting function on analysis of reports						
Review procedures on treating costs as expenses or capital expenditures						
Automate system for estimating product costs						
Increase degree of component standardization as opposed to special design						
Improve accuracy of production time forecasts						
Clarify parts identification method						
Check staffing of product engineering and use of outside consultants						
Use microfilm for reducing records-management space and costs						
Make parts lighter through use of different materials						
Examine production tolerances for possible reduction						
Alter design to reduce scrap materials						

Check product for temperature and/or pressure specifications						
Substitute less expensive metals or plastics						
Attend vendor trade shows to save research money						
Visit key resources' plants to check facilities, quality control, distribution, financing						
Revitalize proven techniques that are not being used						
Intensify value analysis in product design						
Reduce special packages and/or labels without affecting aesthetics						
Question whether new products will add volume or detract from existing items						
Determine timing of new product introduction to consumers						
Check out economies in packaging, handling, distribution						
Have representative consumers field-test product						
Employ direct charges or allocation for data-processing services						
Pinpoint standard costs for products and component parts						
Assure that cost-accounting records agree with other financial items						
Maintain control over major expense and/or capital categories						
Report frequently on actions concerning controllable expenses						
Use cost-avoidance techniques to prevent expenditures						
Involve a steering committee on high-cost projects						
Have cost-accounting participate in production contract preparation						

185

EXHIBIT 11.18 Productivity Improvement and Cost Control

Action Focus	N/A	Strong	Satisfactory	Needs Some Improvement	Weak: Needs Major Improvement	Action Plan, Responsibility
Create a productivity-awareness culture at all levels						
Publish productivity goals in company media						
Establish a performance-measurement and improvement system						
Set up a research/exchange network to exchange information						
Select quality-assurance checkpoints and performance indicators						
Choose reliable volume figures, including sampling						
Calculate productivity performance and determine trends						
Define goals and "status" (on or off target)						
Use graphics and exception reporting to save time						
Isolate controllable from noncontrollable costs						
Distinguish between profit center and cost center						

7. Design for low-cost tooling.

8. Design for high-speed production.

9. Increase feeds and speeds.

10. Improve the print control procedure.

11. Reduce the number of design changes.

12. Design-in quality.

13. Design to reduce scrap.

14. Design to standardize production processes.

15. Use standard hardware in place of custom hardware.

16. Design to reduce manual production operations.

17. Design to reduce material content.

18. Design to reduce number of fasteners required.

19. Specify alloys to enable faster machining.

20. Specify alloys to cut tool wear.

21. Design the cheapest finish feasible.

Cost-Reduction Ideas for Shipping, Receiving, and Warehousing

1. Use conveyors for moving operations.

2. Use reusable pallets and storage boxes.

3. Keep warehouse locked.

4. Minimize travel distances.

5. Group similar parts together in warehouse.

6. Use hydraulic lifts instead of ladders.

7. Ship and receive in unit loads.

8. Protect product from damage and corrosion.

9. Use maximum height for warehouse storage.

10. Speed handling by improving scheduling.

11. Use proper storage containers.

12. Prearrange movement of materials.

13. Replace obsolete equipment.

14. Combine clerical operations.

15. Place fastest-moving items near dock.

16. Mechanize all movement of material.

17. Keep aisle space down to minimum needs.

18. Practice first-in, first-out.

19. Properly identify all stock.

20. Check all freight rates.

21. Audit freight bills.

22. Use economical small package ship methods.

23. Keep less than truckload to a minimum.

24. Minimize demurrage costs—unload promptly.

25. Keep bills of lading legible.

26. Count number of parts received.

Slash Expenses in Production Planning and Control

Reduce inventories:

1. Reduce number of product lines.

2. Reduce size of purchased lots.

3. Reduce size of production lots.

4. Improve forecasting techniques.

5. Convert obsolete parts to current production.

6. Keep inventories organized.

7. Keep inventory records accurate.

Reduce number of salaried people needed:

8. Keep overtime low.

9. Keep warehouse space filled.

10. Reduce office space.

11. Reduce overhead expenses.

12. Improve package design.

13. Keep written procedures current.

14. Keep work standards up to date.

15. Shrink lead times.

16. Reduce emergency orders.

17. Keep product routings up to date.

18. Provide fast access to stock.

19. Use effective communication systems.

20. Minimize material flow.

21. Maintain fork trucks in good order.

22. Improve inspection techniques.

23. Improve vendor performance.

24. Guard against incorrect engineering drawings.

25. Provide for scrap/rework when planning.
26. Schedule to minimize waiting time.
27. Renegotiate vendor prices.
28. Keep production overruns to a minimum.
29. Recognize production bottlenecks, then eliminate them.
30. Keep accurate records.
31. Load work centers to minimize setups.
32. Minimize sales changes to master schedule.

Reducing Plant and Production Engineering Costs

1. Correct wrong bills of material.
2. Reduce average earnings.
3. Curtail use of fuel and electricity.
4. Correct loose work standards.
5. Keep 90 percent of all production jobs on standard.
6. Keep 80 percent of all indirect-labor jobs on standard.
7. Use allowances in standards sparingly.
8. Ensure use of proper feeds and speeds.
9. Issue frequent labor performance reports.
10. Combine production operations.
11. Change standards to reflect improved methods.
12. Sample production counts for accuracy.
13. Analyze and reduce machine downtime.
14. Standardize equipment parts.
15. Combine or reduce machine setups.
16. Simplify tooling, jigs, and fixtures.
17. Keep accurate and up-to-date equipment records.
18. Lease rather than buy equipment.
19. Mechanize manual operations.

Improve Quality Control

1. Reduce scrap levels.
2. Reduce rework levels.
3. Reduce warranty.
4. Improve tool and gauge inspection.
5. Reduce vendor quality problems.

6. Calibrate testing equipment.

7. Prohibit use of marked-up prints.

8. Scrap all makeshift tooling.

9. Segregate defective stock.

10. Modernize inspection equipment.

11. Review packaging quality.

12. Investigate sales of plant scrap.

Backlog Data in Management Reporting

Many service center operations must be concerned with the amount of work in backlog. Most manufacturing companies keep careful account of the orders in their backlog. Many departments within a company want to see backlog in their staging areas. A given amount of backlog is healthy, and too little can cause interruptions in the workflow, with a resulting loss of person and machine time. *Too much backlog can mean delays in delivery promises or can extend delivery schedules beyond the point of customer acceptance, resulting in lost business.*

It is important, therefore, in many service center operations, that the backlog be reported as part of the management reporting system. Maintenance operations present a good example of this need, as do many clerical operations. *Backlog information must be translated into the hours required to handle the backlog, so that decisions can be made to ensure that the facility is adequately equipped.*

For example: In a department consisting of 10 people with 375 hours available per week, a backlog of 3750 hours would represent 10 weeks of work. Is this an acceptable backlog? *This is a question that can only be answered by management, which therefore has a need to know.*

Conversely, if a department loses time waiting for work, then a backlog should exist to run the department in an economic fashion.

Calculating the Backlog

At face value, calculating the backlog appears to be a relatively simple process. The reasonable expectancy (R/E) per unit multiplied by the number of units in the backlog will give the hours in the backlog. This figure, compared to the person and/or machine hours available to produce it, will demonstrate whether or not the department is in a healthy position. But this is too simple. Additional information is needed.

The percentage of performance of the unit against the standard is required to properly evaluate the backlog. Here's how it works:

Step 1. There are 1,000 tons of work in the backlog. The R/E is 0.4 hours per ton. This means that there is a standard measure of 400 backlog hours.

Step 2.   The departmental performance is running at 85 percent on a historical basis. Therefore, the 400 backlog hours must be divided by
85 percent to determine the actual labor hours required. Thus, 400
divided by 85 percent equals 470.5 hours. This is true value of the
backlog.

Step 3.   There are eight people in the department available 37.5 hours each,
for a total of 300 hours. By dividing the 470.5 by 300, we find that
the department has an actual backlog of 1.57 weeks of work.

The same format could be used to show individual departments with the total representing a larger entity. This format allows for the pyramiding of the reports.

The economic staffing level (ESL) is shown in number of people and regular hours.
This figure is the budgeted figure for the department. If the budget has been based on
a variable volume, that is, hours per ton, the figure may well be valuable. If the budget
has been developed on an average basis and is not readily subject to change, then this
will be a fixed figure. In the example shown earlier, the figure of 14 people at 37.5
hours per week is a fixed staffing figure.

The actual hours worked are shown in regular and overtime categories to alert management to any serious or continuing overtime situations. In this case, a 3-day absence
caused 22.5 lost hours. Because 7.5 hours of overtime were used, the total actual hours
of 510 resulted in a net loss from the staffing level of 15 hours. This would not be considered serious, since it is a loss of less than 3 percent compared to a plus or minus 5
percent goal.

The hours on schedule represent the actual hours spent on scheduled (measured)
work. *The scheduled hours produced are the result of the volume produced times the R/E.
Percentage performance is determined by dividing the scheduled hours produced by the
actual hours on schedule. The nonscheduled hours is the difference between the actual
hours on schedule and the total hours worked and is shown in hours and as a percentage.*

In the example used, the goal for performance is 90 percent so the department is
below par. The goal for nonscheduled hours is 5 percent, so we have a double-below-
par situation.

The backlog is shown in tons and hours. In the total column or in any area where the
backlog is made up of a variety of different units, the unit column is not used. The
3,500 units represent 1,400 hours of work at an R/E of 0.4 hours per unit.

The required hours needed to complete 1,400 hours of work, based on a *performance factor* of 83.8 percent is 1,671 hours. Because 1 given week's performance may
not be indicative of the general performance of the department, it is recommended that
a 5-week rolling average be used for this calculation.

Another factor has been introduced here—the percentage of nonscheduled hours.
Again, a 5-week rolling average is recommended, although in the example, the current
figure is used. To calculate the hours required, an additional 9 percent is added, which
makes the hours required 1,821.

12

INVENTORY CONTROLS

PROPER INVENTORY INVESTMENT

Five Variables

There are five variables to be considered when trying to simulate or calculate the proper inventory level:

1. Ability to forecast customer needs, as represented by the forecast error;
2. Desire to give prompt delivery service, as represented by the planned in-stock service level;
3. Accuracy of inventory perpetual records, compared to actual balance on hand, as represented by percent of parts that deviate;
4. Amount of "vertical" integration of the product line, as represented by the amount of manufactured versus purchased parts; and
5. Completeness of documents; as represented by accuracy of bills of material, route sheets, and so on.

Proper Inventory Level

The purpose of establishing an inventory investment standard is to set a level to prevent the build-up of extra inventory that, at some point, would become excessive and eventually obsolete material. There are three methods applicable for determining that proper level.

Day's Usage Method. The calculation worksheet shown on the following page should be completed by the materials manager and submitted to the vice president of manufacturing for approval. The recent historical and/or forecasted "dollar usage per day" should be obtained by taking the total inventory issues in dollars last, and dividing by the number of work days. Insert this number next to the appropriate "type inventory." By using the desired "days supply" column, an extension is made to determine the "standard in dollars." The "actual dollar inventory" should then be posted and the "deviation" from the "standard in dollars" determined.

Forecasted Sales Method.   Although the second procedure is more judgmental, you can establish target levels by ascertaining the amount of inventory desired by sales to meet anticipated customer orders. To use this method, take the historical sales last year, establish months' supply targets, and calculate dollar inventory by various categories.

Calculation Method.   The preceding two methods can easily be utilized. However, it often is desirable to perform a more complete target determination. This procedure is described below.

At any given point, for the items in stock, some will be at maximum amount (e.g., the reorder quantity of 6,000 items, plus safety stock of 600 for a total of 6,600), some at the reorder point (1,800), some at the safety stock level (600) and, of course, all sorts of other levels. The average quantity on hand for an item can be determined by dividing the reorder quantity by two and adding to it the safety stock quantity. If we reordered 6,000 sheets of paper, the average quantity on hand would be 3,600 (6,000 ÷ 2 + 600 safety stock). If we determine the average quantity on hand plus the safety stock quantity and multiply this amount times the unit cost for each item on hand, we then can determine the dollar inventory target standard for all items kept in the stockroom, merely by adding each item's average quantity on hand. This determination can be done by the various inventory groups—raw material, product line, storage location, and so forth.

Most organizations have to maintain additional inventories for the special needs of their customers. This material can be for sales promotions, unusual emergency requirements, prebuilding for seasonal goods, hedges for possible strikes, reserves for special customers, and so forth. Even the most perfect inventory control systems end up with surplus (slow-moving items), as well as obsolete material due to changing customer needs, or even design engineering needs.

One of these groups is the "desired" inventory, two more are "permissible," and the last two are "not desired." Group 2 is under the control of manufacturing or operations, while Group 3 is the responsibility of the sales or special users department. Thus, with permission from management, special inventories can be maintained over and above the normal inventory item balances in Group 1. (Refer to Exhibits 12.1 through 12.4.)

Five Inventory Groups for Determining Proper Investment Targets

Group 1: Normal, Planned Inventory (Desired).   To calculate the inventory for this group, you obtain the reorder quantity and safety stock for each of the departments allowed to maintain inventory. Each reorder quantity is divided by two to get the average on-hand amount.

The planned safety stock is added to this amount to get a unit total, which is multiplied by the unit cost to obtain the dollar value. Then, all dollar values are added by department to get departmental and grand totals for Group 1.

Group 2: Manufacturing Preference Items (Permissible).   Some departments in the company are permitted by management to maintain certain items where no

EXHIBIT 12.1 Calculation Worksheet

Type Inventory	Dollar Usage per Day	×	Days Supply	=	Standard in Dollars	Actual Dollar Inventory	Standard to Actual Deviation	
							Less	More
Raw materials								
Local suppliers	$ 1,760		30		$ 52,800	$ 41,673	$ 11,127	
Distant vendors	4,150		70		290,500	402,693		$ 112,103
Purchase components	2,180		60		130,800	196,532		65,732
Work-in-Process—Parts	1,870		30		56,100	187,961		131,861
Manufactured components	4,700		45		211,500	399,711		188,211
Work-in-Process—Assembly	9,600		60		576,000	781,003		205,003
Finished assemblies	16,100		30		483,000	716,943		233,943
Replacement parts	4,360		90		392,400	181,296	211,104	
Totals	$44,720		49		$2,193,100	$2,907,812	$222,231	$ 936,943
						Net		$ 714,712
						Absolute		$1,159,174

194

stock-out can be permitted. The projected dollar value of these items should be obtained and listed by each storing department.

Group 3: Sales Department Preferences (Permissible).   In any organization, some departments require what we call "preference" items. The actual dollar value of these permitted items on sales and management approval, such as special finished goods for a favorite customer, should be listed on the worksheet.

Group 4: Surplus Inventory (Not Desired).   There is no perfect inventory system; in any organization, surplus or excess material will develop through the normal chain of events. Surplus inventory is defined as good, usable inventory for which you have too much on hand. The maximum amount of inventory on hand for any item should be the reorder quantity plus the safety stock. Thus, surplus inventory is that amount on hand that exceeds the reorder quantity plus safety stock dollar value—so list the actual dollar value by department and total of all surplus material.

Group 5: Obsolete Inventory (Not Desired).   This last group includes items no longer required, due to changes in supplies used and/or equipment required. In this group—also by department—you should list the actual (book or original) value of all obsolete material by department and in total.

In summary, the inventory standard target is the total of Groups 1, 2, and 3. Groups 4 and 5, by being identified, can eventually be disposed of through exchanges, substitution, scrapping, and so forth. The total actual inventory of $3,107,019 (at first-in–first-out [FIFO]) represents a turnover of 2.2 times, since the annual inventory usage was $6,979,316 worth of material. However, if the investment was decreased to the target of $2,168,470, turnover increases to a more respectable 3.2 times.

Work-in-Process Inventory Target

This calculation (which is necessary for most companies) can be made by determining two statistics: (1) the value of the average daily usage (called day's supply), and (2) the average manufacturing actual cycle time in days. The work-in-process target is then calculated.

Work-in-Process Material Target Calculation

1. Divide annual value of raw material and purchased component issues by the number of work days in a year to get "average daily usage" of these materials. For example:

$$\frac{\$6,978,733}{240} = \$29,078$$

2. Determine the average production "cycle time" (sometimes called the "manufacturing lead time"). We'll use 9 days in this example.

EXHIBIT 12.2   The Five Inventory Groups

PLANNED

Desired

Group 1   • Normal inventory items

EXCEPTION

Permissible

Group 2   • Manufacturing preference: Long runs, vendor rework, emergency items, new products strike hedge

Group 3   • Sales preference: Stocking plans, favored company, promotion, credit holds

Not Desired

Group 4   • Surplus: Excess of current needs
Group 5   • Obsolete and phased out material

---

3. Multiply the average daily usage times the average cycle time to obtain the work-in-process inventory target:

$$\$29,078 \times 9 = \$261,702$$

How to Calculate Excess and Obsolete Inventory

The question often raised is how to establish the "classical" procedure to calculate obsolete inventory. You should not have the finance department responsible for the determination of the proper obsolete inventory reserve, for the following three reasons:

1. It removes the responsibility for obsolete inventory from operations, where it belongs.

2. It lessens the responsibility of marketing to provide a forecast or historical customer demand for each item expected to be ordered in the future.

3. It eliminates the independent check-and-balance review, which is a prime duty of the finance department.

The following details the proper method to select the items and make the obsolescence calculation. Since any obsolete calculation is very sensitive to (and dependent on) a correct forecast, this procedure begins in marketing. Projections for future customer demands (orders) come from a combination of:

• A forecast for assembly products;

• Historical activity for spares; and

• The existing open customer orders.

EXHIBIT 12.3 Inventory Target Worksheet

| | Normal Planned (Desired) Group 1 | Exception Inventories (Permissible) | | | Exception Inventories (Not Desired) | | |
	Average	2 Mfg. Preference	3 Customer Preference	Total Target	4 Surplus	5 Obsolete	Grand Total
Type Inventory	Average	Mfg. Preference	Customer Preference	Total Target	Surplus	Obsolete	Grand Total
Raw material							
Purchase components							
Work-in-process							
Finished goods							
Total							
Calculation	a $+$	b $+$	c $=$	d $+$	e $+$	f $=$	g

EXHIBIT 12.4 Inventory Targets

| | Normal Planned (Desired) Group 1 | Exception Inventories (Permissible) | | | Exception Inventories (Not Desired) | | |
	Average	2 Mfg. Preference	3 Customer Preference	Total Target	4 Surplus	5 Obsolete	Grand Total
Type Inventory	Average	Mfg. Preference	Customer Preference	Total Target	Surplus	Obsolete	Grand Total
Raw Material	$ 481,616	$ 41,600	$ 0	$ 523,216	$221,064	$ 47,683	$ 791,963
Purchase components	775,503	61,100	0	836,630	214,336	47,145	1,098,111
Work-in-process	462,037	0	0	462,037	110,325	19,642	592,004
Finished goods	126,087	50,000	170,500	346,587	78,611	199,742	624,940
Total	$1,845,270	$152,700	$170,500	$2,168,470	$624,336	$314,212	$3,107,018
Calculation	a $+$	b $+$	c $=$	d $+$	e $+$	f $=$	g

197

This information is given to manufacturing, which makes a gross requirement master schedule for the life of the inventory specified by finance. Manufacturing compares the schedule needs versus the inventory on hand, and makes a "Tentative Obsolete List." Since the obsolete item determination is dependent on the forecast, a double-check should now be performed to ascertain if any item/product was inadvertently missed. The finalized, recommended list should then be given to finance.

REDUCING INVENTORY TO THE CALCULATED LEVEL

The raw material, work-in-process, and finished-goods inventories in most companies are excessive, usually at least 20 percent too high. The challenge is to reduce carefully the inventory investment with the following steps.

Create an Inventory-Reduction Team

The initial set-up is to establish the inventory-reduction team that will review all areas and activities affecting the factory and warehouse inventory levels. The team is not assigned any operating responsibility for the inventory-control function, but is to serve as a strong assistance to the production and inventory-control departments. The team objectives are to:

- Review and analyze specific inventory-management problems;
- Suggest immediate and obvious steps to balance and reduce inventories;
- Assist in formulation of inventory-management programs;
- Develop necessary procedures to implement recommended changes;
- Provide systems and procedures needed to carry out inventory policies as established by the inventory policy committee;
- Recommend changes for improvements to the inventory policy committee; and
- Provide for accomplishment of corporate inventory objectives, while improving the level of service to customers.

Although the ideal time to reduce inventory is during good economic conditions (it is much easier to use up the excess and write-off the obsolete inventory), most companies undertake inventory-reduction programs during a poor business climate. The efforts should be on both a broadly gauged (macro) basis and a specific item (micro) approach. Timing is short, intermediate, and longer range. Usually, a substantial decrease can be achieved after 3 months of work, followed by a relatively slow period—in terms of reduction—for the next 3 months (the first plateau). Good reductions are then achieved during the seventh to twelfth month (a second plateau), and then steady but smaller decreases until the optimum level is reached at about 18 months after starting.

Short-Range Reductions

An example of the initial efforts that gain short-range reductions can be classified into three groups. The first are tasks that give tangible results, such as:

- Review order before final release;
- Reschedule orders-in-process;
- Cancel or reschedule slow-moving products;
- Cancel or reschedule open purchase orders; and
- Fill branch requisitions from plant inventory.

The second group includes work that cannot be readily measured. These include:

- Hold up purchased materials for delivery;
- Review steel and shop order coverage;
- Return rejected material rapidly;
- Audit inventory analyst's decision; and
- Return supply inventory from field warehouse to central warehouse.

In the third group, on-the-job training of employees should be increased, policies reviewed and emphasized, and supervision efforts magnified.

Intermediate-Range Reductions

Intermediate-range results can be achieved by using these 39 reduction techniques:

1. Buy at a smaller economic order quantity or at the EOQ—if you weren't before.
2. Reduce the protective, safety stock level.
3. Reschedule shop or purchase orders to later deliveries.
4. Telegram vendor to stop delivery for "X" days.
5. Substitute one type of raw material on hand for another.
6. Clean up the shop, scrapping or reworking old material.
7. Reject all overshipments on purchased items.
8. Police the overissues of material.
9. Buy more items on a short-range basis.
10. Reduce ordering costs.
11. Review high order points and high order quantities.
12. Use old stock first.
13. Use just-in-time (JIT) quick delivery flow principle, telling suppliers the day and time to deliver.

14. Deliver by truck or air freight, not by railroad car.

15. Review all A items daily, B items weekly, and C items monthly for excess coverage.

16. Review weekly all purchase orders valued above $300.

17. Cancel all unneeded shop and purchase orders.

18. Modify excess or obsolete parts into another part number.

19. Arbitrarily reduce lot sizes and requisitions by "X" percent.

20. Maintain list of items in all warehouses and move goods from one warehouse to supply another.

21. Accelerate the scrap-processing program.

22. Speed up the receiving inspection process.

23. Rework rejected material rapidly.

24. Send to customers a list of certain items you wish to sell at special prices in a "preinventory clearance" sale.

25. Obtain material from vendors on a delayed-invoice-payment basis.

26. Use the run-out ratio to prioritize various items in process.

27. Use the critical ratio to provide last-minute priority for production sequence.

28. Break critical machine capacity bottlenecks.

29. Review the posting accuracy on ledger cards.

30. Cancel excess "float" on orders.

31. Use line balancing, milestones, or Gantt charts for control of in-process items.

32. Study purchasing statistics for poor vendor deliveries or quality.

33. Speed up sales order entry and engineering document processing time control.

34. Cease supplying old service parts; send customer blueprints instead so they can produce the parts themselves.

35. Set up more blanket orders.

36. Conduct group brainstorming meetings for idea selection.

37. Decrease time span between filling of order and replacement of stock sold.

38. Utilize where-used lists.

39. Control the inventory investment carefully on single-customer-use items.

Exhibits 12.5 through 12.17 illustrate various ways to analyze your inventory carrying costs. Pick the analysis method that is right for you. After you have had a chance to evaluate the results review pages 179–191 and choose strategies that will reduce inventory for your operations. Keep in mind that the balance between inventory turns and holding the correct amount of inventory should be considered and performed accordingly.

EXHIBIT 12.5   Results of Three Inventory-Reduction Programs

Program	Inventory Type	Duration of Program— Months	Value of Inventory ($000)		Reduction		Turnover	
			Start	Finish	Dollars	Percent	From	To
1.	Raw material	12	$ 4,358	$ 3,050	$1,308	30.0	2.4	3.4
2.	Raw material WIP & FG	9	2,500	2,005	495	19.8	2.8	3.5
3.a	Raw material	24	2,022	1,518	504	24.9		
b	Work-in-process	24	3,200	2,210	990	30.9		
c	Finished goods for prod assembly	24	2,884	2,285	599	20.8	2.4	3.0
d	Finished goods for service	24	2,561	1,669	892	34.8		
e	Branch plant RM & WIP	24	6,931	5,942	989	14.3		
Subtotal			$17,598	$13,624	$3,974			
Grand Total			$24,456	$18,679	$5,777	23.6	2.5	3.3

201

EXHIBIT 12.6   Calculation of Cost Factor for Carrying Inventory in Your Company—A Worksheet

Warehouse Space $ _____
    The annual expense of warehouse space in your company. If all
    your space is owned, then it's the cost you'd expect to pay to
    lease equivalent space in your locale.

Taxes $ _____
    Actual taxes paid in the last fiscal year on your inventory. Taxes
    on buildings should be part of the warehouse space cost figure.

Insurance $ _____
    Insurance premiums paid in the last fiscal year on the inventory.
    Again, insurance for buildings is part of the warehouse space cost
    calculation.

Obsolescence/Shrinkage $ _____
    How much inventory value was written-off at the end of last year,
    either because your physical inventory count came out short, or
    because certain material was determined to be nonsalable?

Material Handling $ _____
    The total annual expense in labor and material handling
    equipment (lift trucks, etc.) needed to receive and put away all
    incoming merchandise, or to move it around during the year.
    Customer order-filling expense is not included.

Cost of Money $ _____
    Your current interest rate for borrowing money (whether you
    actually borrowed or not) applied to the average value of the
    inventory throughout the year.

    Total Costs $ _____

$$\frac{\text{Total costs}}{\text{Average inventory value}} \quad \frac{\$ \text{_____}}{\$ \text{_____}} = \text{_____}\%$$

Note: The answer represents your *cost* for carrying $1 of inventory for a year. Acceptable range of
answers: 25% to 35%.

EXHIBIT 12.7 Cost of Carrying Inventory—An Illustration

Warehouse space	$130,200
($10,850 per month × 12)	
Taxes	65,000
Insurance	40,000
Obsolescence/shrinkage	60,000
Material handling	64,800
Cost of money	240,000
(12% × $2,000,000 Inventory)	
Total Annual Costs	$600,000

$$\frac{\text{Total costs}}{\text{Average inventory value}} \quad \frac{\$600,000}{\$2,000,000} = 30\%$$

Note: This company spends .30¢ for every $1.00 of inventory carried for a year. Since, on the average, they have $2,000,000 in inventory throughout the year, the costs listed amount to $600,000. The 30% *rate* is used in other calculations in order to keep the total costs as low as is practical, consistent with the Costs of Ordering and with the service objectives. Rather than making this calculation, you may elect to use 20% plus prime rate.

EXHIBIT 12.8 Computing Your Company's Inventory Turn Rate—A Worksheet

Single Location:
  1. Cost of goods sold (from stock only) this month $ _____
  2. Cost of goods sold—Annualized (No. 1 × 12) = $ _____
  3. Current inventory in dollars $ _____

Calculation:

$$\frac{\text{Annualized cost of goods sold from stock}}{\text{Current inventory in dollars}} = \underline{\hspace{2cm}}$$

Central Warehouse That Supplies Other Branches:
  1. Cost of goods sold (from stock only) this month $ _____
  2. Cost of goods sold—Annualized (No. 1 × 12) = $ _____
  3. Transfers-out to other branches this month $ _____
  4. Transfers-out—Annualized (No. 3 × 12) = $ _____
  5. Current inventory in dollars $ _____

Calculation:

$$\frac{\text{Annualized cost of goods sold from stock and annualized transfers-out}}{\text{Current inventory in dollars}} = \underline{\hspace{2cm}}$$

Note: The answer represents how many times per year your inventory investment is "turned" or utilized through sales or, for a warehouse, supplying needs of other branches. It's a measurement of inventory use. Acceptable answers depend on the gross margin distributors develop. At 30% gross margin, 5 to 6 turns per year is considered good. At 20% margin, the turn would have to be 6 to 8 for good performance.

Here's an average performance for a distributor:

$2,000,000 in cost of goods sold from stock for a year.

$1,000,000 invested in inventory.

The turnover rate is 2.0 ($2,000,000 ÷ $1,000,000 = 2.0)

Let's see what happens to profit if cost of goods sold stays the same, but inventory control performance improves the turn rate:

$$\frac{\$2,000,000 \text{ CGS}}{\$666,666 \text{ INV}} = 3.0 \text{ turns}$$

Inventory savings = $ 333,333

At 30% carrying cost per year, that would save:

$100,000 in *Net profit*

$$\frac{\$2,000,000 \text{ CGS}}{\$500,000 \text{ INV}} = 4.0 \text{ turns}$$

Inventory savings = $ 500,000

At 30% carrying cost per year, that would save:

$150,000 in *Net profit*

$$\frac{\$2,000,000 \text{ CGS}}{\$400,000 \text{ INV}} = 5.0 \text{ turns}$$

Inventory savings = $ 600,000

At 30% carrying cost per year, that would save:

$180,000 in *Net profit*

How many additional sales dollars would have to be generated to produce $180,000 Net profit?

- If it were Gross profit, then a 30% margin would bring $180,000 from $600,000 additional sales, but,
- To get $180,000 *Net profit,* the additional sales needed would likely be nearly $2,000,000!

EXHIBIT 12.10   Service Level Measurement—An Illustration

Week: 11-6-87

Sales orders received	160	
Number of line items		482
Transfer requests	72	
Number of line items		216
(1) Total number of line items		698
(2) Number of lines filled complete		446

Calculation:

$$\frac{\text{Lines filled complete (2)}}{\text{Total No. of line items (1)}} = \frac{446}{698} = \frac{64\%}{\text{Service level}}$$

Note: This company is filling 64% of the "demand" against their *stock items*—represented in sales orders from customers and transfer needs to other branches . . . the very purpose for which the inventory was established.

Admittedly, this measurement is quite harsh. It gives no credit for a line filled partially, as, for example, filling 82 out of an order for a 100 quantity.

It is, however, a defendable measurement. No one could argue that the figures are "padded." And who's to say what negative impact a partial shipment has on a customer? Find out where you are under this measurement and then watch it improve as new controls are put in place.

EXHIBIT 12.11   Calculation of Usage Rate

Current Year

Regular item:

Mar.	Apr.	May	June	July	Aug.	Sept.	
29	17	37	15	20	20	↑	Usage Rate = 23

You're Here
Now

Last Year's Equivalent Months

Seasonal item:

Sept.	Oct.	Nov.	Dec.	Jan.	Feb.	Mar.	
↑	67	84	119	137	127	77	Usage Rate = 102

You're
Here
Now

Add to this base rate, the growth or decline percent of this line, product group, or business in general—last year to this year.

Usage Rate is expressed in number of units sold/transferred (moved) per month. This rate is then used in both the order point and order quantity calculations for proper control of the stock item.

Usage Histories That Need to Be Qualified: Some Examples

Potential Problems

Mar.	Apr.	May	June	July	Aug.
12	14	10	6	18	118

Nonrecurring sale in August for 100 pieces

Usage rate: 30/month

Revised rate: 13/month

Mar.	Apr.	May	June	July	Aug.
7	13	10	0	0	0

Out of stock since May

Usage rate: 5/month

Revised rate: 10/month

Mar.	Apr.	May	June	July	Aug.
50	0	0	50	0	0

One dominant customer!

Usage rate: 17/month

Revised rate: Not figured (Ordering controls set to fit customer's buying pattern)

Mar.	Apr.	May	June	July	Aug.
0	0	0	0	1	0

Low usage item! Sell very low number per year.

Usage rate: .17/month

Revised rate: Not figured (Order point set at zero;) (Order quantity set at one.)

206

EXHIBIT 12.12   Basic Order-Timing Control: The Order Point

Basic Formula:

$$\text{(Usage rate} \times \text{Avg. Lead Time)} + \text{Safety allowance (50\%)}$$
$$\text{Example: } 100 \times 1 + 50 = 150$$

Complicated Formula

$$\text{Usage rate} \times \text{Average lead time}$$
$$+ \left(\text{Usage Rate} \times \text{Lead Time} \times .7 \times \frac{\text{Maximum lead time} - \text{Average Lead Time}}{\text{Average lead time}} \right)$$

- - - - - - - - - - - - - Delivery Delay % - - - - - - - -

- Safety Allowance -

$$\text{Example:} \quad 100 \times 1 + \left(100 \times 1 \times .7 \times \frac{1\frac{1}{2} \text{ Months} - 1 \text{ Month)}}{1 \text{ Month}} \right)$$

$100 \times 1 + (100 \times 1 \times .7 \times .5)$
$100 + (100 \times .7 \times .5)$ Maximum lead time is the
$100 + (70 \times .5)$ worst delivery experienced
$100 + 35$ on this item during the
$135 = \text{Order Point}$ last year.

What the Order Point Does

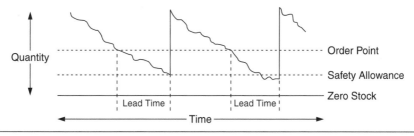

EXHIBIT 12.13   A Higher Order-Timing Control: The Line Point

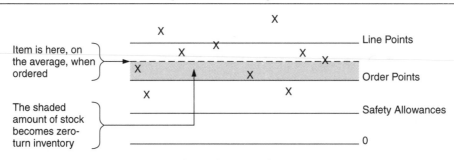

Line Point Formula

Line Point = Order Point + (Usage Rate × Review Cycle)

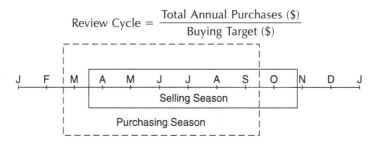

Review cycles for seasonal product lines vary when you are *in* or *out of* the purchasing season. As you enter the season, the review cycle shortens and all item line points change. As you leave the purchasing season, the review cycle lengthens and line points change once again.

Definition of a seasonal product line: 80% of the annual sales occur in 6 consecutive months.

EXHIBIT 12.14   Cost of a Replenishment Cycle ("R" Cost)

One-Half the

Total annual expense of setting-up and maintaining records
  of stock on hand. This includes the cost of all personnel,
  office space, telephones, supplies, computer time if you're
  automated, etc. $ _____

The portion of the Purchasing Department's annual expense
  expended on purchase orders for stock merchandise. Again,
  this includes the personnel costs, office space, long-distance
  calls, computer time, etc. $ _____

Annual expense of expediting stock merchandise $ _____

That portion of the Accounts Payable Department's annual
  expenses devoted to processing, clearing questions on,
  paying, and writing/calling vendors about invoices for stock
  merchandise. This should be about 50% of the total cost of
  the department (people, office space, supplies, telephones,
  computer time, etc.) $ _____

The *fixed* portion of the Receiving Department's annual
  costs devoted to filing, posting to, making receiving copies
  of purchase orders for stock merchandise. Receiving must
  perform some steps to every P.O., regardless of size, number
  of dollars involved. $ _____

                              Total costs in these categories $ _____

1. Number of purchase orders issued for stock merchandise
   in a full year   _____

2. Average number of line items on a purchase order for
   stock items   _____

   Total lines ordered in a year (No. 1 × No. 2)   _____

   Calculation: $\dfrac{\text{Total Ordering Costs}}{\text{Total Lines Ordered}}$: $ _____ = $ _____

Your answer represents the number of dollars you will spend   "R" COST
in your company each time you go through the ordering cycle
on one stock item.

EXHIBIT 12.15   Internal Cost and Turnover Control
Economic Order Quantity (EOQ)

Formula: $$EOQ = \sqrt{\frac{24 \times \text{Cost to replenish (R)} \times \text{Monthly usage rate}}{\text{Cost of carrying inventory (K)} \times \text{Unit cost}}}$$

Examples:

High Cost & Usage Item		Low Cost & Usage Item	
Usage rate	100	Usage rate	10
Unit cost	$10	Unit cost	.15¢
Carrying cost	35%	Carrying cost	35%
Cost to order	$ 5	Cost to order	$ 5

$$\sqrt{\frac{24 \times \$5 \times 100}{.35 \times \$10}} \quad = EOQ = \quad \sqrt{\frac{24 \times \$5 \times 10}{.35 \times .15¢}}$$

$$\sqrt{\frac{12000}{3.5}} \quad = EOQ = \quad \sqrt{\frac{1200}{.0525}}$$

$$\sqrt{3428.57} \quad = EOQ = \quad \sqrt{22857.14}$$

$$59 \quad = EOQ = \quad 151$$

Little over 2 weeks' supply   15 Months' supply

What the EOQ Does

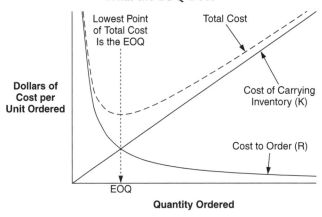

210

EXHIBIT 12.16   Buying in Accord with Inventory Class

Classification Steps

1. For all stock items, or a 10% random sampling, multiply the annual usage in units by unit cost to determine the annual dollar amount moving through the inventory for each item.

    100 Units sold in a year × 4.20 Cost = $420

2. Sequence all items according to the dollar-movement answers. The best items with most dollars moving through the inventory are at the top of the list. Zero's are all at the bottom.

3. Decide where the "Dead" item breakpoint is to be. Suggestion: Any item that sells less than $10 at cost for a whole year is considered "D" Class (Dead, Defunct, Dog, etc.)

4. Remove all D items from the classification exercise. They are now to be handled under the Disposition Program.

5. Assign each item remaining on the list (after the D's are removed from the bottom) an Inventory Class as follows:

Top	7½% of the items		Class 1
Next	7½%		Class 2
Next	10%		Class 3
Next	10%		Class 4
Next	8%		Class 5
	8%		Class 6
	8%		Class 7
	8%		Class 8
	8%		Class 9
	8%		Class 10
	8%		Class 11
Last	9%		Class 12
	100%		

The percentages are of the total number of items on the list. If, for example, you had 5,000 items remaining in the study after taking out the D's, Class 1 would have 7½% of 5,000 or 375 items. Class 2 would also have 375. Class 3 would have 500 items, etc.

6. If you have used a 10% random sampling of your stock items to work out the inventory classes, you must now determine the breakpoint for each class in terms of annual dollar-movement through the inventory.

    The breakpoint, for example, between Class 2 and 3 might turn out to be $1,827 moving through the inventory in a year.

7. When the breakpoint between each class is known, you may assign any and all other stock items to their proper class, simply by determining the annual sales X unit cost for each one.

    Annual sales (250) × unit cost ($.05) = $12.50

This item will likely be Class 12 if you removed all items selling less than $10 in a year. The breakpoint between Class 11 and 12 might be much further up the list of remaining items . . . perhaps somewhere around $30 per year.

EXHIBIT 12.17   Inventory-Control Survey

Action Focus	N/A	Strong	Satisfactory	Needs Some Improvement	Weak: Needs Major Improvement	Action Plan, Responsibility
Calculate degree of investment of inventory versus earning assets						
Use proper mix of raw materials, work-in-process, finished goods						
Improve accuracy of sales forecasts for proper service levels						
Tighten controls over movement, processing, storing of parts and materials						
Set lead time for systematic replenishment						
Calculate sufficient inventory for satisfactory customer service						
Coordinate inventory control with manufacturing process						
Pinpoint cost of capital relative to excess inventories						
Improve timing of raw material deliveries to plant						
Use Economic Order Quantity (EOQ)						
Use optimum # of annual purchase orders calculation						
Employ reorder point-order up to level system						
Compute carrying costs: capital						
Compute carrying costs: inventory service (taxes, insurance)						
Compute carrying costs: storage space (warehouses, etc.)						
Compute carrying costs: inventory risk (obsolescence, damage, pilferage, etc.)						
Computer carrying costs: inventory risk (security, relocation costs)						
Integrate with order entry, sales analysis, cost accounting						

Item			
Improve database management: adding, deleting, changing records			
Use exception reporting back-order reports, automatic order generation			
Explore personal computer with electronic spreadsheets for "what if" simulations			
Try computer simulations of "goal-seeking" for optimum stock levels			
Employ electronic coding for identification and/or physical inventories			
Use optical scanning for inventories, distribution, document preparation			
Conduct cycle inventories rather than all at once			
Store supplies, raw materials off site (occupancy, labor costs)			
Generate automatic or on-line requests for materials replenishment			
Profitably dispose of scrap/surplus to dealers			
Contribute scrap/surplus to charitable institutions			
Contribute scrap/surplus to educational institutions			
Periodically review inventory budget versus actual			
Take action on production workers' waiting time for raw materials			
Provide special care for delicate components			
Place fast-moving parts near production area			
Use inventory locator file to easily find desired item			
Emphasize increasing rate of inventory turns			
Correlate physical inventory to accounting records			
Report slow-moving items, obsolete products, and overstock			
Clear up written instructions for inventory taking and maintenance			

INVENTORY CONTROL GUIDELINES WORKSHEET

	Yes/No	Commentary

1. Is materials handling a specialized activity in the company or unit; that is, at least one person engaged full time in the activity?

2. If yes, are direction and quality of materials handling services the responsibility of one person?

3. Does production planning give warehouse personnel sufficient advance notice of items and stock activity?

4. Are warehouse personnel notified in advance of planned inventory changes?

5. Is there any indication that the company carries varieties of stocks that lend themselves to standardization?

6. If yes, is any kind of value engineering being practiced or planned?

7. Is there any evidence of an excessive accumulation of materials awaiting repair, rework, or return to vendors?

8. Do inventory records appear to serve a useful purpose beyond accounting; for example, are they used for purchasing materials or for rescheduling production?

9. Does someone have the obligation to keep current on new methods of materials handling?

10. If yes, is that person encouraged to look in other industries for equipment that could be slightly altered to meet the company's needs?

11. Do materials appear to be standing around piled up unnecessarily on the receiving platform?

12. Do production workers stand around waiting for materials to arrive?

13. Are materials moved more often than necessary?

14. Do skilled workers handle materials; that is, is expensive labor used for unskilled—and often unnecessary—manual jobs?

15. Are delicate parts frequently damaged in transit?

16. Are production areas cluttered with parts and materials to be used or moved to the next operation?

	Yes/No	Commentary
17. Are all materials unloaded mechanically or with machine assistance?	_____	_____
18. If no, do materials that are unloaded manually have to be handled in that manner?	_____	_____
19. Are prepackaged cartons for simplifying counts and materials handling being used?	_____	_____
20. Are identical items stored in one location to minimize time-consuming searches by stock handlers?	_____	_____
21. If the warehouse is on more than one floor, are fast-moving stock items concentrated on one floor near the shipping area to minimize travel, retrieval time, and elevator usage?	_____	_____
22. Are storage areas and shipping areas close together, so that the storage area can act as an effective feeder to the shipping docks without costly backhauling between storage area and resultant double-handling?	_____	_____
23. If no, can the storage and shipping areas be brought closer together?	_____	_____
24. If yes, does the change appear to be economically justified?	_____	_____
25. Are lifting areas well illuminated?	_____	_____
26. Are all bins clearly labeled to facilitate order-picking?	_____	_____
27. Are materials so placed as not to overflow from one location into adjoining aisles, which would require rehandling to free blocked items?	_____	_____
28. Is merchandise that can be stored uncartoned, rather than cartoned, so stored? (If no, materials handling and production costs may be much higher than necessary.)	_____	_____
29. Are materials available to workers without waste motion?	_____	_____
30. Are bags of incoming materials palletized to avoid handling individual bags?	_____	_____
31. Is there a central locator file?	_____	_____
32. Are large portable bins available to avoid repeated handling of small containers?	_____	_____

	Yes/No	Commentary

33. Are dump trucks in lieu of standard trucks used in unloading bulk commodities? _____ _____

34. Is crane capacity adequate to lift the heaviest jobs? _____ _____

35. Are all the main lifting areas covered by craneways? _____ _____

36. Can forklift trucks be used with benefit in the warehouse and plant? _____ _____

37. If forklift trucks are used, are a sufficient number and variety on hand? _____ _____

38. When material is received, is it properly typed and routed? _____ _____

39. Is material examined for conformance to specifications when received? _____ _____

40. Does storage space throughout appear adequate? _____ _____

41. If materials must be moved from one machine to another, are they moved mechanically? If not, are they best moved manually? _____ _____

42. Is scrap disposed of mechanically? _____ _____

43. Are aisles clear, smoothly paved, and well lighted so that traffic can flow smoothly? _____ _____

44. Are storage areas well lighted? _____ _____

45. Are storages areas marked off into sections? _____ _____

46. If yes, are sections numbered or lettered for identification? _____ _____

47. If yes, are records kept of what is stored in each area, so that parts and products can be located rapidly? _____ _____

48. Are products stored in the most easily handled forms and in units in which they will be shipped? _____ _____

49. Are aisles wide enough to permit free movement of handling equipment? _____ _____

50. Are storage areas located as close as possible to the production areas they serve? _____ _____

51. Is there an adequate supply of fire extinguishers? _____ _____

52. Is warehouse space being utilized for storing materials that are outside the intended scope of storage? For example, is scrap being stored at substantial costs? _____ _____

53. Are costly, long-carried items stored far from exits? _____ _____

Yes/No   Commentary

54. Is a burglary alarm system used for protection
through all doors and through all windows?   _____   _____

55. Is there a regular schedule for cleaning the plant?   _____   _____

56. Does the person approving rates have a rate
and routing guide covering incoming and
outgoing items?   _____   _____

57. If yes, is the guide kept up to date?   _____   _____

58. If yes, is it adequate; that is, does it cover the usual
raw material purchase and shipment of
finished goods?   _____   _____

59. Are quantities checked to the proper receiving
or shipping document?   _____   _____

60. Are the rates checked to the guide and
shipping order?   _____   _____

61. Are the extensions checked?   _____   _____

62. Are bills paid within the specified
time limit?   _____   _____

63. Are there controls such as to prevent duplicate
payment of freight bills?   _____   _____

64. Are controls over payment of freight charges
adequate but not excessive?   _____   _____

65. Have arrangements been made to utilize average
demurrage agreement credits?   _____   _____

66. What corrective action has been taken to reduce
demurrage expense?   _____   _____

67. Examine loss and damage claims and try to
ascertain if there is a pattern for such claims.
Can they be eliminated?   _____   _____

68. Are claims settled promptly?   _____   _____

69. Has the company used the services of an
independent freight audit agency as a supplement to
or instead of its own freight department?   _____   _____

70. Is inventory a significant company investment?   _____   _____

71. Can the quality of inventory management
significantly affect the firm's earnings?   _____   _____

72. Are all material purchases delivered to central
stores as opposed to direct delivery to
production units?   _____   _____

Yes/No   Commentary

73. If yes, are the stores' records maintained by employees functionally independent of the storekeepers? _____ _____

74. Is one person responsible for inventory management? _____ _____

75. Is the gross inventory turnover known? _____ _____

76. Are the turnover rates for the various inventory classes known? _____ _____

77. If yes, do they appear reasonable as measured against industry standards, previous levels, and so forth? _____ _____

78. Are perpetual inventory records maintained with respect to raw materials and supplies, work-in-process, and finished stock? _____ _____

79. Are inventory records maintained on bins or in stock areas? _____ _____

80. Are all inventory items ordered, stored, issued, and controlled on the same basis? _____ _____

81. Are security measures that effectively control pilferage of expensive items in force? _____ _____

82. Are material items properly identified by part number? _____ _____

83. Are vendors' counts double-checked by the receiving department? _____ _____

84. Does the company have adequate storage facilities? _____ _____

85. Does the company carry varieties of stocks that lend themselves to standardization? _____ _____

86. Is there any evidence of an excessive accumulation of material, that is, material awaiting repair, rework, or return to vendors? _____ _____

87. Do inventory records appear to serve a useful purpose beyond accounting; for example, are they used for purchasing materials or for scheduling production? _____ _____

88. Are perpetual inventory records checked by physical inventories at least once each year? _____ _____

89. Is there written approval by a responsible employee of adjustments made to perpetual records based on physical inventories? How much was the last adjustment? What was done about it? _____ _____

Yes/No   Commentary

90. Does the system include provision for periodic reporting to a responsible employee of slow-moving items, obsolete items, and over stock? _____ _____

91. Are the following classes of inventories under accounting control: (a) consignments out, (b) materials in hand, of suppliers, processors, and so forth, (c) merchandise shipped on memorandum, (d) consignments in? _____ _____

92. Is merchandise on hand that is not the property of the company (customers' merchandise, consignments in, and so forth) physically segregated, clearly marked, and under accounting control? _____ _____

93. At year-end inventories, are adequate written instructions prepared for guidance of participating employees? _____ _____

94. At year-end inventories, are the following steps checked on a sample basis: Quantity determinations, summarizations, additions, and summarizations of detailed sheets? _____ _____

95. Are records kept for manufactured parts in subassemblies? Do the records appear justified? _____ _____

96. Has the overall inventory been reconciled? _____ _____

For example:
Beginning inventory
   (at cost) xxx
  Purchases xxx
   Total available xxx
  Less sales (at cost) xxx
  Less scrap (at cost) xxx (xxx)
   Ending inventory xxx

97. Has the effect of local personal property taxes been considered in the storage of inventory? _____ _____

98. Does the company know the cost of maintaining inventory records (personnel, space, data processing)? _____ _____

99. If inventories vary substantially over the year, is a reporting form for insurance coverage used? _____ _____

Exhibit 12.18 illustrates a method to reduce your inventory monthly. The purpose of the technique is to help reduce inventory carrying costs and maintain higher inventory turnover.

EXHIBIT 12.18   Quick Calculation of Inventory Targets

Inventory Class	How Determined (Annual Part Issues)	Last Year's Issues	Turnover Desired	Inventory Target	Actual	Excess
A	$5,000 and above	$4,745,936	4X	$1,186,484	$1,398,156	$ 211,672
B	$1,200–$5,499	1,405,864	3X	468,621	776,753	308,132
C	Below $1,200	827,518	2X	413,759	932,158	518,399
	Totals	$6,979,318	3X	$2,068,864	$3,107,067	$1,038,203

Note: One of the worst mistakes an executive can do is to arbitrarily set a specific inventory turnover as a target—without first calculating the proper level, based on the company's service level objectives.

INVENTORY RECORD ACCURACY ANALYSIS WORKSHEET

One way to get an overall idea of the impact of inventory value and inaccuracy is to utilize the following bits of data collected during and at the completion of the annual physical inventory. In doing any inventory calculations, use the FIFO, not year-end last-in–first-out (LIFO), inventory value.

Data Worksheet

Data Code	Explanation	Typical Data	Your Company
	Inventory Value		
A	Inventory investment (before physical inventory)	$3,107,018	_____
B	Book to physical net adjustment (last time taken)	($ 37,284)	_____
	Record Accuracy[a]		
C	Perpetual book and actual storeroom balances quantities are *within 10 percent* of each other	67%	_____
D	Perpetual book balances exceed *actual stock by more* than 10 percent	21%	_____
E	Actual stock quantities exceed *perpetual book balance* by *more* than 10 percent	12%	_____
	Total of C, D, and E	100%	100%
	Turnover		
F	Actual overall annual inventory turnover	2.246	_____
G	Desired overall annual inventory turnover[b]	3.218	_____
	Carrying Costs		
H	Company's current bank loan interest rate	10.0%	_____
I	Material handling, storage, insurance costs, and so forth	10.7%	_____
J	Total Inventory Carrying Costs	20.7%	_____

Data Code	Explanation	Typical Data	Your Company
	Purchases		
K	Annual Purchases—Production Materials	$6,979,316	_____
L	Annual Purchases—Miscellaneous Items	$1,369,637	_____
M	Total Purchases	$8,348,953	
	Tax and Profits		
N	Present Company Federal Income Tax Rate	42%	_____
O	Company profits last year	$615,000	_____

[a] Random sample permissible to obtain percentages.
[b] Obtain from company executives.

Then use the data obtained in the first step to estimate the impact on increasing company profits through better inventory control. This is accomplished using this calculation worksheet.

How to Estimate the Impact on Profits through Improved Inventory Control

Step 1: Begin by posting the data obtained from the Data Collection Worksheet.

1. Inventory investment (before physical inventory adjustments)   ($3,107,018) (Data A)

2. Physical inventory adjustment (plus or minus)   ($37,284) (Data B)

3. Subtotal (add or subtract lines 1 and 2) $3,069,734

4. Target inventory level

$$\frac{2,246}{\text{(Data F)}} \div \frac{3.218}{\text{(Data G)}} = .6979 \times \frac{\$3,197,018}{\text{(Data A)}} = \$2,168,388$$

5. Subtotal (subtract line 4 from 3) to obtain "Excessive Inventory" $ 901,346

Step 2: Determine the cost of inaccurate inventory records and excessive inventory.

13

PRODUCTION PLANNING
AND CONTROL

Production planning and control is the very essence of an operation. The purchase and use of materials, the movement and control of parts in operations, the warehousing and shipment of products to customers—these activities constitute the basic determinants of success in manufacturing. An effective production-planning-and-control function enables an organization to meet customer delivery requirements, maintain low inventories, and minimize production costs. And the core activity of production planning and control is forecasting.

Forecasting determines how much material will be purchased, stored, and processed, how large inventories will be, how well customer delivery commitments will be met, and how many people will be employed in operations. Forecasting of orders is the first activity of the production-planning-and-control systems, and its success—or lack of it—has made or broken the careers of many managers.

The most established procedure used to forecast orders is the weekly or monthly meeting between sales and operations managers. It is usually at these meetings that forecasts are made, based on sales expectations.

The problem with this method is universal; sales managers—invariably optimistic and concerned about satisfying customer commitments for fast delivery—almost always project greater sales levels than those which actually occur. The reason is that an optimistic outlook on sales will keep the plant producing at high enough levels to satisfy an increase in customer demand.

Of course, when the anticipated increase turns into a small trickle, the person held responsible will not be the sales manager. Inevitably, the manager will be blamed for high inventories and overstaffed shifts. Regardless of fancy platitudes, issued from above, concerning the responsibility of sales for issuing realistic forecasts, it will *always* be the job of management to hold down inventory and manpower costs in relation to sales. Unfair as that might be, that is the way it really is! So it behooves every manager to learn how to forecast realistically. One such method, and one I have come to admire for its relative precision, is called *cycle forecasting*.

CYCLE FORECASTING

Cycle forecasting, a technique developed almost 25 years ago by the Institute for Trend Research, recognizes that there will almost always be peaks and troughs in business orders, and that those peaks and troughs can be roughly predicted. Regardless of product or technology, cycles occur, and they appear to occur within all economic and political institutions.

Cycle forecasting predicts when those orders will expand and when they will contract. It is based on the fact that, throughout economic history, cycles have been artificially induced by businesspeople and consumers, either through their optimism or pessimism regarding the prevailing economic climate. Cycles occur, in other words, when people defer purchases because of fear, and later make those same purchases because of their belief that business conditions are improving. Exhibit 13.1 depicts cycle forecasting calculations.

In Exhibit 13.1, the plant has been using cycle forecasting for many years to predict inventory and manpower requirements. Start by listing actual monthly order rates in dollars for several years. The next column, "Moving Annual Total," shows the current 12-month total. As these numbers are accumulated, the total for current month is added and the total for the same month during last year is dropped. The moving annual total for January 20X0, for example, was calculated this way:

Total for 1/X9:	$18.50 Million
Plus 1/X0 orders:	1.85 Million
Subtotal:	$20.35 Million
Less 1/X9 orders:	1.13 Million
Moving annual total—1/X0:	$19.22 Million

Finally, each current moving annual total is divided by the year-ago moving annual total, to derive the next column (Order Level) as shown here for January 20X1:

$$1/X1 \text{ Order level} = \frac{1/X1 \text{ Moving annual total}}{1/X0 \text{ Moving annual total}}$$

$$1/X1 \text{ Order level} = \frac{\$25.46 \text{ Million}}{\$19.22 \text{ Million}} \times 100 = 132.5\%$$

The order level tends to reduce the impact of seasonal variations and other factors affecting incoming orders such as order-processing delays. The resultant order level trend clearly illustrates basic changes in the ordering cycle alone. (See Exhibit 13.2.)

Compare actual orders for 20X1 with their corresponding order levels for the same months to see the differences. April and May, for example, show actual declines in the number of orders received, while their corresponding order levels are steadily increasing, signaling an upturn in the order cycle. This trend is verified by the higher number of actual orders received from September through December.

If the company had reduced its purchasing and manpower levels, based on decreasing incoming orders experienced in April and May, the plant would have been in poor

EXHIBIT 13.1 Cycle Forecasting Calculations

		Orders*	Moving Annual Total*	Order Level (%)
1990	J	1.13		
	F	1.42		
	M	1.66		
	A	1.46		
	M	1.50		
	J	1.68		
	J	1.58		
	A	1.39		
	S	1.66		
	O	1.57		
	N	1.64		
	D	1.81	18.50	
2000	J	1.85	19.22	
	F	2.03	19.83	
	M	2.49	20.66	
	A	2.06	21.26	
	M	2.03	21.79	
	J	2.11	22.22	
	J	1.94	22.58	
	A	1.91	23.10	
	S	1.95	23.39	
	O	2.44	24.26	
	N	2.12	24.74	
	D	2.50	25.43	
2001	J	1.88	25.46	132.5%
	F	2.59	26.02	131.2
	M	3.14	26.67	129.1
	A	2.91	27.52	129.4
	M	2.87	28.36	130.2
	J	2.95	29.20	131.4
	J	2.62	29.88	132.3
	A	2.60	30.57	132.3
	S	3.45	32.07	137.1
	O	2.90	32.53	134.1
	N	3.40	33.81	136.7
	D	3.38	34.69	136.4

Note: All numbers marked * expressed as millions of dollars.

EXHIBIT 13.2   Comparison of Open Orders and Order Levels

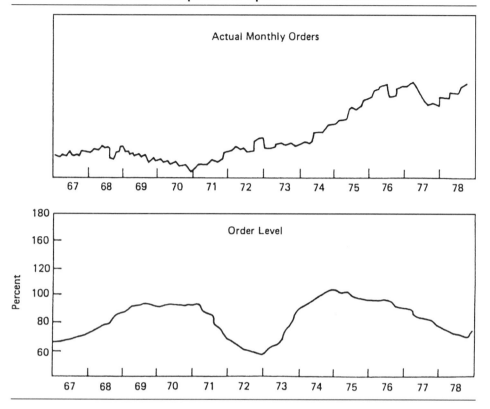

position to handle the larger influx of orders 6 months later. They could have failed to honor customer commitments, or they might have been forced to extend customer delivery dates while they built-up inventories and hired and trained additions to the workforce.

The Business Cycle

Cycle forecasting is predicated on the inevitability of peaks and valleys in the business cycle. As seen in Exhibit 13.3, there are six distinct phases, each recognizable, and each possessing its own unique characteristics:

1. *Expansion.* This phase occurs during a period of optimism. It is recognizable by gains in employment, business increases, and a rapidly improving gross national product (GNP). Productivity increases and purchasing agents contract for additional orders.

2. *Maturity.* The end of the expansion period is marked by narrower gains on the chart for a period of approximately 3 months, and most gains thereafter are balanced by some downturns. The curve "flattens out." During this period,

EXHIBIT 13.3   The Business Cycle

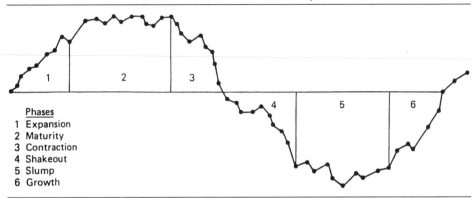

Phases
1 Expansion
2 Maturity
3 Contraction
4 Shakeout
5 Slump
6 Growth

employment and business activity remain high, demand triggers inflationary price increases, and plants are near full capacity.

3. *Contraction.* Three consecutive months of decline on the chart mark the start of a period of business contraction. Purchasing levels drop-off slightly, inventories increase, plants stop hiring people, overtime is drastically reduced, and businesses curtail capital improvement plans. Business, though, continues to be good, but not at the level of the preceding period.

4. *Shakeout.* When the order level drops below 100, and subsequent points on the chart continue to fall, the business cycle has reached its shakeout period. This phase is recognizable by plant layoffs, sales declines, inventory reductions, decreases in the prime rate, and a general sense of pessimism. Business plans are generally curtailed and unemployment levels begin climbing.

5. *Slump.* This is the roughest period of all; if business conditions are severe enough a depression ensues. Plant layoffs continue, employment rates begin to alarm the politicians, capital improvement plans are virtually nonexistent, and inventories continue to climb to discouraging levels.

6. *Growth.* Usually, three successive points of growth on the chart signal the faint beginnings of a period of economic growth and recovery. Plant layoffs stop and some companies begin to slowly rehire skilled employees. Purchasing agents see the first glimmer of hope through small increases in buying levels. Inventories begin to decline and business makes new capital improvement plans. The GNP begins to rise.

A normal business cycle lasts about 4 years, with 2½ years below 100. Obviously, the duration of a business cycle is influenced by a great many variables, such as whether the country is at war or peace, the strength of the dollar both home and abroad, the type of product being manufactured, and literally dozens of other factors. *The business cycle curve, therefore, must be individually interpreted by each company using its own product demand and in the context of its own situation.*

Use of the Business Cycle

The manager can use the business cycle curve to plan ahead. Listed below are typical actions that can be taken by the manager during each of the six phases of the business cycle:

1. *Expansion*

> Build or expand manufacturing facilities
>
> Install new machine tools
>
> Expand the labor force
>
> Build inventory
>
> Subcontract work
>
> Write-off obsolete inventory losses
>
> Develop new vendors
>
> Start training programs

2. *Maturity*

> Sell surplus machinery
>
> Maintain—but not increase—inventories
>
> Freeze all expansion plans
>
> Freeze salaried hiring
>
> Develop plans for business downturn
>
> Plan to reduce subcontract work
>
> Get machinery in top condition
>
> Work overtime

3. *Contraction*

> Begin layoffs
>
> Start reducing inventories
>
> Stop training programs
>
> Reduce purchasing levels
>
> Establish tight budgets
>
> Avoid long-term purchasing contracts
>
> Reduce fixed costs wherever possible
>
> Begin cost-reduction program
>
> Stop all overtime

4. *Shakeout*

> Continue layoffs
>
> Continue reducing inventories
>
> Reduce purchasing levels further

Freeze capital improvement programs

Get tougher on customer returns

Reduce indirect-labor activities

Reduce management deadwood

Combine functions

5. *Slump*

Stop layoffs. Hold on to skilled people

Consider eliminating a shift

Set tighter budgets

Make new expansion plans

Begin purchasing capital equipment

Keep cost-reduction programs moving

Locate better vendors

6. *Growth*

Begin rehiring skilled employees

Build inventories

Move ahead with expansion plans

Place added purchasing orders

Prepare training programs

Hire new salaried employees

Introduce new products

CONTROLLING OUTPUT THROUGH WORK MEASUREMENT

One of the most important decisions a manager will ever make concerns the selection of the work measurement system he will adopt to control output. Common to all is the proper use of a work measurement system to control and improve manufacturing output. Without such a system, output, at best, would be sporadic and, generally, inconsistent. A work measurement system, tailored to the individual organization, is what puts it all together.

Types of Work Measurement Systems

The predicament of the manager is this: Which work measurement system should be selected? The options are these:

1. No work measurement system;
2. Measured daywork;
3. Short-interval scheduling;

4. Incentive systems; and

5. Profit-sharing plans.

1. *No Work Measurement System.* The first option, "No work measurement system," is not as ridiculous as it may appear to be at first sight. Many businesses have operated successfully without application of any work measurement at all, and some will continue to do so in the future.

In a business owned by the workers themselves (there are quite a few of these companies operating successfully), work measurement is generally not required, because all employees are motivated to produce high quantities of output. Obviously, their success is geared to high-production quantities and low costs, provided that sales demand remains high.

Companies that have low labor content in their products normally have production machinery available that set the work pace. Automated equipment, for example, where labor is used to load hoppers only, establishes how high production will be. The influence of operators on output for such machinery is minimal. Under this circumstance, work measurement will not pay for itself. Only 10 to 20 percent of manufacturing companies can sustain relatively high output without the use of some form of work measurement.

2. *Measured Daywork.* Under measured daywork, work standards are established for production operations, but no financial inducements are offered to operators to meet or exceed those standards. The attainment of work standards is left to the varying abilities—and interests—of individual foremen. With measured daywork, skillful supervisors can convince operators to meet established standards; other foremen either cannot or will not. If a foreman knows how to use the standards to increase the work measurement system, then chances are measured daywork will control and improve production output. That is not usually the case.

Measured daywork, however, is normally preferable to no work measurement system at all. It has demonstrated its ability, over the years, to increase output in the range of 20 to 60 percent; but it should be pointed out that many of its successes were attributable, in part, to methods improvements, which accompanied the installation of the measured daywork system.

3. *Short-Interval Scheduling.* Short-Interval Scheduling (SIS) is just as it sounds, scheduling short intervals (i.e., a day or less). SIS combines the best features of a measured daywork system with a proven control technique that sharpens the ability of foremen and managers to increase output. SIS is measured daywork at its best. It is highly recommended that any major application of measured daywork be implemented through the framework of SIS to achieve maximum savings.

4. *Incentive Systems.* For most production operations, incentive systems appear to offer the best chance for increasing labor performance when compared with other work-measurement programs. The chief advantage of the incentive system is that it offers financial rewards for operators who achieve output above established work standards.

5. *Profit-Sharing Plans.* These plans enable all hourly people in manufacturing, both direct labor and indirect labor alike, to share the rewards of increased productivity. They are based on plant-wide productivity improvements. If a plant, for example, had labor content equal to 30 percent of its cost of sales, and known productivity improvements resulted in a reduction of that labor content to 25 percent of its cost of sales, then both management and labor would participate in the profit gain.

The prime advantage of profit-sharing plans is that it includes all hourly employees in the plant, while management does not have to spend money needed to support an incentive system or measure daywork plan.

The basic detraction from this type of plan is that it does not usually produce output improvements anywhere in the range of incentive systems and, in fact, may not even have the savings potential of an effective measured daywork system.

In summary, listed below are the conditions favoring each type of work measurement system:

No Work Measurement System

1. Worker-owned business;
2. Mostly automated machinery;
3. Low labor content;
4. Strong desire for labor peace (assuming company is profitable); and
5. Management convinced (often wrongly) that administrative costs of work measurement exceed benefits.

Short-Interval Scheduling

1. High labor content;
2. Company losing money;
3. Large indirect labor force; and
4. Measured daywork system in place ineffective (or none being used).

Measured Daywork

1. High labor content;
2. Mostly machine-produced product;
3. Strong, well-trained foremen;
4. Strong interest of upper management;
5. Large indirect-labor force; and
6. No work measurement system in place currently.

Incentive Systems

1. High labor content;
2. Well-trained industrial engineers;
3. Many manual operations;
4. Strong desire of management for extra production; and
5. Expressed desire of union and employees for incentive earnings.

Profit-Sharing Plans

1. Large indirect-labor force;

2. Company unwilling to commit resources to support other work measurement systems, but needs to increase output; and

3. Management–employee–union spirit of cooperation very high.

CONTROL OF QUALITY

Quality today is the last frontier for profit improvement and cost reduction, and nowhere is this more so than in manufacturing. Improvements in manufacturing have focused on manpower reductions, tooling and methods improvements, incentive systems, materials requirement planning (MRP) programs, and a host of other approaches and programs designed to reduce costs and improve manufacturing profitability. But relatively little has been accomplished in the area of quality to achieve the same goals. While some progress has been made, the full potential of quality as a contributing factor to manufacturing success has not been realized. Effective quality techniques and controls can contribute both to improved profitability and repeat sales (through enhanced customer satisfaction).

To be successful, the quality program needs to encompass the following elements:

- A cost-of-quality reporting system that indicates the success (or failure) of the quality program;

- A thorough and ongoing and detailed evaluation of the quality system;

- A quality plan, which lists all improvements needed to upgrade quality, including objectives, responsible parties, and timetables;

- A company (or divisional) quality board to establish quality policy, and which concerns itself with major quality problems and opportunities;

- A successful vendor quality program;

- An effective production quality program; and

- A responsive quality audit of outgoing products to customer (responsive in the sense that it is timely and evokes immediate corrective action of problems found).

Let's examine each of the above elements in some detail.

Cost of Quality

Cost of quality means exactly what it says—a detailing of all quality costs. (See Exhibit 13.4.) Unfortunately, in many organizations, many of the elements of the true cost picture are omitted. Some companies claim only scrap and rework costs, while others include cost of inspectors, and so on. To be properly inclusive, an effective cost-of-quality report should include the following elements:

1. *Warranty costs* are those costs that reflect failure of the product to perform its intended function (or those which displease the customer aesthetically). Included are those costs attributable to customer complaint investigations and of returned goods inspection, sorting, and testing.

2. *Scrap costs* are incurred when parts and materials are deemed to become totally worthless (disregarding scrap value) because of quality problems. Scrap costs should always include materials, labor, and overhead apportioned to the product.

3. *Rework costs* also include material, labor, and overhead that results when defective product is sorted, inspected, tested, and reworked to recover the parts or materials for usable inventory. This does *not* include costs billable to vendors for their quality errors.

4. *Appraisal costs* are those associated with inspecting the product to assume compliance with company specifications for purchased parts and materials, and finished product. Also included are costs to inspect the process and costs to determine vendor quality capability. Since both of these latter costs directly influence the quality of products, they are considered part of appraisal costs.

5. *Administration costs* are essentially quality-control budgetary costs less inspection labor. Typical administrative costs are salaries for quality-control managers, foremen,

---

EXHIBIT 13.4   Cost of Quality—Division Level Performance

A. COQ Summary

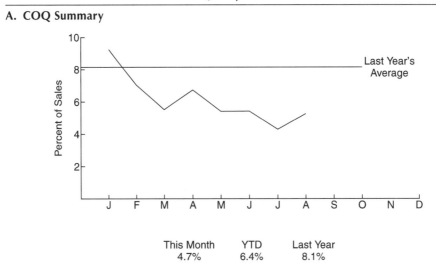

	This Month	YTD	Last Year
	4.7%	6.4%	8.1%

B. Major COQ Categories

COQ Category	Dollars		Percent	
	This Month	**YTD**	**This Month**	**YTD**
Warranty	$ 3,200	$ 45,600	.4	.4
Scrap	8,800	88,500	1.1	1.8
Rework	7,200	57,300	.9	1.3
Appraisal (Inspection)	14,400	160,950	1.8	2.1
Administration	3,120	26,910	.4	.6
Engineering support	805	14,025	.1	.2
Total COQ	$37,525	$393,285	4.7	6.4

technicians, and engineers, and support costs such as testing costs, gauging costs, calibration costs, and other miscellaneous costs reflected in the quality-control budget.

6. *Engineering costs* are those costs incurred in both marketing and engineering to improve product quality. Typical engineering costs are:

Design reviews: These are costs incurred in the review of new products or major design changes of existing products to improve quality and eliminate quality problems prior to the release of product drawings.

Product qualification: This refers to costs incurred in the testing, pilot plant, and qualification of new products or for major changes in existing product lines.

Design changes: These costs occur when design changes are necessary to correct original design inadequacies.

Section "A," "COQ Summary" of Exhibit 13.4 shows Cost of Quality (COQ) as a percent of sales. Since COQ numbers, by themselves, are absolute numbers, they are meaningless until related to some base figure such as sales. This is because a company with $100,000 quality costs and a sales base of $1 million has a COQ of 10 percent, while another company with $50,000 quality costs and a sales base of $250,000 has a 20 percent COQ.

The divisional COQ summary publishes statistics for the current month, year-to-date (YTD), and last year's average. The chart also illustrates monthly COQ readings and the COQ trend.

The next section, "COQ Categories," lists costs for all COQ categories and indicates what their percent of sales are for the current month and YTD. This refinement of COQ dollars shows where the "COQ dollars are." It helps managers to focus on meaningful categories for quality cost reduction.

The last section of the report, "Highlights," indicates the major actions, improvements, and problems of the month. It is a good tool for quality-control people to get their message across and get management's attention.

Quality is much more than designing, manufacturing, and servicing a product that meets company specifications. Ask any manufacturing manager. Quality, today, is the final frontier of reducing costs in manufacturing. Every other aspect of cost reduction has been approached: design, production, purchasing, inventory, manufacturing engineering, and production planning and control. What is left is quality. Quality has the potential to strip millions of dollars of costs given the right perspective, a good and effective operating plan, and aggressive execution. Although it is hard accurately to assess cost of quality for most companies that do not have an effective quality program, it is *not* unusual to see figures at 10 percent of the sales range. If a company sells $20 million, for instance, quality costs in an uncontrolled situation could *easily* be as high as $2 million. Quality costs, for many different reasons, remain undiscovered and unchallenged in the overwhelming number of manufacturing companies operating today.

Effective quality practices, then, have the potential of slashing manufacturing cost significantly. To be considered in this category, the manufacturing quality program must contain the following four elements:

1. A painstakingly thorough analysis of the capability (see Exhibit 13.5) of the manufacturing quality program, and a candid assessment of its effectiveness;

2. A quality plan that describes all of the fundamental techniques which must be adopted to improve the effectiveness of manufacturing quality;

3. Reporting systems capable of characterizing, on a timely basis, all of the strengths and weaknesses of the quality effort; and

4. A responsive and timely quality audit of product being delivered from manufacturing into customer's hands—a tool that manufacturing management can use to launch a well-targeted quality-improvement program.

Analyzing the Quality System

The first step to be undertaken is an assessment of the capability of the quality function in manufacturing. This involves the answers to many detailed questions, along with evaluation of the effectiveness of the function. The evaluation takes the form of a rating technique, which allows manufacturing management to assess strengths and spot weaknesses. The rating technique is shown below:

Effectiveness Quartile	Points	Rating Explanation
85–100%	10	Highly effective
50–84%	6	Acceptable results
25–49%	3	Marginal results
Under 25%	0	Poor results

Notice that the ratings are based on *results;* this tends to rate the activity realistically rather than on any apparent degree of sophistication.

The final results of the quality capability study shown in Exhibit 13.5 culminate in a numerical rating, which assesses the strength of the quality system. A review of the system's maximum points is given below (of course, the minimum point would be zero):

Function Evaluated	No. of Questions × 10 =	Maximum Points
Organization and Administration	4	40
Receiving Inspection	7	70
Operator Workmanship	8	80
Manufacturing Quality	15	150
Packing and Shipping	6	60
Gauge Control and Calibration	9	90
Warehousing and Delivery	8	80
Quality Reporting	8	80
Purchasing	6	60
Quality Planning	8	80
New Product Quality	5	50
Process Audit	6	60
Product Audit	10	100
Total	100	1,000

EXHIBIT 13.5   Quality Capability Survey

Organization and Administration

1. Is the quality organization organized properly to accomplish its objectives?
2. Is there a quality plan, and is it working?
3. Is there a quality manual that explains all techniques, practices, and procedures used by QC?
4. Are QC employees trained well, and do they know their jobs?

Receiving Inspection

5. Are product drawings used up-to-date?
6. Are all tests performed written in a procedures manual?
7. Are records maintained by vendor showing quality history for each?
8. Is there rapid feedback of rejected material to vendors via the purchasing department?
9. Is there evidence of vendors correcting quality problems?
10. Is rejected material segregated from accepted stock, and is it locked-up?
11. Are sample plans meaningful and easy-to-use by inspectors?

Operator Workmanship

12. Are production operators well trained in product quality techniques?
13. Do they sample-inspect their own production?
14. Do they have adequate gauges for measuring their own work?
15. Are there written inspection procedures and quality standards for operator use?
16. Are inspection results told to operators?
17. Is their performance adequately adjusted to improve quality at individual workstations?
18. Are operators who produce faulty work given additional guidance and counseling to improve their performances?
19. Does each operation have adequate process instructions and product drawings?

Manufacturing Quality

20. Are tests and inspections in the form of written instructions to inspectors?
21. Is first piece inspection practiced on operations where the setup of the machine determines the quality of the parts, such as metal stampings?
22. Is roving inspection used to gather quality data (as it should be) instead of control of operations?
23. Do all production batches funnel through a finished-batch-inspection station (tollgate)?
24. Are the inspections made sensitive and timely enough to detect shifts in the production process?
25. Is corrective action of substandard operations timely and effective?
26. Is defective material subjected to material board review prior to disposition?
27. Are production operators made aware of defective parts they have produced?
28. Are routine investigations made of recurrent defective parts and operations by QC?
29. Is defective material reworked by the same operator who produced the defective material?
30. Are inspection buy-off stamps used for accepted product?
31. Does the combination of operator and inspection sampling provide needed quality protection?
32. In assembly operations, is analysis made of defective parts, to determine which department (and operation) is the cause?
33. Are quality standards the same between fabrication, machining, and assembly operations?
34. Do inspections and tests simulate end-use of the assembled, finished product?

Packing and Shipping

35. Are written packing and shipping specifications available and used?
36. Are packing and shipping containers and methods adequate to prevent corrosion and damage?

(continued)

EXHIBIT 13.5 *(Continued)*

37. Are picked parts checked against master parts shipping list to assure correct parts and quantity shipment?
38. Are shipping cartons well identified to prevent mix-ups in deliveries?
39. Are all appropriate documents included with the shipment?
40. Is release to ship authorized by QC?

Gauge Control and Calibration
41. Are gauge masters traceable to the National Bureau of Standards?
42. Is there a written system for gauge control and calibration?
43. Are production gauges, as well as QC gauges, calibrated?
44. Are the frequencies of calibration adequate?
45. Are gauge calibration records maintained?
46. Are all gauges marked with the last date of calibration?
47. Are all new gauges calibrated before their use in production?
48. Are calibration tests conducted under the proper environment of temperature and humidity?
49. Are employee-owned and subcontractor gauges calibrated?

Warehousing and Delivery
50. Are handling methods for stock in place so that damages are minimized?
51. Are all parts bins and storage locations adequately marked to identify stored parts?
52. Are handling, storage, picking, and delivery operations specified in writing?
53. Are export packaging requirements identified?
54. Are receiving and shipping operations adequately separated to prevent mixes?
55. Is defective stock quarantined?
56. Is accepted stock under lock to prevent contamination, pilferage, and loss of control?
57. Is release to stock authorized by QC?

Quality Reporting
58. Is cost-of-quality information published on a timely basis, and does it identify all major costs?
59. Are performance reports (batch acceptance and sample percent defective) reported at all key operations?
60. Are quality records retained for sufficient lengths of time to satisfy all regulatory and company requirements?
61. Are quality reports used effectively for quality improvement?
62. Are records maintained in a protected area?
63. Are the results of inspections and tests recorded in a manner suitable for defect analysis?
64. Are scrap and rework data summarized and then used to reduce defect levels?
65. Are suitable summary reports prepared for top management, so they can monitor and control quality improvement?

Purchasing
66. Does purchasing have the latest drawing revisions to give to vendors?
67. Are vendors aware of the company's quality standards for purchased parts and materials?
68. Are quality standards included in purchasing contracts?
69. Do vendors submit their test results with shipments?
70. Are vendors promptly made aware of rejections?
71. Do vendors move quickly to correct their mistakes?

Quality Planning
72. Are written tests and inspection methods prepared for all new products and processes?

EXHIBIT 13.5 *(Continued)*

73. Does quality engineering plan the inspection stations in the manufacturing process, including location, sample technique and sizes, gauging, methodology, and reporting practices?
74. Does quality engineering review all new tooling in the plant to assure its ability to consistently produce acceptable products?
75. Is quality taken into account in work standards so operators can (a) sample their own output, and (b) recognize that incentive payments will not be made for defective product?
76. Does the paperwork process allow for traceability of defective work to individual operators and workstations?
77. Does quality engineering train inspectors, operators, and foremen in effective work habits aimed at producing a top-quality product?
78. Has quality engineering determined the best testing equipment and gauging to be used in product inspection?
79. Has quality engineering assured the availability of test and product specifications, visual standards, models, and samples?

New Product Quality
80. Are critical quality characteristics specified on engineering drawings?
81. Have quality standards and inspection requirements been planned for the new product, along with tooling and gauging?
82. Have potential quality problem areas been identified and corrected?
83. Are design reviews made sufficiently ahead of production to allow QC to adequately prepare for manufacturing quality requirements?
84. Are prototypes run in production so manufacturing and quality capability can be improved?

Process Audit
85. Are process audits made that evaluate the capability of the manufacturing process to provide a consistently high-quality product that meets company expectations?
86. Is this process audit conducted by people outside of the manufacturing organization to assure its impartiality?
87. Are the audits made at random so no preparation can be made by production people?
88. Are reports made to the functions that are in the best position to correct problems?
89. Is the corrective action timely and effective?
90. Are steady improvements being made?

Product Audit
91. Are audits made of completed and approved products ready for shipment?
92. Are the auditors apart from the regular QC organization to assure their impartiality?
93. Do field service and marketing people participate in the audit so the "view" is tilted toward customer acceptance?
94. Are prepared checklists made which list those quality characteristics wanted on machines by customers?
95. Are those characteristics weighted to show the differences among critical, major, and minor defects?
96. Is a final numerical rating achieved so that comparisons among audits and trends can be observed?
97. Do manufacturing people from diverse functions participate in the audit so they can learn the importance of quality?
98. When defects are discovered, are they quickly corrected in the manufacturing process?
99. Are these product audits summarized for management review?
100. Do all QC people rotate turns in conducting product audits so they can keep in touch with customer expectations?

Finally, total points are correlated to the following ratings:

Rating	Points
Highly effective	840–1,000
Acceptable	491–839
Marginal	251–490
Poor	0–250

The Quality Plan.   To be really successful, a company just completing its quality system evaluation must identify its weaknesses and establish a plan to overcome them. Problems are identified, actions are specified, persons responsible for the actions are identified, and dates for completion of the actions are indicated. (See Exhibit 13.6.)

The quality plan should *always* have the blessing and support of top management if anything is to get done. This point is particularly relevant when it is recognized that manufacturing people alone cannot make all the needed improvements; engineering and marketing people are also involved.

The Quality Board.   Any ongoing quality program needs direction. It is simply not enough to turn full responsibility for quality improvement over to the quality-control manager; too many other people are involved. The quality-control manager cannot design, manufacture, or sell and service the product. These jobs rightfully belong to engineering, manufacturing, and marketing. These are the people who have the primary influence on quality and, consequently, they affect quality results the most. They must become involved.

EXHIBIT 13.6   Quality Plan

Problem	Action to Be Taken	Persons Responsible	Date for Completion
No identification of quality costs	Develop a COQ report	QC Manager	3/81
Inspectors are confused about relative seriousness of quality characteristics	Identify critical quality characteristics on engineering drawings	QC Supervisor and Engineering Manager	1/82
Excessive defective parts are escaping the machine shop	Improve sampling plans used by inspectors	Quality Engineer	6/81
There is no early warning of quality problems found by customers	Start a finished-goods audit	QC Auditor	2/81

Each company or division of a company needs a quality board to direct the quality efforts of its people. The quality board should become involved with quality in the following areas:

Quality policy;

Quality improvement; and

Major quality problems.

The quality board, then, assumes the mantle of responsibility for the quality success of the company. Their job is to monitor major actions and results to assure the right things are done by the right people at the right time. It assures direct involvement in quality of every operating and support arm of the company.

The quality is very important to the manufacturing manager. There is a tendency in any manufacturing company to lay the total blame for poor quality on the doorstep of manufacturing. In almost every case that is not true. Sloppy design practices, misunderstandings between marketing people and customers regarding product needs, poor service—these and a host of other factors are directly attributable to engineering and marketing. The quality board provides an opportunity to objectively analyze quality problems and assign responsibility for corrective action to the right parties.

The quality board should generally have this composition:

General manager—Chairman

Quality control manager—Secretary

Operations manager

Engineering manager

Marketing manager

It is essential that the general manager assume responsibility for quality results by chairing the quality board. His leadership will also preclude the dominance of vested interests above actions best for the company.

Vendor Quality. Experience shows this measurement is the simplest and best to use for evaluation of vendor quality. Other complex ratings have been developed by quality practitioners but tend to become so hard to understand that they lose their meaning. The use of acceptance rates, shown below, tells it all about vendor performance.

$$\text{Percent lot acceptance} = \frac{\text{No. of lots accepted}}{\text{No. of lots inspected}} \times 100$$

The control of vendor quality also demands some other activities:

1. Use of vendor history files to list lot acceptance rates by part numbers on dates received, rejections made, visits to and by vendors and listing of problems

discussed, actions taken by vendors to correct quality problems, and a summary of their effectiveness.

2. Insistence by *purchasing* people that vendors correct quality problems, that timetables be established for corrective action, and that vendors will be eliminated as a source of supply if quality does not improve.

3. Evaluation of new suppliers' quality capability and their full understanding of the company's quality requirements.

4. Fast correction of rejected quality parts by vendors, through rework of shipment of replacement parts.

Production Quality Program. There are just a few basic ways that parts and materials can be inspected in processing. These are discussed below.

First-Piece Inspection. When the quality of the production run is dependent on the machine set-up, a first-piece inspection needs to be made. Almost any operation utilizing tools, dies, jigs, and fixtures needs a first-piece inspection. This type of inspection is usually best performed by a combination of set-up people *and* machine operators, the operators rechecking and verifying the adequacy of the set-up made by set-up people. Inspectors (quality-control people) are best left out of this sequence, unless the first-piece inspection demands specialized testing equipment. Once production people come to depend on inspectors to check set-ups, they will not pay as close attention to the job. If they are held responsible for set-ups, they will do a better job and higher quality will result.

Roving Inspections. Here, inspectors move from machine to machine during the production run, checking. When production is generating either very-high-quality or very-low-quality parts, this type of inspection is very effective. If quality is high there is no sense in using other more costly methods of inspection. Roving inspection is generally the least expensive method of inspection; a few inspectors can cover a lot of territory. If quality levels are very poor, roving inspection will quickly detect failures, and inspectors will then be able to quarantine defective lots. The high rejection rate assures that defects will be found.

Tollgate Inspection. For most operations, quality is neither very high nor very low; it falls somewhere in the middle. In this case inspectors, using the roving inspection method, are less likely to detect poor-quality parts. When this is the case, tollgate inspection is called for.

In tollgate inspection, all completed lots of parts are funneled through a stationary inspection point at the end of each department. The product flow shown below illustrates tollgate inspection:

Grinding department $\rightarrow$ Grind pins
                          Tollgate
Milling department $\rightarrow$ Mill slots in pins
                          Tollgate
Polishing department $\rightarrow$ Polish pins
                          Tollgate
                          Deliver to assembly dept.

Tollgate inspection is obviously most applicable to operations grouped together. For example, if all grinding machines are in one department, a tollgate inspection can follow grinding. If many different types of operations are combined in one production department, tollgate inspection will probably be placed after key operations. To have it follow, each and every operation would be too costly. For example:

Small parts department   →   Automatic chucker—Thread fitting

Chamfer machine—Chamfer fitting

Tapping machine—Tap

Tollgate

Deliver to assembly department

Automatic Inspection—In this type of inspection, equipment inspects parts. This method of inspection is the fastest and most reliable, but also the costliest. It is generally applied to high cost, tight-tolerance parts, where assembly operations are highly dependent on good parts.

Operator Inspection—It is *always* best to have operators check their own parts, whenever possible, using an established sampling plan. This is probably one of the best inspection methods. It assures the interest of operators in quality, and reduces the number of inspectors needed in operations. Operator inspection is generally used in partnership with either roving or tollgate inspection.

Finished Goods Audit. The finished goods audit is a final inspection of the product the way the customer sees it when he gets to use it. It is always conducted on product ready for shipment, and it is a reflection of (1) the quality level of products reaching customers, (2) the effectiveness of operations in building a high-quality product, and (3) the effectiveness of the quality organization in releasing only high-quality products for customers. The finished-goods audit is composed of quality characteristics important to customers and, hopefully, those same quality characteristics which are inspected in processing. The finished-goods audit allows operations management the opportunity to preview quality problems customers will find, and gives operating personnel the opportunity to correct those problems before the finished-goods warehouse is flooded with defective products.

Developing a Quality Plan. Once the capability of the quality system has been evaluated, the weaknesses of the function must be addressed to improve quality results. The plan prioritizes needed action, establishes key events, sets timetables, and shows specific individuals responsible for corrective action. (See Exhibit 13.7.) A quality plan can be made for almost any period of time, but, in the opinion of a great many users it should cover a period of 2 to 3 years, normally an optimum period. Anything shorter will probably not be inclusive enough to cover the many key events that need to happen. Anything longer is speculative. Too many things can change in 4 or 5 years; the planning of events that far down the road is vague, at best.

The Best Early-Warning System.   Early-warning systems are designed to do just that—provide an indication of your product's outgoing quality level, as well as

EXHIBIT 13.7   Machining Subcontractor Quality Plan

Problem	Key Event	Date Completion	Responsibility
High in-plant failures of vendor material	Establish effective receiving inspection system	3/91	J. Barnes, Quality Engineer
High rejection rates in coils and bars	Implement a statistical Bar X & R program	5/91	M. Jones, Quality Engineer
Many false readings of inspection gauges resulting in rejection of acceptable coils	Train inspectors to read and handle testing gauges	6/91	P. Shore, Assistant Quality Manager
Management complaining about poor quality reports	Start improved quality reporting system	7/91	S. Pauley, Quality Control Manager

highlight current quality problems. In most cases it is months, and sometimes even years, before products reach customers' hands. If companies rely mostly on warranties and complaints to assess customer satisfaction, the pipeline between the plant and the customer might be clogged with products that have a multitude of defects, undiscovered by the factory, and inordinately costly in terms of repair costs and irritated customers.

Many firms conduct product audits to assess product quality levels, but few conduct them properly. They are seeking the best early-warning system to suit their particular needs but, for one reason or another, they fail to do the right things.

A well-designed product audit is the best method yet devised to provide early warning of outgoing quality levels and problems. To be successful, however, it should contain the following five elements:

1. Products must be selected randomly after they have been accepted by the line quality assurance organization and are ready for shipment to distributors or customers. The product audit is, after all, an indication of the effectiveness of the quality assurance organization as well as the operating effort.

2. The product auditor must be independent of the line quality assurance organization that accepts the product. Ideally, the product auditor should work directly for the general manager, but, in practice, that arrangement would be too cumbersome. Not enough direction would be provided by the general manager. He is too busy. There is nothing wrong with having the product auditor report directly to the top quality person in the organization. It is important, however, for him to be independent of the line quality assurance organization responsible for product buy-off and free from any pressure from it or from operating people.

3. The quality characteristics being rated during the product audit must be the same characteristics that are important to the customer. *This is an extremely critical point that is most often missed by the majority of early-warning systems.*

Most quality systems are geared to product specifications; acceptance is based on whether or not the product meets specifications. But the customer is totally indifferent to his supplier's internal specifications. What he wants is a product that functions properly, is aesthetically pleasing, and is safe to use. While product specifications are generally defined in terms of customer needs, that is not always the case. As products mature, they become subject to all sorts of compromises and modifications. Engineering changes, for example, are made to reduce costs. These changes may substitute materials that may not be acceptable to some customers; or part functions may be modified to accommodate manufacturing operations, and those changes might affect product function in customers' hands. All kinds of changes occur. Eventually, some product specifications become monsters on their own. They become self-perpetuating, with no consideration of their intended purpose—that is, to consistently produce customer satisfaction.

Quality characteristics for product audits, therefore, should be established *jointly* by quality assurance *and* marketing. Salesmen and servicemen, in particular, will be most sensitive to customer wishes and customer needs. Many times the listing of quality characteristics important to customers will come as a surprise to quality assurance people, simply because they have been trained to think in terms of specifications and, as we have come to see, specifications drift over a period of time. The exercise of establishing meaningful quality characteristics will generate positive changes in product specifications.

4. The quality characteristics should be rated as to their importance. There are four classifications of defects ranging from "very serious" to "incidental." Each class is assigned a weight in points, with the most points assigned to the most serious classification of defects. During the product audit each characteristic is evaluated and actual points are assigned. Should the product auditor decide to assign partial points to a 50-point characteristic, he can do so, provided that, in his judgment, some, but not all, of the quality characteristics have been attained. At the conclusion of the audit, standard points and actual points are totaled and divided to establish the rating.

5. Defects found during the product audit must be aggressively traced and eliminated. This is the most important segment of the audit. While it is relatively easy to reinspect the finished product for defects found in the audit, it is much more difficult—but more necessary and more rewarding—to eliminate the cause of defects. The constant recurrence of the same defects signals higher rework or scrap costs, more defective products finding its way to customers, and, most importantly, a discouraged and dispirited management team that becomes increasingly frustrated watching the same defects recur.

A product audit constructed with the elements just described will be a powerful tool for management to use to upgrade quality levels and assess the effectiveness or the organization. A smart management team will take full advantage of this early-warning system.

Points

100 Class A—Very Serious

1. Will surely cause an operating failure of the unit in service that cannot readily be corrected in the field.
2. Will surely cause intermittent operating trouble, difficult to locate in the field.
3. Will render unit totally unfit for service.
4. Is liable to cause personal injury or property damage under normal conditions of use.

50 Class B—Serious

1. Will probably cause an operating failure of the unit in service that cannot readily be corrected in the field.
2. Will surely cause an operating failure of the unit in service that can readily be corrected in the field.
3. Will surely cause trouble of a nature less serious than an operating failure, such as substandard performance.
4. Will surely involve increased maintenance or decreased life.
5. Will cause a major increase in installation effort by the customer or serviceman.
6. Has defects of appearance or finish that are extreme.

10 Class C—Minor

1. May cause an operating failure of the unit in service.
2. Is likely to cause trouble of a nature less serious than an operating failure, such as major degrees of substandard performance.
3. Is likely to involve increased maintenance or decreased life.
4. Will cause a minor increase in installation effort by the customer or serviceman.
5. Has major defects of appearance, finish, or workmanship.

1 Class D—Incidental

1. Will not affect operation, maintenance, or life of the unit in service (including minor deviations from engineering requirements).
2. Has minor defects of appearance, finish, or workmanship.

A quality control analysis is shown in Exhibit 13.8. If the analysis indicates several weaknesses, management should develop action plans based on priorities.

EXHIBIT 13.8 Quality Control

Action Focus	N/A	Strong	Satisfactory	Needs Some Improvement	Weak: Needs Major Improvement	Action Plan, Responsibility
Call customers to find out how your products are working						
Designate a quality-control manager and hold accountable						
Measure cost of quality by component						
Emphasize prevention rather than appraisal						
Calculate rework expenses over time to determine trend						
Employ Quality Circles productively						
Try a "bragging session" to highlight success stories						
Reward superior suppliers of quality materials						
Train resources in quality improvement						
Use statistical sampling for inspection						
Establish upper control limits and exception reports for rejects						

EXHIBIT 13.9   Maintenance Labor Report—Week Ending 3/24

Craft	Number of Men	Total Hours Worked	Planned Hours		Unscheduled Hours	Earned Hours	Percent Labor Performance	Percent of Time on Standards
			Routine	PM				
Machinists	10	430	205	40	185	220	89.8	60.0
General maintenance	6	210	180		30	190	105.6	85.7
Electricians	6	240	100	40	100	130	92.9	58.3
Pipefitters	4	130	60		70	50	83.3	46.2
Truck mechanics	2	80			80			
Total Department	28	1,090	545	80	465	580	92.8	57.3

246

CONTROL OF MAINTENANCE

The control of maintenance operations is essential to good plant performance. Reports designed to disclose all important aspects of maintenance are needed by operations managers in order to stay on top of maintenance costs and performance. These reports are:

- Labor performance (see Exhibit 13.9);
- Schedules missed (see Exhibit 13.10);
- Craftsman performance (see Exhibit 13.11); and
- Machine maintenance costs (see Exhibits 13.12 and 13.13).

Labor Performance

Labor performance in maintenance operations is one of the most difficult of all operating jobs to achieve. The work is highly nonrepetitive, there is a good deal of judgment involved for most maintenance tasks, there is still a good deal of art involved in the application of crafts rather than science alone, and—last but not least—most maintenance workers consider themselves a cut above most plant workers and resent the intrusion of management-control systems in their work, similar to control systems the ordinary plant operator is exposed to.

EXHIBIT 13.10   Schedules Missed Report for Maintenance Work Orders—Week Ending 3/24

Work Order Number	Work Description	Planned Hours	Earned Hours	Percent Labor Performance
80-12	Repair 6″ drill press	50	40	80.0
80-28	Install monorail system	121	86	71.1
80-34	Rebush boring mill	168	122	72.6

EXHIBIT 13.11   Craftsman Performance Report—Week Ending 3/24

Craftsman Name	Current Week Performance				YTD Performance	
	Planned Hours	Earned Hours	Percent Labor Performance	Percent of Time Standards	Percent Labor Performance	Percent of Time Standards
Jones	32	30	93.8	80.0	91.7	51.5
Rawlins	18	16	88.9	45.0	90.5	46.7
Fanton	22	17	77.3	55.0	86.9	48.3

EXHIBIT 13.12   Maintenance Work Classification

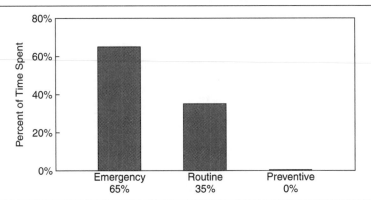

EXHIBIT 13.13   YTD Machine Maintenance Costs—Week Ending 3/24

Machine	Maintenance Labor Costs	Material Costs	Total Costs	Replacement Costs
Grinder #2R	$280.50	$ 6.75	$ 287.25	$12,500.00
Miller #3F	660.35	225.30	885.65	16,750.00
Tapper #4G	106.50	85.90	192.40	17,200.00
Reamer #7T	675.90	910.32	1,586.22	10,900.00

For all of these reasons alone, control is important. In fact, a maintenance organization exposed to the discipline of effective control techniques costs significantly less to operate when compared with an uncontrolled department. That is a matter of record.

The first two columns of the weekly report shown in Exhibit 13.9 indicate the type of craft and the number of people in each craft, while the third column lists the hours each craft and the entire department worked during the week.

The next two columns show just how many of these hours worked were spent on planned activities for both routine and preventive maintenance (PM). Planned activities, in hours, are those activities planned ahead of time by maintenance supervisors, to which work standards have been applied.

The next column, "Unscheduled," reflects those hours spent on emergency and unplanned maintenance work. Adding this column to the two previous columns under "Planned Hours" results in the hours listed in the "Total Hours Worked" column.

"Earned Hours," the next column, shows hours earned on work standards. The next column, "Percent Labor Performance," is derived by dividing earned hours by planned hours, as follows:

$$\text{Percent labor performance} = \frac{\text{Earned hours}}{\text{Routine} + \text{PM hours}} \times 100$$

The final column shows how much time was actually spent on hours being measured by work standards. Since hours on work standards is equivalent to planned hours, time on standards is derived like this:

$$\text{Percent of time on standards} = \frac{\text{Routine} + \text{PM hours}}{\text{Total hours worked}} \times 100$$

Notice that only 57.3 percent of all maintenance time was spent on planned work with work standards. This is not unusual. The object, of course, is to approach 100 percent, but it will never quite be reached, because the nature of maintenance work is that emergencies will always occur, and that emergency work is unplanned and essentially hard to measure for work standards.

Returning to labor performance, it can be stated that 92.8 percent for the entire department is a respectable performance, and that an examination of labor performance for individual crafts does not reveal any exceptionally poor performances, although the 83.3 percent performance of the pipefitters, and 89.8 percent performance for machinists can certainly be improved.

Schedules Missed

Analysis of the maintenance labor report is likely to indicate areas of performance, which management will want to examine closely.

This report automatically prints out those work orders whose earned labor performance falls below a stated percentage. Management selected 90 percent as the lowest percentage it considers acceptable performance. Any work order performance level slipping below that point is programmed to be displayed automatically on a computer report.

The schedules missed report describes work order performance as contrasted with the maintenance labor report, which describes labor performance by craft. Between the two, maintenance management is given sufficient information to detect weak spots, make corrections, and control overall performance. Both reports, then, attack collective labor performance from different angles.

The schedules missed report starts with a listing of the delinquent work order numbers and a description of the tasks contained in the work orders. It then goes on to list planned hours, earned hours, and percent labor performance, as shown in the maintenance labor report.

Craftsman Performance

While the maintenance labor performance report and the schedules missed report focus on overall work order and departmental labor performance, the craftsman performance report details individual craftsman performance.

The left-hand column lists each craftsman's name, and the following columns calculate his labor performance and percent of time on standards for both the current week and YTD. This report shows maintenance supervisors which craftsmen need additional training and direction. The YTD columns allow supervisors to track individual performance over the course of the year. Craftsman Ferguson, for example, had a labor performance of 77.3 percent for the current week and is only at 86.9 percent for the current year—a poor performance.

Machine Maintenance Costs

Machine maintenance costs report is seen in Exhibit 13.13. This report shows how much it costs to maintain individual pieces of production (or support) machinery. The columns of the report show, from left to right, machine, labor costs, materials costs, total costs, and replacement costs. By comparing total costs with replacement costs, manufacturing and maintenance managers can determine when the purchase of new machinery is more economical than repairing existing machinery.

This report also helps managers spot developing problems in machinery. It helps managers recognize the principle that, when maintenance costs increase, so does machine downtime, and that maintenance costs can be reduced significantly when machinery failures are minimized. Smart maintenance managers recognize that a thorough preventive-maintenance operation on production machinery, coupled with the replacement of parts that exhibit high failure rates, are the prime ingredients in the reduction of machinery maintenance costs.

How One Company Saved 30 Percent by Installing a Maintenance Work Classification System

A service center in New England classifies all maintenance work in one of the following categories:

- *Emergency.* Work needed to immediately restore production such as machine breakdown, loss of air supply, or electrical failure. This category of maintenance receives preference over the other described below.

- *Routine.* Work needed to improve the functional characteristics of a working piece of equipment. A slitter, for example, currently producing at 60 percent efficiency can be scheduled for upgrading to increase its efficiency rating to 80 percent. This type of maintenance work can be scheduled to repair at the convenience of both production and maintenance people.

- *Preventive.* Service of machines and equipment before they need repairs. Preventive maintenance aims to increase equipment uptime through scheduled, periodic servicing including adjustments, lubrications, and overhauling.

The company at one time had an uncontrolled maintenance function. Early analysis of the amount of time spent on each of the three categories of maintenance revealed, graphically, what is shown in Exhibit 13.12.

The company soon installed a maintenance work order system coupled with effective time estimating of work to be done by craft, Gantt chart scheduling of longer-term maintenance work, and training for crafts members in these techniques. The results,

EXHIBIT 13.14   Maintenance Results—Two Years Later

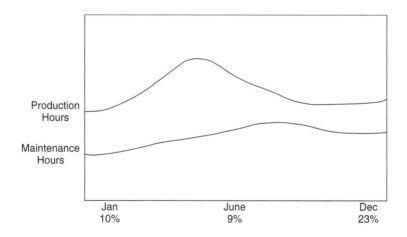

within a period of 2 years, are displayed in Exhibit 13.14. Their estimated savings in dollars by craft exceeded 30 percent for total maintenance dollars. Dollars expended were reduced by $275,000 per year.

Measuring Maintenance Effectiveness with Three Control Charts

It is not enough simply to install effective disciplines within the maintenance activity. Controls must be established to monitor progress. A company in the Midwest uses the following controls to maintain the large savings in labor it achieved.

1. *Maintenance hours as a percent of production hours.*

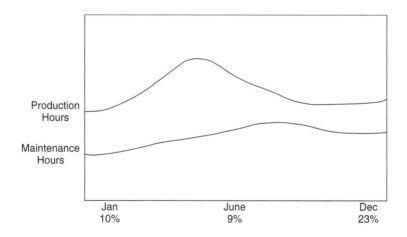

In this case, maintenance hours showed an unfavorable trend. Not enough dollars were shaved from the maintenance budget to keep in pace with the downturn in production hours beginning mid-year.

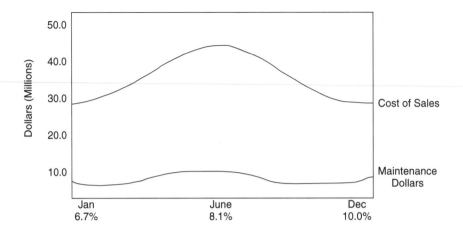

2. *Total maintenance dollars as a percent of cost of sales.*
   Here, too, the trend is up, although the total percentage average (about 8 percent) is considerably below the prior year's performance of 12 percent. Again, industry or regional averages are not really significant. What counts is *improvement*. So long as a company's maintenance department's control indicators are constantly improving, criticisms cannot be leveled.

3. *Maintenance supply costs as a percent of total maintenance dollars.*

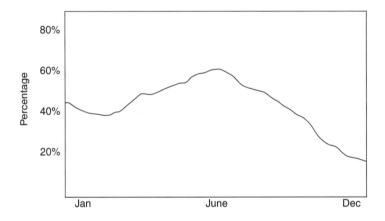

Here, a steady and noticeable trend is evident. Maintenance management exercised good control over the expenditure of maintenance supply costs.

Exhibit 13.15 on pages 254–255 is a maintenance checklist.

COST-SAVING MEASURES FOR CONSERVING ENERGY

This section presents some important fundamentals, pointing out places to look for conservation opportunities, showing how to set up an energy-conservation program, and examining alternate sources of energy, all the while keeping an eye on the bottom line. While delving into the particulars of these topics, you are advised to keep some basic truths in mind.

- *Conservation* is the most powerful tool. Almost every manufacturing plant abounds with opportunities to reduce energy consumption without switching fuels, and without making major changes in equipment or process.

- Oil and gas are fuels of *convenience,* and when the price of the convenience exceeds its value there should be no hesitation to replace them.

- Energy problems have not changed the *rules* of economics, only the numbers. Equipment additions that will cut the use of energy must still be economically justified and proposed operating changes must be shown to enhance, not reduce, profitability.

Plant buildings may house offices, laboratories, warehouses, and production operations. Heating will usually be required in the winter months and, for some of the building space, air conditioning in the summer. Look for energy-conservation opportunities in the following key areas.

How to Stop Unwanted Air Movement

Reduce the infiltration of outside air (or flows between parts of a building) by following the four steps:

1. Applying caulking and weatherstripping to holes in the building walls and to poorly sealed windows and doors. Look for holes around window and door frames and where pipes and conduit pass through walls.

2. Installing strip curtains in doorways and wall openings, such as those for a conveyor, which must be left open for traffic but, at the same time, allow unwanted air currents to move. The strip curtains will part to allow personnel and objects to pass, but close up again as soon as they are through.

3. Sealing off doorways in plant areas that must handle frequent traffic by installing impact doors consisting of two flexible sections, each covering half of the opening. The sections part when contacted by a moving object, such as a lift truck, automatically resealing after it passes.

4. Installing dock seals and shelters at the warehouse loading docks. They consist of blocks of flexible foam insulation covered with a resistant fabric, and placed on the outside wall of the dock in an inverted U at the dock opening.

EXHIBIT 13.15 Maintenance Checklist

Action Focus	N/A	Strong	Satisfactory	Needs Some Improvement	Weak: Needs Major Improvement	Action Plan, Responsibility
Categorize productive versus nonproductive hours						
Check maintenance assignments and degree of supervision						
Improve workload identification, measurement, management						
Use planning, scheduling, and control techniques (e.g., PERT/CPM)						
Increase accuracy/timeliness of maintenance information						
Increase Engineering's role in plant planning, installation						
Investigate pros and cons of contract maintenance						
Perform major maintenance at regular intervals						
Teach production workers simple preventive maintenance						
Establish standard times and costs for routine repairs						
Take appropriate action on major cost variances						
Emphasize preventive maintenance philosophy at all levels						
List machines that shut down key parts of production						
Use colored tags to mark equipment needing repair or service						
Recharge batteries on vehicles such as materials handlers, etc.						
Combine and/or consolidate vehicle delivery routes						
Place computer equipment away from open windows (sunlight, dirt, temperature, humidity changes)						
Keep computers away from electrical machinery to prevent interference						
Cover printers, consoles, floppy disks, personal computers, etc.						
Enforce no smoking rules in computer centers						

254

Install anti-static mats; spray carpeting							
Periodically clean read/write heads with special diskettes							
Put printing elements (including daisy wheels) into cases							
Clean print wheels, chains, and platens periodically							
Use nonabrasive solutions and lint-free cloths on terminal screens and keyboards							
Maintain floppy disks in envelopes and avoid writing on them							
Keep staples, paper clips off disks to keep from demagnetizing							
Identify equipment with high price tags							
Report on machine conditions at shift end							
Condense maintenance list and post at selected machines							
Ensure that vehicles are serviced at or better than prescribed intervals							
Use mobile repair kits (bicycles, etc.)							
Employ activity analysis and auditing							
Standardize and document maintenance instructions							
Provide pocket pagers or walkie-talkie devices to summon personnel quickly							
Fit machinery with attachments to record running time cumulatively							
Have operators record problems on special forms at the machinery							
Consider reconditioning used equipment							
Sell obsolete machines to scrap dealers							
Remind operators of machine cost, use a sign showing replacement value							
Have Engineering approve or originate design specs for buildings and equipment							
Request a formal work order to improve planning and chargebacks							
Examine "backlog report" for critical items to be expedited							
Perform periodic safety checks							

255

The truck is backed up to the dock so that the edges of its sidewalls and roof contact the blocks, sealing off air flow from the outside while the truck is being unloaded.

Techniques for Blocking Solar Radiation

When buildings must be kept as cool as possible by natural means, or when they require expensive energy for air conditioning, use these five techniques to reduce the heat load imposed by incident sunlight:

1. Change the color of exterior surfaces exposed to sunlight. Light colors reflect more of the sun's radiation, with aluminum and white-colored surfaces reflecting most of all. One building owner in the Southwest found that the use of white roof gravel would reduce absorbed heat from sunlight by 42 percent.

2. Be sure that windows are provided with shades or blinds, that their reflecting surfaces are kept clean, and that they are used.

3. Provide exterior shading of walls and windows with awnings, canopies, overhangs, and plantings.

4. Install reflective or tinted glass in windows to reflect incident sunlight or to block those wavelengths that produce the greatest heating effect.

5. For larger buildings, adjust the responses of heating and cooling systems to the variation in loads in different parts of the building. As the sun moves through the sky in a normal workday, various parts of the building receive different amounts of solar heat. People working in the north end of the building may complain, winter and summer, that they are "always cold"; those on the south side may have just the opposite complaint. Concentrations of people and the activities they perform may vary in different parts of the building at different times of the day. The solutions can be as simple as putting separate zone controls in those parts of the heating and cooling systems, serving various parts of the building and as sophisticated as installing entirely new control systems operated by computers, which constantly monitor changing conditions and direct the most economical response to them.

Tips for Using Solar Radiation

In those areas, and at those times of the year when heating loads are the most important energy consumers, the sun's energy can be used in these ways to help carry the loads:

1. Reverse as many as practicable of the techniques mentioned above to block solar radiation—use darker exterior colors, remove exterior and interior shading of windows and doorways.

2. Install skylights, so that sunlight can help with the lighting load. A refinement is to add light-sensitive dimmer switches to the artificial lighting controls, so that

they contribute more light when the sunlight is weak and less when it is strong, maintaining a constant level of light in the illuminated areas.

3. More elaborate passive-solar-heating systems can be installed. Their fundamental components are (a) an unoccupied area of the building, (b) a large roof or wall section fitted with glass or other transparent material through which the sun's rays can pass to heat the air in the unoccupied section creating a "greenhouse effect," and (c) a means of circulating the air thus warmed to the occupied sections of the building. Control systems can be as simple or as complex as desired.

How to Reduce Conduction/Convection Losses

The object here is to cut down the losses or gains of heat through walls, roofs, and floors—the "building envelope"—primarily through the use of insulation.

1. *Roofs.* The upsurge in fuel costs which occurred in the early 1970s have caused building designers to take a more careful look at the amount of roof insulation provided. One owner of an industrial building complex built on the U.S. Gulf Coast found that, by increasing the standard one inch of roof insulation to three inches, he could cut heat gain or loss by 20 percent, and thus achieve the best balance between additional construction cost and fuel savings.

2. *Walls and floors.* Uninsulated concrete floors laid on ground can be expected to have a heat loss of about 2 BTU per hour per square foot, assuming room temperature at 70°F and the ground at a constant 50°F. Uninsulated brick and concrete walls exposed to outside temperatures down to 0°F can be expected to lose 15 BTU per hour per square foot; insulation thicknesses of $1\frac{1}{2}$ inches, once considered adequate for industrial buildings, have been increased in some cases to two or three times that amount, depending on the cost of fuel, and the severity of the climate.

3. *Windows.* Ordinary window glass comes in thicknesses of $\frac{1}{16}$ or $\frac{1}{8}$ inch. Even if the thermal conductivities of glass and building brick are roughly the same, a $\frac{1}{8}$-inch thickness of glass will conduct 96 times as much heat as the same area of a 12-inch brick wall. That is why many newer industrial buildings (especially if they are conditioned) are designed without any windows at all. "Double glazed" or *thermal pane* windows, which consist of two (sometimes three) sheets of glass separated by dead air space, can be used (when the building must have windows) to reduce heat loss or gain, but their high cost has tended to limit industrial applications.

4. *Ceiling height.* In buildings (particularly older ones) with high ceilings, a great deal of energy can be wasted in heating successive layers of warm air, which rise to the ceiling, until they fill the air space down to the level at which personnel are comfortable. One way to avoid this loss is to install a false ceiling at normal room height, cutting off the space above from the flow of air. If this cannot be done for some reason, another solution is to install fans in the upper air space to direct the warm air back to the lower levels.

Lighting Conservation Measures

Look for energy savings in these areas:

1. *Reduced illumination.* Do you really need all that light? One company found that it could reduce the "normal" standard of illumination of 100-foot candles to 70, without interfering with worker effectiveness; it also provided three levels of lighting in office and general work areas, and added "task lighting" at specific workstations. The drop from 100- to 70-foot candles resulted in a reduction of 30 percent in energy consumption.

2. *Fluorescent lighting.* Fluorescent lamps will provide the same illumination as incandescent types, for about one-third of the energy consumption.

3. *Windows.* Ordinary window glass comes in thicknesses of $1/16$ or $1/8$ inch. Even if the thermal conductivities of glass and building brick are roughly the same, a $1/8$ inch thickness of glass will conduct 96 times as much heat as the same area of a 12 inch brick wall.

4. *Heat from lights.* In buildings that have extensive lighting systems, advantage can be taken of the heat given off by the lamps. Blowers are set up to move air across the banks of lights, and the air thus warmed is distributed for space heating. Economies are realized, not only in the reduction of heat that must be supplied from other sources, but also in the prolonged life of the lamps, which results from their operation at lower temperatures. In the cooling season, this warm air is diverted to the exterior of the building, reducing the load on the air conditioning system.

Three Ways to Save Energy with Heating and Cooling Systems

Here are three ways you can work with the system you have to save energy:

1. Adjust temperature settings in unoccupied spaces. There will be a number of areas of the plant not occupied at all during some parts of a 24-hour day, or occupied only sparsely and intermittently. Heat control settings should be lowered and cooling control settings raised in such areas, and automatic controls are usually the cheapest method of adjustment. Of course, nothing beats shutting them down altogether—there is no greater energy saving than zero consumption—but the savings must be compared with the costs of wear and tear caused by frequent start-ups and the extra energy required to bring the space back to its normal controlled temperature.

2. Lower control settings in winter, raise them in summer. In times of energy shortages, Americans are asked to heat occupied buildings only to 68°F, and cool them to 78°F. While these temperatures may not be comfortable for everyone, you can set up a test program, to see how closely these settings can be approximated without an undue number of complaints.

3. Establish adjustment and preventive-maintenance programs. Make sure that fuel–air ratios, dampers, vanes, and valves are properly adjusted on a regular basis; that heat exchange surfaces are cleaned; and that filters and belts are replaced or adjusted.

Energy Savings in Plant Operations

Steam generation and distribution: Conservation in the steam system starts with the question: How much of the energy paid for in the purchased fuel is lost? Look for ways to recover it in the answers to the following questions:

- How much energy is going up the stack?
- How much energy is lost in steam leaks and malfunctioning steam traps?
- How completely used is the steam you generate?
- How much energy is lost through poor insulation?

Electrical system: Most plant managers are not building new plants and must address the problem of conserving electrical energy in an existing installation. The first and probably most remunerative action to take is to look at is the plant *power factor,* which is the ratio of the electric power company.

Plant processes: No matter what industry your plant is a part of, it probably has its own literature—books, trade magazines, and technical journals. Your technical staff should review the literature for energy-conservation ideas specific to your industry. At the same time, here are some general lines of attack that can be pursued in most plants.

1. *Don't throw away energy you have already paid for.* Too often a hot process stream at the end of the production process is cooled with water or air, and its heat rejected to the atmosphere. With heat-exchange equipment, this energy can be recovered and used profitably, for example, to preheat cold feed streams or provide hot water for various purposes. And, do not forget that heat can be reclaimed from hot solid products, as well as from fluids—usually by air (or other gas) streams which, when warmed, can be fed to furnaces and burners, cutting their energy consumption, or for space heating. The same idea applies to energy in the form of pressure; one plant, which operates a large air compressor for process use, achieved flow control by blowing off some of the compressed air to the atmosphere. As part of an energy-conservation program, it connected the compressor vent to the plant's utility air system, allowing it to shut down completely that system's smaller compressor, and found a process use for the remaining vented air. In the first year alone, cost savings were four times the capital costs incurred in making the necessary changes.

2. *Keep heat-transfer surfaces clean.* Process streams can deposit undissolved solids on heat-exchanger surfaces by a silting process, or dissolved materials can precipitate on them, along with decomposition products. More efficient use of these heat-transfer surfaces may be achieved by more thorough cleaning of the stream before it starts through the process, or, if the product can tolerate it, addition of antifouling chemicals to resist deposition on heat-transfer surfaces. If neither of these works, periodic shutdowns to permit physical scraping and brushing may be necessary. If one of the heat-transfer surfaces consists of fins exposed to the air, they should be periodically washed or blown to remove dust and grease accumulations.

3. *Consider energy consumption when purchasing new process equipment.* Makers of industrial equipment have been giving more attention to the energy efficiency of their products since the high-priced energy era began. Request energy-consumption information from the manufacturer whose equipment you are considering, and include energy usage per unit of output in the purchasing decision.

4. *Look for energy-saving opportunities in the way process and utility flow streams are controlled.* Prior to the arrival of expensive energy, industrial practice was to pump liquids and gases at higher pressure than needed, and insert a throttling valve in the line to reduce flows to desired levels. Although not as obvious to the naked eye as a stream leak blowing to the atmosphere, throttling valves waste energy by converting it to heat, which is dissipated in the flow stream or lost to the atmosphere. One way to reduce these losses is to install variable-speed motors on the pumps and blowers in the system, whose output can then be adjusted to changing flow demands, reducing the need for throttling. For an elaboration on this and other ideas for saving process system energy, see F. G. Shinskey, *Control Systems That Save Energy,* in Elias P. Gyftopoulos and Karen C. Cohen, eds., *Industrial Energy Conservation Manuals: No. 2* (Cambridge, MA: MIT Press, 1982).

Heat pumps: Under favorable conditions, the heat pump can deliver four times as much energy as it absorbs in running the compressor, which makes it an attractive energy-conservation device. In the winter mode, however, when it absorbs heat from the outside air, its efficiency drops off rapidly if the outside temperature falls below freezing. An ideal situation for the heat pump exists when a large supply of noncorrosive underground water is available (which will have a steady temperature close to 50°F) for the external heat exchanger. Then the working fluids can reject heat to the water (summer) or absorb heat from it (winter) at good efficiencies.

Although heat pump systems have been designed and built since the 1930s, they did not come into widespread use until the era of high energy prices, and their application has been mostly for residential and commercial space heating and cooling. Some industrial applications have been reported in low-level heating processes, and in distillation and evaporation.

Switching fuels: A recent U.S. Department of Energy survey found that 70 percent of large industrial boilers in the United States were capable of burning more than one fuel, and the most popular combination was the ability to burn natural gas or fuel oil.

Natural gas is the most widely used industrial boiler fuel, because it is clean-burning and requires the least operator attention and the least capital investment in burning equipment. However, industrial users may find that for economic reasons or through a requirement of the gas supplier, they must contract for gas on an "interruptible" basis. This means that, during periods of peak demand, the gas company may require industrial users to stop using it, forcing plants either to shut down or switch to an alternative fuel.

For boilers capable of using only natural gas, the addition of an alternative fuel is easiest when the new fuel is oil. Although gas-only and oil-only boilers are built somewhat differently, the design parameters are usually within 20 percent, and only minor modifications to the internal structure of the boiler are needed as the alternative burning equipment is added. But the process is not entirely without complications: Fuel oil tanks will need to be installed; soot blowers may need to be installed to remove ash deposits from the boiler tubes; and the smokestack may need to be lengthened to reduce the air pollution effects at ground level.

Converting a gas boiler to use coal as an alternate fuel is a much more difficult problem. Here the design parameters vary by 50 percent, and extensive changes to the furnace and the boiler tubes will be required. Installation of a soot blower will be mandatory. Before proceeding very far with such a project, a thorough study should be undertaken by a competent engineering group; they may ultimately recommend installing a second coal-fired boiler alongside the gas boiler, rather than trying to modify it. Another possibility would be to consider a coal-water slurry as the fuel, rather than dry coal; conversion to this fuel might involve much less modification of the original boiler.

How to Set Up a Successful Energy-Conservation Program

By looking back through this chapter, you can see that energy conservation is (1) an *engineering* problem that involves replacing and redesigning equipment; (2) a *maintenance* problem, in keeping insulation, steam systems, and other possible energy-loss sources in good repair; (3) an *operating* problem, requiring energy-conservation discipline among the people who throw the switches and open the valves that control energy flow; (4) a *cost* problem, because so much capital and operating expense is involved; and (5) a *management* problem, because all these elements must be combined into a coordinated effort to achieve visible results.

Five Steps to Take in Beginning Your Program.　These are the five basic steps to take in setting up an energy-conservation program.

Step 1: Make an energy survey of the plant. (See Exhibit 13.16.) This step readily breaks down in two phases. Phase One will consist of a physical inspection of the plant and an examination of its records to answer the following kinds of questions:

- How much energy is being used?
- What kinds of energy are consumed?
- Where in the plant is it being consumed?
- Are there leaks, sloppy operating practices, or other energy-losing situations readily observable?

Phase Two consists of examining the information obtained in Phase One to answer these questions:

- Which units are operating at the lowest levels of efficiency and, therefore, offer the greatest opportunities for energy conservation?

EXHIBIT 13.16 Energy-Saving Survey

Department ——————— Surveyed by ——————— Date of Survey ———————

Fuel Gas or Oil Leaks	Steam Leaks	Compressed Air Leaks	Condensate Leaks	Water Leaks	Damaged or Lacking Insulation	Excess Lighting	Excess Utility Usage	Equipment Running and Not Needed	Burners Out of Adjustment	Leaks of or Excess of HVAC	Location	Date Corrected

- Are there cost-saving or security of supply benefits to be obtained by changing or adding to the types of energy purchased by the plant?

- What additional electric meters, steam flow meters, and other types of instrumentation must the plant install to be able to measure the effects of energy-conservation measures?

Step 2: Identify capital projects that will improve the plant's energy position. Typical projects would include (1) modification of existing equipment, such as adapting boilers to use alternate fuel; (b) replacement, such as retiring production equipment that may be still operable, but is obsolete in terms of energy consumption; and (c) installing new equipment, such as heat exchangers and electric capacitors, to make more efficient use of energy. (See Exhibit 13.17.)

Step 3: Identify operating changes. These are the measures that can be taken without changes to plant equipment, and might include shutting down certain energy-consuming units for part of the day, operating equipment at lower temperatures and pressures, and modifying operating procedures and rules, so that a higher degree of energy conservation discipline is actually obtained. (See Exhibit 13.18 on pages 266–271.)

Step 4: Establish goals for energy improvement. Steps 1 through 3 provide the tools for making things happen to improve the plant's energy situation. Now it is up to management to establish the goals which the program is expected to accomplish. They must be expressed in clear, measurable terms (preferably units of energy consumption), have a stated time period for accomplishment, and be realistic—too difficult, and a sense of frustration will set in; too easy, and no one will be motivated to work very hard.

Step 5: Train and motivate plant personnel at all levels. Everyone in the plant must understand what it is you are trying to accomplish, why you are conducting the program, and what it means to them to contribute all they can, if the program is to be successful.

How to Organize Your Plant's Energy Program. This job cannot be accomplished by appointing a "plant energy committee," having it meet once a month, and hoping that something comes of it all. The job of upgrading the plant to optimum efficiency with respect to energy consumption is clearly one for the line organization, and only that group can be expected to accomplish the program's goals.

In a small plant, the plant manager himself may head up the energy-conservation group. In larger plants, an assistant plant manager or operations manager may be available to take charge; if so, that manager must carry the full delegated authority of the plant manager to implement the program. Each production, utility, and staff department head is automatically a member of the conservation group, and is responsible for carrying the program in his department.

None of this is to say there should not be staff assistance. A Plant Energy Coordinator can be appointed, whose job is to assist the line organization by keeping records of progress, disseminating information and new ideas on conservation techniques, reminding line managers of upcoming deadlines, preparing reports of the program's progress, and participating in the training effort. In the larger plants, this may constitute a full-time

EXHIBIT 13.17   Energy-Conservation Capital Projects

Department _____   Form Completed by _____   Date _____

Project Number	Project Description	Energy Savings BTU/Year	Capital Cost $	Ratio BTU/Year Savings $ Capital	Percent ROI	Priority	Status

job. Some plants have found it useful to have each department head appoint a subordinate to handle the working details of the conservation effort, and to have these people form a liaison group, which meets regularly to exchange ideas, identify problems, and report progress. The important point is to not allow the Coordinator or the liaison committee to become bogged down in trying to carry out conservation projects themselves.

Keeping Track of Progress.   The program will require its own special record-keeping system in order to provide a coherent picture of past performance and provide a justification for future activity. Follow these steps in setting up the system:

Step 1: Adopt a standard energy use statistic for all departments of the plant. The unit that probably has the widest applicability is BTU per unit of production (pounds, tons, or item count). Users of various forms of energy such as steam, electricity, and natural gas, would convert all their consumption rates to BTU and divide the number of BTU by the production units. A cautionary note is in order here, however, which is best illustrated by an analogy from ordinary life. If an automobile is driven over a 50-mile course at 65 miles per hour (mph), it will consume considerably more gasoline per mile than if it were driven over the same course at 40 mph. Production equipment may react in much the same way—consuming more energy per unit produced if it is driven over the same course at 40 mph. Production equipment may react in much the same way—consuming more energy per unit produced if it is driven harder to meet special time or quality requirements. Provisions must be made for these variations in the record-keeping systems, if valid performance comparisons are to be made.

Step 2: Establish uniform recording methods for all departments. Not only should they report for the same time periods and in the same units, but they should use the same energy-conversion factors and the same formulas for calculating such measures as boiler and process equipment efficiency. The record-keeping system may also have to conform to rules issued by corporate headquarters, if the company owns more than one plant. (See Exhibits 13.19 on page 272 and 13.20 on page 273.)

Step 3: Establish a baseline for energy consumption before undertaking energy improvement projects. The energy survey mentioned above should provide sufficient data to establish the preprogram energy consumption levels of the various plant units.

Step 4: Computerize. The number of items to be kept track of, the calculations and data manipulation required, and the frequency of reporting all make the energy reporting system a natural application for the computer, especially for the mini-computer. An undue amount of energy reporting in industry is still being done manually—in small manufacturing units, because no computer is available, and in large operations, because access to the mainframe is not readily available and sufficiently informal. The declining costs and rapidly expanding power of mini-computers make them a tool for energy-management programs that should not be overlooked.

Inform the Players.   General support for the program will lag if only a few insiders know what is going on. Management will demand matter-of-fact reports, which report the energy usage and dollar-value achievements of conservation measures employed by the program, as well as any progress made toward security of operation—the ability to keep the plant running if one of its sources of energy is suddenly cut off or curtailed.

EXHIBIT 13.18   Energy-Saving Plans of Action

Action Focus	N/A	Strong	Satisfactory	Needs Some Improvement	Weak: Needs Major Improvement	Action Plan, Responsibility
Energy						
Stop leaks of heat and air conditioning						
Reduce temperature on thermostats during certain periods						
Insulate walls, floors, pipes, etc.						
Use solar heating where applicable						
Print employee reminders to put lights off						
Use automatic light dimmers and/or shutoff switches						
Employ timers to shut off equipment after prescribed time						
Appoint departmental "energy-watchers" to coordinate program						
Use alternate fuels including production by-products (waste)						
Audit energy bills and meters						
Examine equipment power requirements						
Upgrade wiring						
Use heat exchangers, etc.						
Track energy bills for unusual increases in costs						
Use different temperature standards for winter versus summer						
Keep doors and windows closed						
Encourage employees to wear suitable clothing						
Install air seals at loading dock entrances						
Check energy efficiency ratings of electrical equipment						
Convert lighting fixtures to more efficient types (mercury, sodium)						
Remind employees to shut off vehicle engines when not in use						

			Item
			Obtain heating and air conditioning from a single unit
			Recognize outstanding employees with appropriate awards
			Upgrade furnaces for greater fuel efficiency
			Seal up cracks around windows and doors, change to double insulated
			Plug up leaks in steam lines
			Clean and service boilers, fans, and blowers
			Use window coverings and insulating film to reduce energy consumption
			Try spring loaded faucets to shut off water automatically
			Reduce hot water temperature; avoid mixing with cold water
			Consider premium awards for energy suggestions
			Reduce exterior lighting to minimum safe levels
			Use variable speed motors where applicable
			Clean or replace air filters
			Convert from ambient to task lighting
			Turn off vending machine lights
			Employ a variable air volume system
			Use infra-red scanning to locate sources of heat loss
			Take advantage of off-peak utility discounts; shift work accordingly
			Machines and Equipment
			Pinpoint pros and cons of equipment purchase vs. rental vs. leasing
			Train machine operators thoroughly; maintain progress reports
			Evaluate availability and reliability of vendor service
			Keep detailed records on dependability of spare parts
			Provide backup priority list for critical equipment
			Replace inefficient machines with newer ones

(continued)

267

EXHIBIT 13.18 *(Continued)*

Action Focus	N/A	Strong	Satisfactory	Needs Some Improvement	Weak: Needs Major Improvement	Action Plan, Responsibility
Conduct safety training on hazardous equipment to reduce accidents						
Question equipment features for cost effectiveness						
Use posters and other media to dramatize need for equipment care						
Chart workflows to isolate wasted steps						
Chart workflows to see if straight-line method is used						
Project cash flow through relationship to Purchasing subsystem						
Provide for just-in-time applications to reduce inventories						
Allow random stores feature to handle multiple locations						
Automatically select vendors to keep acceptable mix of resources						
Maximize cash discounts and vendor credits						
Enter input on-line to reduce data entry costs						
Post financial information directly to journals, ledgers						
Prepare balance sheets, P&L, budgets as by-products of system						
Generate all mandated and optional payroll forms, reports						
Provide proper audit trails for internal and legal purposes						
Allow downloading to personal computer for electronic spreadsheets, etc.						
Produce depreciation schedules for fixed assets (land, building, equipment)						
Integrate with comprehensive order-entry system						
Evaluate sales performance by person, geographic area, customer, product						
Age accounts receivables, print reports on inactive or delinquent customers						

Integrated Manufacturing Information Systems				
Meet raw material requirements of production process				
Prevent excess inventory accumulations				
Provide current, accurate stock status				
Highlight significant variances between book and physical inventories				
Indicate fast and slow sellers				
Produce preprinted count tags				
Allow flexibility in count cycles (annual, monthly, cyclical, etc.)				
Generate timely, accurate master production schedules				
Permit modeling ("what if") to simulate effects of changes				
Calculate bills of material value				
Compare planned versus actual labor hours in detail				
Schedule parts shipments on a planned rather than crisis basis				
Avoid extra shifts and overtime by adjusting capacity				
Check off receipts to appropriate purchase order				
Packaging/Materials Handling				
Improve product protection: more durable packaging				
Improve product protection: more weather resistant packaging				
Study distribution center layouts and space requirements				
Study distribution center systems for materials handling				
Make packaging more attractive at same or lower cost				
Enhance identification of cartons' contents to save time in picking stock				
Material Handling/Warehouses				
Adjustable shelves to allow for different package sizes				
Adjustable shelves for volume peaks and valleys				

(continued)

269

EXHIBIT 13.18 *(Continued)*

Action Focus	N/A	Strong	Satisfactory	Needs Some Improvement	Weak: Needs Major Improvement	Action Plan, Responsibility
Adaptable loading dock ramps for different heights of vehicles						
Gravity feed instead of manual movement of inventory						
Ball-bearing conveyors						
Kit of commonly used items (tape machines, cutters, package markers)						
Clear assignments for production employees' simple equipment maintenance						
Solicit suggestions from employees						
Receiving/Shipping Emphasis on quality control to reduce damaged shipments						
Suppliers show weight on cartons to speed stocking						
Legibility of shipping addresses to reduce handling time						
Standards for receiving and storage time of inventory						
Manufacturing Resource Planning Measure current system effect on expense reduction						
Check present system effect on cash flow improvement						
Evaluate MRP Re: productivity						
Feasibility of MRP for better systems and data processing						
Practical use of simulation ("what if")						
Reduce excess paperwork						
Tighten controls on inordinate overtime						
Decrease routine Purchasing expenses						
Interact with Product Engineering on better bills of material						
Coordinate production plan (units) with business plan ($)						
Measure goals, actuals, variances of production						

Item				
Take action on significant variances				
Order materials on planned (not crisis) basis				
Track number of inventory turns versus comparable periods				
Compare inventory mix to customer demand				
Check if customer delivery dates are met				
Make provision for standard versus actual costs				
Assign accountability for production plan				
Prepare production timetables for 12–24 months				
Review frequency of production plan relative to sales forecast				
Check practicality of inventory lead times, safety stock				
Evaluate master schedule for proper units by product				
Verify performance of facilities planning				
Employ dispatch list for production work centers				
Set production priorities wherever appropriate				
Integrate MRP with accounts payable to properly reimburse vendors				
Provide for reports of stock status and back-orders				
Interact with payroll system to pay employees accurately				
Set up easily understood parts numbering system				
Examine input/output costs this year versus last year				
Consider pilot versus parallel system for conversion				
Brief supervisors/managers on benefits, operation of MRP				
Identify and rectify production bottlenecks				
Transportation/Construction				
Reduce freight rates through conversion to full carloads				
Traffic department scheduling to lower distribution costs				
Audit of freight bills to uncover overcharges				
Preventive maintenance of company vehicles				
Standards for construction of distribution facilities				
Standards for creation of parking lots, building security				

271

Form Completed by _____   _____ Date _____

EXHIBIT 13.19   Monthly Plant Energy Consumption Log

Year	Electric Power		Natural Gas			Fuel Oil			Coal			Total BTU	Number of Units Produced	BTU per Unit of Production
	kWh	BTU/kWh	BTU	k cu ft	BTU/k cu ft	BTU	gal	BTU/gal	BTU	Tons	BTU/lb	BTU			
Jan.															
Feb.															
Mar.															
Apr.															
May															
June															
July															
Aug.															
Sep.															
Oct.															
Nov.															
Dec.															
Year															
Jan.															
Feb.															
Mar.															
Apr.															
May															
June															
July															
Aug.															
Sep.															
Oct.															
Nov.															
Dec.															

EXHIBIT 13.20   Energy-Conservation Project Evaluation Summary

Capital _____ or Expense _____

Department _____

Date _____

Project No. _____ Person Responsible _____

Project Title _____

Description of Project _____

_____

_____

_____

_____

_____

_____

_____

_____

Location _____

_____

_____

Financial Evaluation

  Estimated

      Energy saving (electric power kWh/yr, steam lb/yr, etc.)

        Utility or Raw Material   Saving

        _____   _____ /yr

        _____   _____ /yr

        _____   _____ /yr

      Total energy saving   _____ MBTU/yr

      Total energy cost saving   _____ $/yr

      Other cost saving due to:

      _____   _____ $/yr

      Additional cost due to:

      _____   _____ $/yr

      Net cost saving   _____ $/yr

      Cost of project   _____ $

The general plant population will want something more informal and easier to understand. Some useful ways of communicating, to keep interest alive, are monthly newsletters, plant billboards, signs in each department showing past usage and future goals, foremen's meetings, and department or plantwide general meetings.

Newer Developments in Energy Supply

Solar Energy.   Some very broad definitions of solar energy have appeared, including not only the direct energy received from sunlight but extended also to include indirect effects, such as wind, ocean waves, and biomass conversions. This section will deal only with the direct use of sunlight.

The main limitations on the application of solar energy to industrial uses have not been technological factors, but cost. Although a number of pilot units have been constructed that demonstrate the technical feasibility of generating hot water and steam, industrial development has awaited very large reductions in the capital cost of the required equipment. The following are main types of solar devices, which may find ultimate industrial/commercial use.

Flat-plate-solar collector: This, which resembles a large window frame lying on its side, usually mounted on a roof or similar structure, so that it faces the sun. At the top of the frame are one or two sheets of glass or plastic, through which the sun's rays pass. Below that is a flat metal plate painted black. If water is the working fluid to be used, the metal plate is attached to pipes or tubing containing water. Below them is a thickness of insulation supported by a base plate. The radiant energy is received by the blackened plate and converted into heat, which is transmitted to the water; the transparent plates prevent the loss of this heat back to the atmosphere by convection and, to some extent, by radiation. Flat-plate collectors have been commercially applied to residential hot water heating, and could be applied for the same purpose in industrial situations, where they are cost effective. They are, however, generally limited to producing fluid temperatures below 200°F.

Thermal power central receiver system: This system consists of a steam boiler mounted on an outdoor tower. It is surrounded by a field of mirrors, shaped to focus the sun's rays on the boiler, and equipped with mechanisms that allow them to follow the sun as it moves through the sky. Steam is generated in the boiler and can be used for process purposes or to drive an electric power generator. Much higher temperatures—up to 2000°F—can be generated. These systems require a great deal of land space, and will probably find their greatest use in the Southeast.

There is an obvious gap between the need of a manufacturing plant for a steady supply of energy and the fluctuation of energy available from sunlight, caused by changes in the length of day and variable cloud cover. Solar power systems, therefore, usually require a conventional backup system (electric power from a utility or fossil-fuel-burning equipment), or a means of strong surplus solar energy for later use (electric batteries, or, in a hydroelectric system, a pumped storage facility).

Fuel Cells.   Basic courses in chemistry often include a demonstration in which an electric current is passed through water, decomposing the water into its constituent elements, hydrogen and oxygen. The fuel cell works in just the opposite way—hydrogen is passed over one electrode of a cell, oxygen over the other, and electricity is produced. Thus, the fuel cell is a means of converting chemical energy into electrical energy, and, in practical applications, it produces heat as well. The oxygen can be supplied pure or contained in an air stream. The hydrogen is obtained from natural gas, oil refinery products (naphtha), or coal; since this brings us right back to the use of fossil fuels, the question may well be asked, "Why bother with the fuel cell—why not just burn the fuel directly?"

The answer lies in efficiency of the process. The efficiency of fuel utilization in a fuel cell will run from 10 to 40 percent higher than in a conventional system. The higher number applies when both the electricity and heat generated in the cell are used. The electricity is generated as direct current (usually at less than 500 volts), and, for plants using that kind of power, there is an additional saving over the efficiency loss suffered when alternating current purchased from a utility is converted to direct current. These devices are expensive, and widespread application will await steep declines in the capital cost of the cells.

Economics: The Bottom Line Still Counts

Throughout this chapter we have dealt with the two basic goals of the energy-conservation program, the first goal being to find ways of reducing the suddenly very high costs of supplying fuel to the plant. This is a cost-reduction effort, and its projects are expected to generate a return on capital investment at least competitive with, if not superior to, other possible cost-reduction opportunities requiring capital. Although the search for new energy-conservation methods is challenging and often fascinating, money is the yardstick that tells us when we have gone far enough.

The second goal is to protect the company against going out of business altogether, if the primary form of energy used by the plant is threatened with interruption or curtailment for any length of time. When survival is the issue the rules can be bent rather sharply, but, even in this situation, there are economic limits. If, for instance, the annualized cost of installing a backup fuel system is greater than the company's expected earning for the next 8 years, then the risk of being shut down for a period may have to be borne. In a less extreme situation, if the cost of the backup system is not actually prohibitive, but would preclude a very attractive investment in production equipment that would increase the company's market penetration, then a more careful study of the risks must be made. It would involve making estimates such as the probability of an energy supply failure occurring and its length, and its severity expressed in dollars—loss of sales, diminished competitive position.

Operating Example: Determining the Cost Effectiveness of an Energy-Conservation Proposal. Following the plant energy survey, a plant manager was presented with the following proposal from his powerhouse superintendent: An economizer can be installed on the main boiler to heat the incoming feedwater and thus recapture some of the heat now going to the atmosphere in stack gases. The installed cost of the equipment is estimated at $302,000. The area engineer estimates that approximately 18,000 barrels of fuel oil will be saved per year, yielding annual cost savings of $223,560. For investment analysis purposes, the plant manager assumes that the economizer will have a useful life of 210 years, with no salvage value and, using the economic justification method, makes the following evaluation:

Return on Investment

Total pretax profit over life of project (10 × $223,560)	$2,234,600
Less depreciation	302,000
Taxable profit	$1,933,600
Income tax at 34%	657,424
After-tax profit	$1,276,176
Average annual after-tax profit (Divide by 10 years)	137,618
Return on investment (127,618 divided by 302,000)	42.2%

Payback Period

After-tax profit	$1,276,176
Plus depreciation	302,000
Cash Flow	$1,578,176
Average annual cash flow (Divide by 10 years)	157,818
Payback period (302,000 divided by 157,818)	
(Investment divided by Annual cash flow)	1.91 yr

With a 42 percent return and a payback period of 2 years, this might be an attractive investment to management. But there could be other economic considerations that would create serious second thoughts about proceeding with it. For instance, if capital funds are very hard to obtain for some reason and only enough money is available for this project or for the installation of new production machines needed to keep the company competitive in its business, then the company may have to forego the energy savings as a matter of survival.

Monitor Fuel-Saving Ideas

- By developing more efficient processes for its use, which takes time and money;
- By rationing or reducing demand for it through pricing, so that only a few can afford to buy it; and
- By operating existing processes more efficiently, which requires the dedicated enthusiasm of all.

Lighting.   Lighting usually represents a small faction of the total energy requirement of a factory, but economies are easy for all to see and can give impetus for conservation of less tangible items. Good lighting design improves productivity, but glare can lead to accidents.

- Make the best use of daylight by keeping windows and roof lights clean, also by suitable arrangement of working places near windows.
- Keep lamps and fittings clean.

- Replace lamps when their efficiency drops through aging.
- Use suitable reflectors and diffusers, which transmit light in the desired direction.
- Avoid dark background colors, which absorb light.
- Have separate switches to control lights near windows.
- Make sure that light is adequate, but that it is switched off when not required. (Frequent switching reduces the life of lamps.)
- Consider automatic switching of lighting.
- Use fluorescent or discharge lamps, rather than filament lamps.

Space-Heating.   Excessive temperature variation with hot and cold spots needs to be controlled by strategically placed thermostats.

- Block off unoccupied working areas and do not heat them.
- Limit maximum temperature to the legal limit of 19°C. Check the accuracy of temperature control. Minimize variation in temperature.
- Use warm air curtains in conjunction with automatic door closing, where possible, to improve comfort without draught or excessive loss of hot air. Dispatch bays are often the cause of excessive heat loss.

Ventilation.   A ventilation system, which includes heating, humidification, and filtration is expensive to install, but a good system will improve the working environment, as well as productivity.

- Avoid drafts by a properly sealed system, sealing doors, windows, etc.
- Doors and windows should normally be closed in cold weather.
- Excessive ventilation, caused by leaving windows open, involves excessive space-heating. Consequently, the number of changes per hour in a room should be restricted.
- In air-conditioned buildings, ensure that the controls for moisture content, temperature, and direction of air flow are effective.
- Avoid air leaks in ducts by sealing them.
- On nonworking days do not switch on air heating and ventilation too soon, but maintain a level just sufficient to give frost protection.
- Switch off the air conditioning system up to 1 hour before the building is due to be vacated for a long period.

Electrical Equipment.   Electricity costs are based on the rate as well as the amount of consumption. This requires a company to balance the costs of the maximum demand and the load factor. Maintaining a high power factor is important in reducing costs, by increasing efficiency of usage.

- Switch off equipment which is not required for any prolonged period.
- Lower the maximum demand by regulating the intermittent use of equipment.
- Match electric motors to their required duties.
- Use higher voltage, where possible, to reduce transmission losses.
- Match the size of transformers to their load requirements.
- Make the best use possible of the three-phase system for power distribution.
- Obtain advice on power factor control and most advantageous tariff.

Thermal Insulation.   The material chosen has to be of low thermal conductivity and suitable for the temperature of operation, so that it does not shrink, melt, or otherwise deteriorate.

- Except for heat-transfer units such as space-heaters and refrigerators, heated and cooled pipes should be lagged.
- Any exposed surface not at room temperature should be thermally insulated. Included should be valves, flues, and chimneys.
- Protect thermal insulation from damp, inclement weather, and mechanical damage.
- Use cavity insulation in buildings.
- Apply thermal insulation to lofts or roofs (100 mm recommended).
- Double-glazing provides thermal saving, also reduces drafts and noise levels.
- Make exterior doors self-closing.
- Consider the use of double doors or revolving doors in the entrances to buildings.
- Consider the replacement or enhancement of thermal insulation for low, medium, and high temperature, using material of low thermal conductivity.
- Cover the surface of a hot liquid with a lid or a floating insulator to reduce the heat loss.
- Apply cold-face insulation to the exteriors of furnaces and ovens.
- Use where possible hot-face insulation inside ovens and furnaces, which are intermittently heated, so as to reduce the heat storage loss.
- Prevent radiation escape by closing apertures such as inspection holes and doors.
- Use polished metal exterior surfaces to minimize radiation loss.

Steam, Compressed Air, and Other Services.   Oversized steam and other heated pipes, even if lagged, may have a low delivery temperature because of heat losses. Undersized pipes also have losses, but, in this case, are due to friction, which has to be overcome by a higher-than-normal pumping pressure, or by a low delivery pressure, which may fluctuate excessively with flow changes. All common services should be regularly inspected for leaks, since they are often not attended for long periods, due to poor accessibility.

- Take particular care to avoid leaks. Check thoroughly for leaks and repair, where necessary.
- Inspect and maintain stream traps.
- Seal off redundant pipework and ducts.
- Ensure that steam mains are properly sized.
- Recover steam condensate and return it to the boiler, if not contaminated.
- Avoid the use of steam-reducing valves for low-pressure steam. Back-pressure engines or calorifiers should be considered.
- Switch off compressed air services when they are not required to run continuously.
- Clean air filters and renew packing to reduce pressure losses.
- Mechanical efficiency falls with use, hence renew valves, springs, rings, glands, etc.
- Avoid overheating air in a compressor, by returning it through a by-pass to the inlet.
- Multiple-stage compressors are more efficient with intercooling between stages; regularly clean the heat exchangers to ensure minimum pumping cost.
- Ensure that fan rotating parts are in balance.
- Fan impellers often become dirty and corroded. Surface cleaning and polishing will improve efficiency.

Boilers for Steam and Hot Water.   Where more than one boiler is in use, it may be possible to shut one down for part of the time. Hot water storage of a boiler will vary with the load on it and is greatly affected by the efficiency of combustion and by the transfer of heat from the waste gases to the water or steam, hence the need for regular cleaning and setting of controls.

- Stagger the demands for steam as much as possible, to give a more even loading on the boilers.
- Avoid boiler safety valves blowing unnecessarily, by proper control of firing.
- Controls should be serviced and adjusted to maintain optimum efficiency, temperature, pressure, etc.
- Is the treatment of feedwater appropriate?
- Do not have excessive blowdown.
- Can the temperature of hot water be reduced with an improvement of efficiency?
- Where superheated steam is appropriate, this should be provided at a high steady temperature.

Combustion.   The efficient combustion of a fuel demands that the combustion apparatus be suitable for the fuel concerned. Solid fuel has to be of the correct size and hardness, and have suitable moisture, ash, volatile matter, and sulfur contents. The ash fusion temperature of coal may be critical, leading to loss of unburned fuel, and problems with fly-ash, grit, and permeability of the fuel bed. Variable quality of fuel poses additional problems. High volatility in fuel can lead to incomplete combustion of waste gases, unless the supply of combustion air is suitably distributed.

- Switch off unwanted burners.
- Excess air in fuel-fired equipment is probably the chief cause of energy waste in industry. Therefore, the control of air–fuel ratio should provide only sufficient of each for complete combustion consistent with proper mixing.
- The percentage of carbon dioxide and the like in waste gases should be monitored regularly to check that combustion is efficient.
- Air leaks in brickwork and flues and around dampers should be stopped.
- Furnace drafting should be balanced; fit flue dampers to isolate boilers not on line to prevent a natural draft pulling in cold air.
- Fuel supplied for combustion should be in the proper condition to achieve optimum heat release.
  Coal—uniform mix of suitable size range, volatile matter, ash and moisture content, hardness, and reactivity;
  Oil—constant temperature to control viscosity, constant pressure; and
  Gas—constant pressure.
- A combination of different fuels calls for mixing control.
- Burners should not overheat. Their efficiency is maintained by adjustment, cleaning, and replacement of worn parts.
- Adequate mixing of fuel and air at the burner is necessary for proper direction of the flame and completion of heat release from the fuel within the combustion chamber.
- Multiple burners and multiple-zone heating need balancing to produce even heating.

Furnaces and Ovens.   For heat-transfer efficiency the hearth area of a furnace needs to be completely covered with the charge, but overloading is undesirable, as it slows the rate of heating. Control of temperature to give uniform heating aids productivity and minimizes rejects. Machinery associated with heating process is itself subject to overheating, and this is often overlooked.

- Hearth coverage is increased by proper loading.
- Doors should be left open for as short a time possible, for loading, and unloading, and should be well maintained so as to minimize radiant heat loss and air in-leakage.
- The mass of carriers, trays, and so on can often be reduced without loss of control.

- Steady operation by planning throughput is desirable.

- Heating cycles, particularly in batch furnaces, should be short but consistent with the maintenance of product quality.

- Consider the possibility of changing to a more efficient form of heating by changing the burners, or fuel, or by using an electrical method.

Reduction of Waste. Hot water wasted means energy wasted. Is the water temperature higher than necessary? Besides placing notices to discourage waste on washroom doors, the fitting of spring-loaded taps and of low-throughput showers, together with a high standard of insulation and maintenance, can be of assistance.

- Closer specification in the use of all materials saves in many ways. Energy is directly saved with those involving a high consumption of energy in their production, such as metals, rubber, plastics, paper, glass, cement, and refractories.

- Sort waste materials at source ready for recycling.

- Incinerate refuse and recover its heat, for example, for space-heating.

- Fermentation of organic waste could provide methane gas as a fuel to drive stationary engines for power.

Waste Heat Recovery. When energy is rejected in the form of pressure, temperature of waste gases and other products, or unburned fuel from one process, it may be possible to harness it to reduce the energy needs of the same or some other process. An investigation is necessary to establish the facts before recovery of energy in the form of preheat of charge, combustion air, fuel, hot water, steam, or unburned fuel is attempted. Waste heat recovery involves capital investment. Criteria on which this investment could be justified are as follows:

- The source must provide sufficient energy at a high enough temperature or pressure, or, in the case of unburned fuel, at a high-enough calorific value.

- The quantity of energy saved must be worth more than the equivalent cost of fuel, which would otherwise be burned directly.

- The energy in the form recovered must be needed for some processes, or adaptable for that need.

- The pattern of energy demand for the waste heat recovery must comply with the pattern of availability (storage of energy in a tank or accumulator, standby plant, or auxiliary fuel firing may be possible).

- There must be space available for the recovery equipment.

- The return on capital must be acceptable.

- A loan for the capital has to be available. Government grants and short-term loans are available for approved energy-saving projects.

General Comments.   An Energy Management Department is usually to be found in a large company; its role will be to promote efficiency in the use of heat and power. A small firm requiring external advice may obtain it from appropriate government departments, advisory councils, energy and fuel suppliers, insulation manufacturers, polytechnics and universities, or research organizations and trade organizations.

- Investigate the various tariffs available for the supply of fuels, to ensure that they are those that best meet the needs of the process.

- Keep a regular record of stocks, purchases, and consumption of energy.

- Provide instrumentation to measure and control the consumption of energy. Regularly maintain and check the calibration of the instruments.

- Examine the records to pinpoint any change in the energy consumption, making use, where appropriate, of computer database packages, to relate energy consumption to production.

- Carry out efficiency tests on machines and other plant equipment to verify that they are not deteriorating.

- Institute or revise planned engineering maintenance, to reduce energy waste, improve safety, and to enhance general working conditions.

- Ensure that energy conservation has due consideration in production planning.

- Encourage all personnel to save energy, by investigating any suggestion that might reduce energy consumption in the long term.

- Be prepared to argue a case for the installation of capital equipment, which can reduce energy consumption; investigate what grants are available from regional and government sources.

- Use persuasion and incentives to achieve desired results and, above all, maintain the pressure for fuel economy.

Appendices

APPENDIX A

PROCESS IMPROVEMENT FLOW DIAGRAMS

Business Process Flow

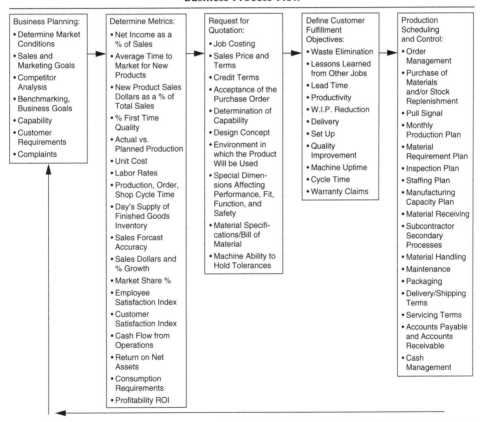

Business Planning:
- Determine Market Conditions
- Sales and Marketing Goals
- Competitor Analysis
- Benchmarking, Business Goals
- Capability
- Customer Requirements
- Complaints

Determine Metrics:
- Net Income as a % of Sales
- Average Time to Market for New Products
- New Product Sales Dollars as a % of Total Sales
- % First Time Quality
- Actual vs. Planned Production
- Unit Cost
- Labor Rates
- Production, Order, Shop Cycle Time
- Day's Supply of Finished Goods Inventory
- Sales Forcast Accuracy
- Sales Dollars and % Growth
- Market Share %
- Employee Satisfaction Index
- Customer Satisfaction Index
- Cash Flow from Operations
- Return on Net Assets
- Consumption Requirements
- Profitability ROI

Request for Quotation:
- Job Costing
- Sales Price and Terms
- Credit Terms
- Acceptance of the Purchase Order
- Determination of Capability
- Design Concept
- Environment in which the Product Will be Used
- Special Dimensions Affecting Performance, Fit, Function, and Safety
- Material Specifications/Bill of Material
- Machine Ability to Hold Tolerances

Define Customer Fulfillment Objectives:
- Waste Elimination
- Lessons Learned from Other Jobs
- Lead Time
- Productivity
- W.I.P. Reduction
- Delivery
- Set Up
- Quality Improvement
- Machine Uptime
- Cycle Time
- Warranty Claims

Production Scheduling and Control:
- Order Management
- Purchase of Materials and/or Stock Replenishment
- Pull Signal
- Monthly Production Plan
- Material Requirement Plan
- Inspection Plan
- Staffing Plan
- Manufacturing Capacity Plan
- Material Receiving
- Subcontractor Secondary Processes
- Material Handling
- Maintenance
- Packaging
- Delivery/Shipping Terms
- Servicing Terms
- Accounts Payable and Accounts Receivable
- Cash Management

Business Improvement Approach

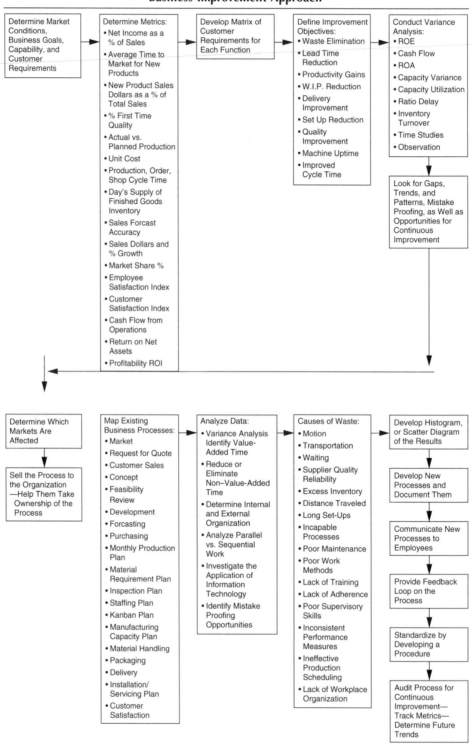

| Determine Market Conditions, Business Goals, Capability, and Customer Requirements | Determine Metrics:
• Net Income as a % of Sales
• Average Time to Market for New Products
• New Product Sales Dollars as a % of Total Sales
• % First Time Quality
• Actual vs. Planned Production
• Unit Cost
• Production, Order, Shop Cycle Time
• Day's Supply of Finished Goods Inventory
• Sales Forcast Accuracy
• Sales Dollars and % Growth
• Market Share %
• Employee Satisfaction Index
• Customer Satisfaction Index
• Cash Flow from Operations
• Return on Net Assets
• Profitability ROI | Develop Matrix of Customer Requirements for Each Function | Define Improvement Objectives:
• Waste Elimination
• Lead Time Reduction
• Productivity Gains
• W.I.P. Reduction
• Delivery Improvement
• Set Up Reduction
• Quality Improvement
• Machine Uptime
• Improved Cycle Time | Conduct Variance Analysis:
• ROE
• Cash Flow
• ROA
• Capacity Variance
• Capacity Utilization
• Ratio Delay
• Inventory Turnover
• Time Studies
• Observation |

Look for Gaps, Trends, and Patterns, Mistake Proofing, as Well as Opportunities for Continuous Improvement

| Determine Which Markets Are Affected

Sell the Process to the Organization —Help Them Take Ownership of the Process | Map Existing Business Processes:
• Market
• Request for Quote
• Customer Sales
• Concept
• Feasibility Review
• Development
• Forcasting
• Purchasing
• Monthly Production Plan
• Material Requirement Plan
• Inspection Plan
• Staffing Plan
• Kanban Plan
• Manufacturing Capacity Plan
• Material Handling
• Packaging
• Delivery
• Installation/ Servicing Plan
• Customer Satisfaction | Analyze Data:
• Variance Analysis Identify Value-Added Time
• Reduce or Eliminate Non–Value-Added Time
• Determine Internal and External Organization
• Analyze Parallel vs. Sequential Work
• Investigate the Application of Information Technology
• Identify Mistake Proofing Opportunities | Causes of Waste:
• Motion
• Transportation
• Waiting
• Supplier Quality Reliability
• Excess Inventory
• Distance Traveled
• Long Set-Ups
• Incapable Processes
• Poor Maintenance
• Poor Work Methods
• Lack of Training
• Lack of Adherence
• Poor Supervisory Skills
• Inconsistent Performance Measures
• Ineffective Production Scheduling
• Lack of Workplace Organization | Develop Histogram, or Scatter Diagram of the Results

Develop New Processes and Document Them

Communicate New Processes to Employees

Provide Feedback Loop on the Process

Standardize by Developing a Procedure

Audit Process for Continuous Improvement— Track Metrics— Determine Future Trends |

APPENDIX B

BUSINESS ANALYSIS

Management auditing is much more than an internal check. Internal check can best be understood as being an internal cross-check which is certainly an important element of most effective systems of management auditing. The system of management auditing is the totality of methods and measures that management has introduced to provide reasonable assurance of the achievement of objectives and the avoidance of unwanted outcomes. As such, management auditing is the essence of good management. The classic view of management is that it comprises effective planning, organizing, staffing, directing, and controlling. Each of these must be done well if there is to be effective management auditing. The following management plan has helped over 600 companies in a variety of industries; you are welcome to use it at your discretion.

MANAGEMENT PLAN

General Operations

1. Establish primary goals of the company—maintenance of status quo, evaluation and recommendations, or take charge through implementation of new game plan.
2. Meet all first-reports, introduce game plan, and initiate implementation of action items on this list.
3. Have all first-reports complete the agenda for the future.
4. Discuss the dozen biggest problems and opportunities from the perspective of all first-reports.
5. If survival mode is required, cut costs immediately where necessary and prudent and in accordance with the company's short- and intermediate-term goals.
6. Identify and implement the top six action items that could measurably increase short-term revenues.
7. In addition to this action list, formulate a short-term game plan for the company, get the company's approval, and communicate the plan to key personnel, suppliers, and lenders.

8. Prioritize the top 10 action items for the whole company and begin implementation.

9. Identify the top goals for the company for the current month, quarter, and year.

10. Set up forecasts so that they provide an early warning of potential risks/opportunities versus reports against budgeted targets. Revise forecasts on an exception basis only and through a single common tool.

11. Focus the forecast analysis and reporting on tactical plan adjustments to meet the budget.

Financial Issues

1. Within the first week, get current and detailed financial statements, itemized payroll, payables, and receivables list.

2. Review budgets of all departments or divisions for reasonableness of assumptions, quality of projections, and relevancy in light of recent corporate changes and goals.

3. Evaluate obvious, and not so obvious, problems and strengths revealed by the financial statements.

4. Do a realistic cash forecast for the next 90- and 180-day periods.

5. Evaluate asset utilization and redeploy if appropriate and prudent in the short term.

6. Review banking and debt obligations for next 90-, 180-, and 365-day periods and ensure no technical or major defaults, if possible. If in default, develop a game plan and/or negotiate a workout.

7. Determine which critical suppliers have suspended support due to lack of payment or other problems.

8. Identify and take steps to immediately defuse all visible, or suspected, ticking time bombs.

9. Know margins by customer and product.

10. Understand your process costs and cost drivers.

11. Develop customer P&Ls.

12. Prioritize opportunities and develop a customer profit plan.

Supply-Chain Management

1. Manage areas like accounts receivable, accounts payable, inventory turns, and cash-to-cash cycle time to improve working capital efficiency.

2. Manage return on assets, capacity and throughput, network optimization, and outsourcing to improve fixed capital efficiency.

3. Keep supply-chain costs low through process cost reductions, shared services, and outsourcing without jeopardizing customer satisfaction.

4. Minimize the company's tax rates by managing asset location, sales locations, transfer prices, and customs duties.

5. Ensure profitability through new product development, maintaining a global presence, after sales service, and perfect order fulfillment.

Regulatory/Legal/Litigation

1. Ensure all payroll taxes are paid and properly reported.

2. Determine what, if any, problems exist with the IRS and state agencies.

3. Ensure the company is in compliance with all required regulatory and licensing agencies and if not, take action to resolve these issues.

4. Identity all outstanding legal issues and litigation risks along with probable, and possible, associated costs.

5. Ensure no securities law violations have occurred. If they have, take immediate steps to remedy them, or mitigate their impact.

6. Ensure any patents, trade secrets, trademarks, and copyrights are properly filed and appropriate protections are in place.

Product Lines/Marketing/Sales/Distribution— Know Your Customers' Needs

1. Analyze product delivery schedules and takes steps to improve meeting commitment dates.

2. Evaluate product development timetables, budget forecasts, and quality of project management systems, procedures, and controls.

3. Evaluate sales, marketing, distribution, forecasts, and trend lines for improvement opportunities in all areas, so as to generate more cash in the short term.

4. Identify both the best customers and the most unhappy customers, as well as the company's image in the marketplace.

5. Complete a competitive analysis for each product line.

6. Evaluate pricing models for each product line and adjust accordingly.

7. Identify product line strengths and weaknesses and develop a short-term action plan to solve the most glaring problems.

8. Identify potential products—6-, 12-, and 24-months into the future—and their possible impact on revenue and expenses.

9. Establish/update/expand Web presence.

10. Evaluate expenditures and effectiveness of marketing and advertising for media, trade shows, market research, focus groups, and public relations, and adjust accordingly.

11. Evaluate sales force, sales-related incentives, sales targets, sales personnel training, special offers, dealerships, telemarketing, and sales support.

12. Evaluate and optimize short-term inventory.

13. Evaluate customer/technical support, warranties, guarantees, and after-sales service.

Personnel Issues

1. Upon arrival, candidly communicate with all company personnel for introduction and conveyance of immediate game plan.

2. Set up suggestion boxes and invite anonymous e-mail to gain insight into less obvious underlying problems.

3. Review major Human Resource department aspects of the company for legal compliance, competitiveness of benefits package, diversity, clarity of policies, and potential costs savings.

4. Evaluate the strengths and weaknesses of all first-reports.

5. Develop 30-, 60-, and 90-day performance plans for all first-reports.

6. Evaluate the organizational structure and effectiveness of the company and reorganize if appropriate, adjusting total payroll if necessary.

7. Identify the best and worst 5 percent of employees in the company—probably replacing the worst 5 percent and ensuring the best 5 percent are motivated enough to stay.

8. Analyze employee turnover rates to identify the fundamental problem areas.

9. Identify key personnel and unfilled job functions, define criteria, and initiate search, within budget constraints.

10. Identify the personality issues and company policies that may be creating a negative impact on both company morale and productivity.

11. Review and modify written delegation of authority for all first-reports.

12. Review all employment contracts or agreements, oral or written, including any severance or termination compensation agreements with salaried, hourly, or collective bargaining employees.

13. Review all bonus, deferred compensation, stock option, profit sharing, retirement programs or plans covering salaried, hourly, or collective bargaining employees.

IPO/Merger/Acquisition/Disposition/Dissolution

1. Identify which mergers, acquisitions, dispositions, and investments make the most sense for the company.

2. Identify the growth issues regarding acquisitions, spin offs, expansion, downsizing, and establishing new and/or closing existing branches and stores.

3. If the decision is to sell the company, establish the price and terms, subject to company approval, prepare a sales summary, and develop a game plan and methodology for sale.

4. Complete a 3-year *pro forma* based on realistic assumptions to determine the future valuation potential of the company and the likelihood of an IPO or merger and acquisition.

5. If the company decision is to dissolve the company, develop a game plan for the liquidation of assets and follow up on a bankruptcy filing.

General/Administrative

1. Evaluate and control travel, entertainment, and all discretionary expenditures and implement new written policies for these issues.

2. Review all facilities and real estate issues, including a review of current lease requirements.

3. Review all equipment leases for cost cutting and improved technology opportunities.

4. Create and update the business plan for current internal clarity and banking or capital formation needs.

5. "Manage by roaming around"—gaining insights into attitudes and problem areas from within all levels of the organization.

6. Evaluate in-place systems and procedures and streamline where appropriate.

7. Evaluate technology implementation and optimize within budget constraints.

8. Visit all branch offices and evaluate their needs, performance, personnel, and cost-effectiveness.

Stockholder Status/Investor Relations

1. Evaluate investor and stockholder relations and communication status and initiate appropriate action.

2. Generate updated lists of all current shareholders and percentage ownership of each.

3. Review stock options or purchase plans and agreements, as well as lists of outstanding warrants and options, including date of grant, exercise price, number of shares subject to option, and date of exercise.

The Next Step

Report to the company the objective status, evaluation, recommended modifications to the short-term game plan, and any cash needs.

COST-SAVING MANAGEMENT AUDIT CHECKLIST

Here is a typical cost-saving management audit checklist for you to use. Use a 1 to 5 scoring system; 1 being least effective and 5 being most effective. 5 = 90–100 percent,

$4 = 80–90$ percent, $3 = 70–79$ percent, and $2 = 60–69$ percent. We know that this a subjective scoring system. A question may be weighted differently based on the circumstances.

Business Efficiency Methods

Planning   *Results*

- Review Operating Statements
- Identify Areas that Offer Best Cost-
  Reduction Potential
- Flow Chart All Major Areas
- Group Related Functions under the
  Same Supervision
- Shorten the Chain of Command
- Define Responsibilities and Authority;
  Eliminate Overlaps
- Decentralize and/or Centralize Operations
  as Appropriate
- Develop a Profit-Planning Program for Employees
- Measure Benefits before Spending
- Make Employees Plan Major Jobs in Advance
  of Implementation
- Defer All New Actions Until the True Needs
  Are Determined
- Reduce All Committees and the Length of
  Each Meeting
- Have an Annual Cost-Reduction Suggestion
  Program

Analyses of Departments and Activities   *Results*

- Are All Departments Necessary? Should Any
  Be Added?
- Are All Officers and Jobs Necessary?
- Is the Company Magazine Necessary?
- Are Company Sponsored Organizations
  Necessary?
- Establish a Word Processing Center
- Reduce Central Filing
- Centralize Office Services
- Evaluate All Major Cost Programs

- Review the Need for Institutional
  Type Advertising
- Eliminate Duplicate Records. Put a Price Tag on
  Each Report Issued (the information will be surprising).
- Review All Scrap; Determine if Any Scrap Value
  Can Be Realized

Personnel   *Results*

- Set a Good Example for Your Staff
- Promote from Within to Improve Morale
- Institute a Hiring Freeze for Short Periods
- Review Manpower Requirements Periodically
- Review All Education and Training Programs
- Have Periodic Performance Reviews
- Request Periodic Time Distribution Reports
  from Employees

Efficiency   *Results*

- Start and Leave Work on Time
- Utilize People to Full Capacity and
  Qualifications
- Permit Carryover of Workload and
  Level Out Peaks
- Reduce Overtime by Better Scheduling and
  Prioritizing Work
- Review All Form Designs for Efficiency
- Review Quality of Office Equipment
- Standardize Equipment
- Use More Estimates in Accounting
- Have Cycle Billings
- Close Manuals Quarterly; Use Estimated P&L
  Statements Monthly
- Reduce Quantity of Reports
- Use Handwritten Instead of Typewritten Memos
- Eliminate Business and Trade Reports When
  Not Necessary
- Make a Periodic Review of Files for Retention
  Necessity
- Establish Convenient Libraries for Manuals

- Use Combination Requisition, Purchase Order, Receiving Reports
- Route Reports Rather than Prepare Multiple Report Copies

- Use Microfilm Files to Save Space
- Use Computer to Assist Auditors
- Use Cheaper Paper in Duplicating Machines
- Use Better Machines for Duplicating to Cut Down on Waste
- Reduce Duplicating by Use of Common Files
- Do More Internal Printing of Forms
- Utilize Copiers at Strategic Locations
- Establish a Form Control Manual; Control Quantities of Forms
- Review All Forms for Necessity and Simplicity
- Review All Stationary Costs
- Reduce the Size of Annual Reports, and the Number of Colors
- Purchase and Issue Office Supplies in Economical Quantities
- Reduce the Kinds of Accounting Paper Carried in Inventory
- Control Supplies and Sundries

Office Facilities   *Results*
- Have Forward Planning of Office Layout
- Have More Modest Offices
- Eliminate Offices for Lower Supervisory Personnel
- Use Proper Wattage and Voltage
- Use Florescent Lighting
- Turn Out Lights When Not in Use
- Establish Janitorial Procedure that Cycles the Workload
- Remove Materials from Desk Nightly to Reduce Janitorial Work
- Set Standards for Floor Space Allowances by Classification of Office Employees

Outside Services   *Results*

- Hire Temporaries for Emergencies;
  No Overtime
- Utilize an Auditor's Free Technical Service
- Cut Out Professional Services Where Possible
- Do Your Own Building Maintenance
- Use Bank Facilities to Accumulate and Pay
  Freight Bills
- Use Bank Facilities to Mechanically Reconcile
  Bank Accounts
- Self-Produce Costly Supplies or Materials Needed

Communications   *Results*

- Review All Communications and Facilities
- Start a Telephone Expense Reduction Campaign
- Reduce Switchboard Hours; Close Board Earlier
- Use One Central Mailroom Only
- Install Inter-Office Mail and Messenger Service
- Mechanize Mail Processing
- Use Lowest Class Mail Rate When Feasible
- Use Lighter Paper and Envelops
- Don't Use Separate Envelops on Inter-Office Mail
- Mail Dividend Check with the Annual Report
- Eliminate the Second Proxy Mailing
- Don't Mail Statements to All Customers
- Reduce Size of Mailing Lists
- Don't Use Express Mail Unless Necessary

Meetings and Travel   *Results*

- Strictly Regulate All Travel
- Cut Out Executive Cars
- Cut Out Company Planes
- Use Coach Instead of First Class Air Travel
- Use the Airport Bus Instead of Cabs
- Stagger Company Hours to Relieve Congestion
  Problems
- Lease Company Cars Instead of Purchasing;
  Use Compacts

- Set Up Your Own Transportation Fleet
- Reduce Meeting and Travel Expense by a Set Percentage
- Eliminate or Reduce Convention Attendance
- Use Lower Priced Hotels
- Make Contact Travel Arrangements with Hotels in Cities That Are Frequently Visited by Company Employees
- Control Moving Expenses of People Transferred
- Eliminate Expensive Stockholder Meetings
- Eliminate Special Stockholder Meetings through Better Planning
- Cut Down on Lunch Time Meetings
- Have Management Meetings at Corporate Offices

Payroll and Fringe Benefits   *Results*

- Schedule Overtime by Priority
- Dock Employees for Being Late
- Have Shorter Lunch Periods
- Eliminate Oddball Deductions for Employees
- Eliminate Paychecks; Have Pay Deposited into Employees' Bank Accounts
- Schedule Varying Pay Rates to Level Load in the Payroll Department and Reduce Staff
- Eliminate Fringe Benefits (picnics, golf outings, etc.)
- Review Employee Stock Option Plans
- Eliminate Holiday Gifts to Employees
- Eliminate or Reduce Coffee Breaks
- Have Suggestion Awards Programs

Funds   *Results*

- Raise Capitalization Limits
- Use Lock-Box Banking
- Keep Petty Cash Funds to a Minimum
- Minimize the Number of Bank Accounts
- Have Bills Paid by Sight Draft
- Use Idle Funds

- Speed Up Billings
- Review Discount Procedures
- Hold Payables for Maximum but Pay for Discount
- Have Salesman and Drivers Deposit Collections Directly into Banks

Taxes and Insurance   *Results*

- Move to Lower Tax Areas
- Renegotiate Real Estate Taxes on Idle Facilities
- Control Inventories to Reduce Property Taxes
- Don't Pay Tax Installments until They Are Due
- Establish Subsidiary Corporations for Branches in Areas That Tax on the Total Company Business
- Review Insurance Costs
- Extend the Use of "Self-Insurance"
- Negotiate Insurance Rates on a Package Basis

Subscriptions and Dues   *Results*

- Reduce Memberships in Outside Societies, Clubs, Associations
- Eliminate Duplicate Memberships in Organizations
- Buy Industrial or Trade Magazines at Wholesale Prices
- Centralize Magazine Services
- Reduce Number of Magazine and Newspaper Subscriptions
- Develop Bibliography of Current Periodicals to Ensure Review of Latest Ideas

Miscellaneous   *Results*

- Assemble All Reports into a Single Manual
- Establish Greater Security to Avoid Inventory Thefts
- Obtain Competitive Bids for Purchases of Materials and Supplies
- Review Purchase Frequency of Supplies and Materials
- Review Technical Magazines Systematically for Cost-Savings Ideas

- Develop Checklist of Cost Saving—Profit Producing Approaches with Key Staff Members

Product Engineering   *Results*

- Make Tolerances More Flexible
- Reduce Surface Finish Requirements
- Eliminate Need for a Specific Part
- Substitute a Cheaper Material
- Reduce the Number of Parts Needed
- Combine Part Functions
- Design for Low Cost Tooling
- Design for High Speed Production
- Increase Feeds and Speeds
- Reduce the Number of Design Changes
- Design in Quality
- Design to Reduce Scrap
- Design to Standardize Production Processes
- Use Standard Hardware in Place of Custom Hardware
- Design to Reduce Manual Production Operations
- Design to Reduce Material Content
- Design to Reduce the Number of Fasteners Required
- Use Specific Alloys to Enable Faster Machining
- Use Specific Alloys to Cut Tool Wear
- Design the Cheapest Finish Feasible

Shipping, Receiving, and Warehousing   *Results*

- Use Conveyors for Moving Operations
- Use Reusable Pallets and Storage Boxes
- Keep Warehouse Locked
- Minimize Travel Distances
- Group Like Parts Together in Warehouse
- Use Hydraulic Lifts Instead of Ladders
- Ship and Receive in Unit Loads
- Protect Product from Damage or Corrosion
- Use Maximum Height for Warehouse Storage
- Speed Handling through Improved Scheduling

- Use Proper Storage Containers
- Prearrange Movement of Materials
- Replace Obsolete Equipment
- Combine Clerical Operations
- Place Fastest Moving Items Near Dock
- Mechanize All Movement of Material
- Keep Aisle Space Down to Minimum Needs
- Practice First-In–First-Out
- Properly Identify All Stock
- Check All Freight Rates/Bills
- Use Economical Small Package Ship Methods
- Keep Less than Truck Load to a Minimum
- Minimize Demurrage Costs—Unload Promptly
- Keep Bills of Lading Legible
- Count Number of Parts Received

Production Planning and Control   *Results*

- Reduce Inventories by Reducing the
  Number of Product Lines
- Reduce the Size of Purchased Lots
- Reduce the Size of Production Lots
- Use Better Forecasting Techniques
- Convert Obsolete Parts into Current Production
- Keep Inventories Organized
- Keep Inventory Records Accurate
- Reduce the Number of Salaried People
  Needed
- Keep Overtime Low
- Keep Warehouse Space Filled
- Reduce Office Space
- Reduce Overhead Expenses
- Improve Package Design
- Keep Written Procedures Current
- Keep Work Standards Up to Date
- Shrink Lead Times
- Reduce Emergency Orders
- Keep Production Routings Up to Date

- Provide Fast Access to Stock
- Use Effective Communications Systems
- Minimize Material Flow
- Maintain Fork Trucks in Good Order
- Improve Inspection Techniques
- Improve Vendor Performance
- Guard Against Incorrect Engineering Drawings
- Provide for Scrap/Rework When Planning
- Schedule to Minimize Waiting Time
- Renegotiate Vendor Prices
- Keep Production Overruns to a Minimum
- Recognize Production Bottlenecks, Then Minimize Them
- Keep Accurate Records
- Load Work Centers to Minimize Setups
- Minimize Sales Changes to the Master Schedule

Plant and Manufacturing Engineering   *Results*

- Correct Wrong Bill of Materials
- Reduce Average Earnings
- Curtail Use of Fuel and Electricity
- Correct Loose Work Standards
- Keep 90 Percent of All Production Jobs on Standard
- Keep 80 Percent of All Indirect-Labor Jobs on Standard
- Use Allowances in Standards Sparingly
- Ensure the Proper Use of Feeds and Speeds
- Issue Frequent Labor Performance Reports
- Combine Production Operations
- Change Standards to Reflect Improved Methods
- Sample Production Counts for Accuracy
- Analyze and Reduce Machine Downtime
- Standardize Equipment Parts
- Combine or Reduce Machine Setups
- Simplify Tooling, Jigs, and Fixtures

- Keep Accurate and Up-to-Date Equipment Records
- Lease Rather than Buy Equipment
- Mechanize Manual Operations

Quality Control   *Results*

- Reduce Scrap Levels
- Reduce Rework Levels
- Reduce Warranty
- Improve Tool and Gauge Inspection
- Reduce Vendor Quality Problems
- Calibrate Testing Equipment
- Prohibit Use of Marked Up Engineering Prints
- Scrap All Make Shift Tooling
- Segregate Defective Stock
- Modernize Inspection Equipment
- Review Packaging Quality
- Investigate Sales of Plant Scrap

Safety   *Results*

- Establish a Plant Safety Program
- Self-Insure Your Company
- Get Free Advice on Safety Issues
- Hire a Nurse to Screen Employees
- Have Workers Participate in the Safety Program
- Use Posters and Awards to Make Employees Safety Conscious
- Get the Union on Your Side
- Use Control Reports to Monitor Progress
- Use Accident Reports to Identify and Correct Safety Problems
- Publish Safety Rules and Discipline Offenders
- Provide Safety Training for All New Employees
- Make Safety the Responsibility of the Line Managers
- Use Self-Inspection Checklists

- Use an Internal Expert on Safety Regulations
- Investigate Accident-Prone Employees
- Provide First Aid Training for Emergencies
- Conduct Housekeeping Tours to Prevent Accidents
- Have the Plant Manager Chair the Safety Committee
- Know How to Use Fire Extinguishers
- Use Lead-Free Paint
- Use Safety Glasses on Every Job

INDEX